THE BARTLETT 2014

**The Bartlett
School of Architecture
UCL**

240 Blackfriars
Photograph by Rob Parrish

Foster + Partners

www.fosterandpartners.com

Bartlett International Lecture Series

Supported by Fletcher Priest Trust

www.fletcherpriest.com

Light first. Social innovation through lighting.

Socially engaged.

Environmental protection, **biological and psychological wellbeing, sustainable economies**: since **1959** we have been committed to positive development of life and society **through light**. We promote **responsible use** of energy with public organisations, protagonists of architecture, industry and trade, to support cities for a real improvement of social life. We want light to convert public places and working environments into centres of life **by integrating** it into the surrounding fabric in order to become places where smiles, encounters, looks and handshakes can still have a **meaning**.

Knowledge-based wellbeing.

A new social and individual wellbeing based on **vital energy**, quality of technologies and **know-how**. This is why we have committed ourselves to the search for **products** and **solutions**, to the increase of the **performance** of lighting systems. We have created an ideal, yet concrete story with political, territorial and international initiatives that is oriented towards the future, attracting and supporting the most **scientifically** and **ethically** advanced positive thrusts of contemporary society.

Is there life on Light?

Light generates **innovation** through mutually integrated technological, industrial and design systems. Breakthrough solutions in our **organisation** are created by **constant dialogue** with the international protagonists of projects and ideas, by discussion with best producers of technologies. There's **a great deal of life** in light.

@iGuzziniUK
#LightFirst

iGuzzini

COMMERCIAL, CHALLENGING, PRACTICAL – THE FOUNDATIONS OF OUR APPROACH. FOR OVER 35 YEARS WE HAVE DELIVERED ACCOUNTING AND BUSINESS ADVICE TO ARCHITECTS WITH A VIEW TO HELPING THEM GROW PROSPEROUS PRACTICES.

WHETHER YOU ARE AN ESTABLISHED PRACTICE OR JUST STARTING OUT, CONTACT US TODAY TO SEE HOW WE CAN SUPPORT YOU AND YOUR BUSINESS.

HW-CREATIVE.COM/SECTORS/ARCHITECTURE

Summer Show Supporter

Rogers Stirk Harbour + Partners

A façade of the World Conservation and Exhibitions Centre at the British Museum, London
www.rsh-p.com

Supporters

We are grateful to our generous
supporters and partners:

**Summer Show Main Title
Supporter 2014**
Foster + Partners

Supporters of the Summer Show
Laing O'Rourke
Rogers Stirk Harbour + Partners
Scott Brownrigg
Wilkinson Eyre

Prizes
Allford Hall Monaghan Morris
Make
Max Fordham
Next Limit Technologies

Bartlett Book 2014
Allford Hall Monaghan Morris

Private Reception
Adrem
Haines Watts

**Bartlett International
Lecture Series**
Fletcher Priest Trust

Bursaries
Leverhulme Trust
Rogers Stirk Harbour + Partners

Lighting Supporter
iGuzzini

**Summer Show Opener's Prize
awarded by Michael Webb**
Wilkinson Eyre

Partner
London Festival of Architecture

Foster + Partners

ALLFORD HALL MONAGHAN MORRIS

iGuzzini

Rogers Stirk Harbour + Partners

SCOTT+ BROWNRIGG

Wilkinson Eyre. Architects

LVA
luis vidal + architects

Kite & Laslett

Contents

Bartlett Summer Show 2013, BSc Unit 3 (photo Virgilio Ferreira)

The Bartlett
School of Architecture

The selection of almost 1000 images in this publication represents only a fraction of the work produced by 500 of our students on the RIBA/ARB validated Architecture programmes this year. It's far from an easy task reducing the selection to this figure, so in truth, the catalogue is only a taster, a bumper volume that captures the flavour of the best work in the year. So to start, we wish to express our profound thanks to all students and staff involved in this effort, it is a hugely demanding task on top of the work involved in building The Bartlett Summer Show.

Our BSc and MArch Architecture students are graduating from programmes supported by Technology, History & Theory, Professional Studies, and the School's renowned Design Units. Their talent and commitment enables us to sustain our reputation as a world-leading and diverse community for creative and critical discourse through all manner of spectacular productions, inspired insights, and ambitious dreams.

Bartlett students go on to work not only in architectural practice, but in roles across the creative and built environment sectors, with many founding their own innovative companies that were spawned here. So looking ahead, a key priority for our future is supporting our students into a changing workplace environment. We will continue to respond to the ways our industry and profession are changing, as well as intellectual, cultural and social transformations. We will look to shine a spotlight on the link between experimental study and innovative practice, and in doing so, seek to develop new steps between our capacity for intellectual creativity and the establishment of new practices, disciplines, businesses and cultures.

2014 marks a very particular year in the School's history. For the eleventh year in a row we continue to hold our position as the UK's top-ranked School of Architecture in the AJ100. Our students currently hold all three RIBA President's Medals, and our staff have been nominated for many prestigious awards including the RIBA Stirling Prize. It is also the year in which we move into refitted temporary premises at 140 Hampstead Road, whilst UCL invests over £40m in extending and refurbishing Wates House. And it is also only two years away from our 175th anniversary, for which we have commenced planning.

The next two years will bring unprecedented opportunities for renewal. Our temporary home will have a radically different environment in spaces 6m tall that offer potential for work of a very different kind. BSc and MArch Units will coexist on the same floor in the largest studio space the school has ever enjoyed, and we will have at our disposal an even better set of workshops than before, as well as essential social spaces that we've not had in a very long time. Change is in the air, and The Bartlett School of Architecture is on the move.

Finally, we warmly congratulate our students and staff, whose fascinating and inspiring work makes The Bartlett such an exciting place. We also extend our sincere thanks to all our consultants, critics, examiners, guest speakers, sponsors, faculty and campus colleagues, and friends.

Professor Frédéric Migayrou
Bartlett Professor of Architecture

Professor Bob Sheil
Director of the Bartlett School of Architecture

Student Prizes 2013-14

Bartlett School of Architecture Medal

For students averaging 80% or higher in professional programmes

MArch Architecture
Rodolfo Acevedo Rodriguez, Unit 12
Alistair Browning, Unit 17
Nick Elias, Unit 10
Siyu (Frank) Fan, Unit 10
Daniel Lane, Unit 11
Thomas Pearce, Unit 23
Francis Roper, Unit 16
Sandra Youkhana, Unit 11

BSc Architecture Year 1

Building Design Prize, sponsored by Make
Sophie Percival
Drawing Design Prize, sponsored by Make
Yuanchu Yi
Model Design Prize, sponsored by Make
Ching Kuo

Herbert Batsford Prize
York (Nerissa) Yeung

Next Limit Prize for Digital Visualisation
Iman Datoo
Bethan Ring

BSc Architecture Year 2

Narinder Sagoo Drawing Prize
Boon Yik Cheung, Unit 5

Victor Kite Prize for Design Technology, sponsored by AHMM
Douglas Miller, Unit 4

BSc Architecture Year 3

Distinguished Work in History and Theory
Matthew Bovingdon-Downe, Unit 5

Environmental Design Prize
Max Butler, Unit 4

Fitzroy Robinson Drawing Prize
To be announced

Making Buildings Prize
Harry (Duncan) Clover, Unit 9
Joshua Toh Kai Heng, Unit 8
Songyang Zhou, Unit 3

RIBA Donaldson Medal
To be announced

Professional Studies Prize
Isobel Parnell, Unit 5
Marcus Cole, Unit 9

Dean's List (First Class Honours in BSc Architecture)
Alexandria Anderson, Unit 1
Laurence Blackwell-Thale, Unit 4
Thomas Budd, Unit 8
Max Butler, Unit 4
Xi Yao (Joyce) Chen, Unit 4
Duncan (Harry) Clover, Unit 9
George Courtauld, Unit 6
John Cruwys, Unit 4
Katie Cunningham
David Flook, Unit 4
Ruochong (Robin) Fu, Unit 9
James Hignett, Unit 1
Konrad Holtsmark, Unit 0
Kar Tung (Karen) Ko, Unit 8
Lisa McDanell, Unit 4
Ian Ng, Unit 8
Emily Priest, Unit 1
Eleanor Sampson, Unit 4
Claire P Seagerm, Unit 1
Joshua Stevenson Brown, Unit 8
Samuel Tan, Uni 6
Ivo Tedbury, Unit 9
Joshua Toh Kai Heng, Unit 8
Eleanor Daisy Ursell, Unit 8
Songyang Zhou, Unit 3

BSc Architectural & Interdisciplinary Studies

Distinguished Work in History and Theory
Stephen Henderson

Dean's List (First Class Honours in BSc AIS)
Stephen Henderson

MArch Architecture Year 4

Design Technology Prize
Marcus Stockton, Unit 11

History and Theory Prize
Nicolas Blomstrand, Unit 11
Andre Kullmar, Unit 17

Rogers Stirk Harbour Bursary
Chris Worsfold, Unit 17

Leverhulme Trust Bursary
Ben Ferns, Unit 12

MArch Architecture Year 5

Ambrose Poynter Prize
Jennifer Dyne, Unit 11

Fitzroy Robinson Drawing Prize
Rodolfo Acevedo Rodriguez,
Unit 12

Leverhulme Trust Bursary
Rodolfo Acevedo Rodriguez,
Unit 12

**Max Fordham Environmental
Design Prize**
Daniel Lane, Unit 11

**RIBA President's Medals
Dissertation Prize Nominee**
Leon Fenster, Unit 12
Thesis Tutor: Prof Murray Fraser

Sir Andrew Taylor Prize
Francis Roper, Unit 16

Sir Banister Fletcher Medal
Nick Elias, Unit 10

**Dean's List (Distinction
in MArch Architecture)**
Rodolfo Acevedo Rodriguez,
Unit 12
Benjamin Murray Allan, Unit 16
William Armstrong, Unit 11
Kairo Baden-Powell, Unit 24
Sonal Balasuriya, Unit 18
Alastair Browning, Unit 17
Ko Wai Cheung, Unit 22
Aleksandra Natalia Cicha, Unit 23
Jason Coe, Unit 12
Daniel Cotton, Unit 24

Anthony D'Auria, Unit 18
Natalia Eddy, Unit 16
Nicholas Elias, Unit 10
Frank Siyu Fan, Unit 10
Leon Fenster, Unit 12
Sarah Firth, Unit 22
Ryan Edward Hakiman, Unit 10
Thomas Hopkins, Unit 20
Mara-Sophia Kanthak, Unit 11
Anja Leigh Kempa, Unit 10
Woojong Kim, Unit 10
Alastair King, Unit 12
Matthew Lacey, Unit 19
Jason Lamb, Unit 10
Daniel Lane, Unit 11
Chun Yin (Samson) Lau, Unit 10
Wai Yue Law, Unit 20
Tess Martin, Unit 21
Joseph Paxton, Unit 11
Thomas Pearce, Unit 23
Joanna Preston, Unit 22
Samuel Rackham, Unit 12
Francis Roper, Unit 16
Javier Ruiz, Unit 20
Sayan Skandarajah, Unit 21
Louis Sullivan, Unit 12
Antonina Tkachenko, Unit 21
Athanasios Varvanas, Unit 18
Daniel Wilkinson, Unit 12
Kirsty Sarah Williams, Unit 17
Emily Yan, Unit 20
Sandra Youkhana, Unit 11
Mika Helen Zacharias, Unit 17
Shuo Zhang, Unit 19

Postgraduate Diploma in
Professional Practice &
Management in Architecture
(ARB/RIBA Part 3)

Ross Jamieson Memorial Prize
Michelle Barlow
Dean Walker

2013 RIBA Medals

**Bronze President's Medal for
Best Part 1 Design Project**
Vanessa Lafoy, BSc Architecture,
Unit 8

**Silver President's Medal for
Best Design Project at Part 2**
Ben Hayes, MArch Architecture,
Unit 17

**President's Medal
for Dissertation**
Tamsin Hanke, MArch
Architecture, Unit 17
Thesis Tutor: Sophia Psarra

**Shortlisted, RIBA President's
Award for Outstanding Master's
Degree Thesis**
Isabelle Priest, MA Architectural
History

**Winner, RIBA President's Award
for Outstanding PhD Thesis**
Dr Ricardo Agarez, PhD
Architectural History & Theory
Supervisor: Prof Adrian Forty

Academic Streams

Director of Design, Professor Christine Hawley

The process of design is at the core of architecture, painting and sculpture, yet today the term extends far beyond the realm of these classical disciplines. Lived experience encompasses all facets of the environment: physical, experiential and climatological. Design at The Bartlett School of Architecture has a dual emphasis on both production and on the ideas that lead to all manner of speculation about the future. We encourage and emphasise experimentation that is informed by social responsibility and stimulated by the creative dialogue between writing and making.

Director of History & Theory, Professor Iain Borden

Architectural history and theory is a staging post, a place of reflection, a continual project. It is omnipresent: every architect, historian, theorist – knowingly or not – uses some intersection of history and theory every time they design, document, discuss or speculate. At The Bartlett, history and theory interjects at all levels, from encounters with buildings to the elaboration of critical processes, from public discussions to individually focused research projects, and from factually-based empirical studies to theorised speculations and creative writing practices.

Director of Technology, Professor Bob Sheil

What is evident in their work is that Bartlett students approach technology, environmental and computing modules as ambitious design challenges, not areas of stand-alone study. This practice is nurtured by an extraordinarily dedicated and diverse staff collective, around 20 in number, in a progression of sequential steps from the deep end of Year 1, to the testing grounds of Years 2, 4, and the laboratories of Years 3 and 5.

Director of Professional Studies, Susan Ware

We question the role and function of the architect in an industry which is in a state of constant change. Students' ambitions and career aspirations are nurtured through innovative Professional Studies courses and informal advice on practice and employment. The school has an outstanding track record in the range of practices that graduates join, ranging from small specialist design practices to multidisciplinary global conglomerates.

Director of Research, Dr Yeoryia Manolopoulou

Our world-leading research emerges from the understanding that architecture is a transdisciplinary subject. It engages with social, political, environmental and urbanist concerns, resulting in diverse outputs: from books and buildings to installations and urban proposals, which exert a considerable international influence on architectural design and scholarship. The School achieved the highest national rating among the Architecture and Built Environment submissions to the UK 2008 Research Assessment Exercise (RAE), with the highest percentage of world-leading 4* staff outputs. Results for the Research Excellence Framework (REF 2014) will be out later this year.

Bartlett Programmes

The Bartlett School of Architecture offers a comprehensive range of architecture programmes. Some are aimed at those seeking to become professional architects, while others specialise in advanced architectural design, history and theory and urban design. All enjoy an international reputation, and attract the very best students from around the UK, Europe and worldwide.

Undergraduate
BSc Architecture (ARB/RIBA Part 1)
3 year, full time (FT) study plus 1 year in practice

Postgraduate
MArch Architecture (ARB/RIBA Part 2)
2 years FT

Pg Dip in Professional Practice and Management in Architecture (ARB/RIBA Part 3)
6-12 months part-time (PT) study plus 24 months in practice

Undergraduate
BSc Architectural & Interdisciplinary Studies
3 years FT / 4 years FT with a year abroad

B-Pro MArch Graduate Architectural Design (GAD)
12 months FT

B-Pro MArch Urban Design (UD)
12 months FT

MA Architectural History and Theory
12 months FT

Pg Cert in Advanced Architectural Research
3 months FT / up to 2 years PT

MPhil/PhD Architectural Design
3 years FT / 6 years PT

MPhil/PhD Architectural History & Theory
3 years FT / 6 years PT

Summer School
2 weeks in August

Summer Foundation
6 weeks from July to August

Bartlett Springboard
3 months

SOTA-Bartlett Pop-up
10-day workshop

We are nearly 175 years old

In 2016 we will be 175 years old.

Thomas Leverton Donaldson was appointed as UCL's first Chair in Architecture in 1841, inaugurating university-based architectural education in the UK, founding what later became The Bartlett School of Architecture.

To celebrate this milestone we are aiming to organise a number of one-off celebrations throughout the year, and in addition, establish a new fund for student bursaries.

The School will be looking for support from friends, alumni, associates, and followers, as the grand occasion unfolds.

More details will be announced soon at
www.bartlett.ucl.ac.uk/architecture

BSc Architecture ARB/RIBA Part 1
30

BSc Architectural & Interdisciplinary Studies
140

Bartlett Summer Show 2013, MArch Unit 20 (photo Virgilio Ferreira)

Year 1

Homing In: The First Year in Architecture

Frosso Pimenides, Patrick Weber

Special thanks to: Abi Abdolwahabi, Richard Beckett, Bim Burton, Emmanuel Vercruysse and Nick Westby from The Bartlett Workshop, and to Rachel Antonio, Danielle Hodgson and Afra van't Land

Thanks to Carol Swords, James Willis, and all the staff of Sir John Soane's Museum and Pitzhanger Manor

Year 1 Staff: Dimitri Argyros, Tim Barwell, Charlotte Bocci, Mary Duggan, Elie Lakin, Lucy Leonard, Brian O'Reilly, Sara Shafiei, Matt Springett

Architectural Media Studies Tutor: Joel Cady

The Bartlett School of Architecture 2014

The Bartlett's BSc degree programme aims to develop a creative, diverse and rigorous approach to architecture and design from the outset. Year 1 is centred on the design studio and is taught to the year as a whole. Students learn to observe, draw, model and design through a series of creative tasks, before embarking on an individual small building project sited in the context of London.

————The main intention of the first year at The Bartlett is to explore 'ways of seeing' – understanding and interpreting objects, events and places, and learning to look beyond the visible into the unseen qualities of things and places. In this way, a place can also be seen as something with its own identity, which each student can interpret. The importance of character and personality is emphasised throughout the design process, whether it concerns analysis, site interpretation or architectural vision. A number of recording techniques are used as a way of clarifying the subject. By being aware of the possibilities and limitations of techniques, each student learns to develop an idea for an architectural proposition critically and independently. The aim is to be serious yet playful, passionate and ruthlessly experimental – always pushing the boundaries of possible realities.

————The life of our first year students is a continuous process of testing, questioning, rethinking and visually communicating a series of design explorations over the course of the year as part of a studio culture, a community and the city of London. It is a journey of learning skills and knowledge that give students the tools to think, experiment, make lots of mistakes, celebrate their failures and, finally, have fun designing.

————Students began the year by exploring their own domestic environments through drawing and making. After this they worked in groups on an installation project in Sir John Soane's country house, Pitzhanger Manor in Ealing. Each of the six groups created a site-specific interpretation of a member of Soane's household. Students worked collaboratively to conceive, prototype, test and craft their 1:1 temporary installations. The individual designs explored the relationship and spaces of the Chambermaid, the Footman, the Housemaid, the Butler, the Cook and the Coachman, and their spatial relationship to the Soane family.

————The second term started with an expedition to Barcelona. Three spaces were explored and recorded in a travel diary. This was closely followed by a trip to Margate and Broadstairs on the Kent coast. After making a short survey exploring the history and topography of the place, each student embarked on the design of a Seasonal Hermitage for a specific site within the fabric of Margate and Broadstairs. The buildings had to accommodate a domestic and a seasonal aspect.

Year 1

Linzi Ai, Richard Aina, Yat Au Yeung, Amelia Black, James Bradford, Hoi Chan, Bingqing Chen, Hoi Cheung, Lester Cheung, Yan Cheung, Jooyoung Cho, Maria Chodzen, Deedee Chung, Conor Clarke, Carrie Coningsby, Alessandro Conning-Rowland, Jack Cox, Charlotte Creber, Iman Datoo, Samuel Davies, Danny Dimbleby, Judy El-Hajjar, Iona Farrar-Bell, Peter Feehily, Alexander Findley, Dan Florescu, Christopher Grennan, Yangzi Guo, Melina Hadjiargyrou, Una Haran, Sarah Hollis, Ana-Maria Ilusca, Marta Jakubowska, Yufan Jin, Maria Junco, Emma Jurczynski, Klaudia Kepinska, Karolina Kielb, Jaejun Kim, Cheuk Ko, Ching Kuo, Yik Lai, Andrew Leather, Kwok Li, Yi Ning Lui, Xiao Ma, Divesh Mayaramani, Benjamin Mehigan, Liam Merrigan, Jun Mo, Iman Mohd Hadzhalie, Michael Mcadam, Adam Moqrane, Maria Moustroufi, Samuel Napleton, Xin Ng, Hoi Ngan, Maryna Omelchenko, Fola-Sade Oshinusi, Yu Pan, Achilleas Papakyriakou, Minesh Patel, Sophie Percival, Joseph Philo Powell, Calvin Po, Sze Poon, Duangkaew Protpagorn, Charles Redman, Manpreet Riat, Andrew Riddell, Bethan Ring, Samuel Rix, Joanna Rzewuska, Shona Sharma, Frederick Sheppard, Issui Shioura, Isaac Simpson, Yip Siu, Benjamin Sykes-Thompson, Sheau Tam, Nihal Tamang, Matthew Taylor, Rachael Taylor, Olufunto Thompson, Minh Tran, Tze-Chuan Tung, Hoang Vu, Fei Waller, Ngai Wang, Chun Wong, Kate Woodcock-Fowles, Ella Wragg, Xinyue Yao, Adeola Yemitan, Sum Yeung, Yuanchu Yi, York (Nerissa) Yeung, Wing Yiu, Yinong Zhang, Meng Zhao, Yehan Zheng

Fig. Y1.1 Soane Installations on site outside Pitzhanger Manor House in Ealing in December 2013. **Fig. Y1.2** 'The Chambermaid'. The installation focuses on the link between the rhythmical repetition in Soane's escapist morning walks to Pitzhanger Manor and the repetition inherent in his chambermaid's tasks: scrubbing and dusting, with a particular focus on the biannual dying of the curtains yellow with turmeric. Operated through a repetitive straining action, it forces the viewer into a crouch position to glimpse the ground at floor level on the Pitzhanger façade. **Fig. Y1.3** 'The Butler'. The installation explores the role of the butler within the household, with a clear distinction between the back and the front. From the back the 'butler' controls what the viewer sees on the front side, guiding them through his daily routine.

Crucial also is the difference between the day, with its endless polishing, and the night-lit experience of the piece, which alludes to Soane's obsession with entertaining his guests. **Fig. Y1.4** 'The Housemaid'. A series of frames assembled as an analogy of the serving experience of a housemaid's daily routine in the Soane family: the opening and closing of shutters, the lighting of fires, and the whitening of the floors. Through the opening of each different frame, a sense of enclosure is created. It is a performance of the invisible hand, with shadows and silhouettes of the user reflected on frames with different symbolic treatment of materials, thicknesses and positions.

Y1.2

Y1.3

Y1.4

Fig. Y1.5 'The Cook'. The installation explores the three distinct conditions of cooking, cleaning and sleeping hidden in Soane's kitchen throughout a daily routine. Inspired by the processes of culinary preservation of the era, it is trying to capture the sensational experience of food through methods of hanging, drying and concealing. Scents are embedded in pockets to represent the effort made to mask repulsive smells; these smells longer upon the user as a live memory of Soane's household. Fig. Y1.6 'The Footman'. This installation shows the paradox between the life and chores of the footman and Sir John Soane. The footman's life, being the dark and hidden underworld, in which the dirty and menial chores must be done, and Soane being the clean and perfectly formed front shown to the public. Soane's relentless control means these

routines fit together in perfect equilibrium of two worlds, one above and one below. Fig. Y1.7 'The Coachman'. This installation explores the peculiar relationship between Soane and the Coachman, focusing on the hierarchy of control between the two. The hand movements of the 'controller' cause the framed views of the 'experiencer' to change, mirroring the control that the coachman has over Soane's environment while travelling. Looking through the viewfinder the 'experiencer' is shown the view of either the Coachman or Soane from their positions when arriving at Pitzhanger. Each of the suspended frames shows the thresholds visible to each. Soane has a clear view, looking straight through the building, whereas the coachman has an obstructed view with the thresholds overlapping.

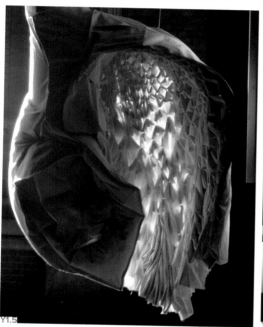

Fig. Y1.8 Judy El-Hajjar 'Fossil Hunter's House in Margate'. The building is constructed of chalk-lined concrete with timber frames housing the fossil collection. Two distinct but interweaving routes separate the public from the private areas. The collector has views to the sea to study the weather. **Fig. Y1.9 Wing Yip Siu** 'A House for the Last Fisherman in Margate and his Seagulls'. Organised as a complex compact tower this dwelling is oriented to the owners fishing grounds and his boat. The project is an exploration of the enduring symbiotic relationship between fisherman and seagulls. The tower accommodates dwelling space for both, as well as a small shop for bycatch. Built from chalk-lined concrete the building will erode over time. **Fig. Y1.10 Samuel Davies** 'A House in Memory of Margate's Lost Butcher'. When a hoard of animal bones were recently discovered buried in Margate harbour, it came to light that a Georgian butchers shop once occupied site. The architecture is drawn out of this memory, a detailed observation of anatomy and the requirements to preserve meat in two ways: one quickly over 30 days and one annually. The building envelope has been designed to catch wind and enhance the dry-curing process through enhanced airflow. **Fig. Y1.11 Yunachi Yi** 'Margate Tailor's Residence'. The building is located within a terrace of historical shop buildings facing the sea. A tailor shop, a dwelling and a studio fills the narrow site and connects the rear street to the promenade. The building is constructed of timber beams and columns forming a matrix with a threadlike sewn cladding forming a rain- and sun-screen.

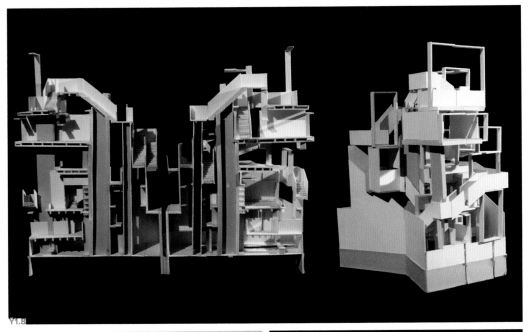

Y1.8

Y1.9

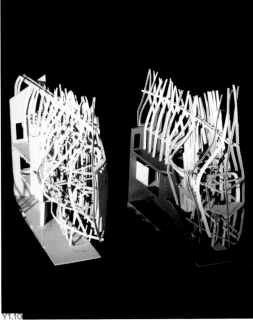

Y1.10

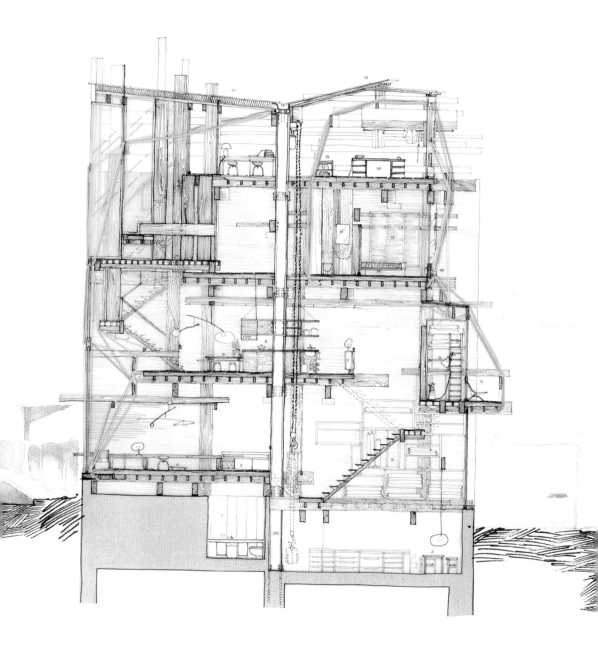

Y1.11

Fig. Y1.12 – Y1.13 Ching Kuo 'The Fisherman's House'. The Fisherman's House in Broadstairs is a dwelling that doubles as a kiosk for the preparation, cooking and selling of the season's bycatch fish. Studies into the filleting of fish have led to the development of a series of vertical slices and folds that act as primary structural steel fixed back into the cliff. Within these frames a secondary timber structure is hung. These house the main accommodation. The photos show a series of development models used to explore the structure and define the inhabited spaces. **Fig. Y1.14 Issui Shihora** 'A House for a Rain Collector'. The project weaves a series of spaces for living with notions of how to collect and celebrate water through large-scale models exploring themes such as lighting and materiality. The private sequence of spaces are arranged at

the core of the building while the public can occupy the ground and the roof. Both public and private are able to experience a sequence of spaces centred around the theme of water. **Fig. Y1.15 Achilleas Papakyriakou** 'A House for a Beachcomber'. The project is driven by a journey both for the public but also for the owner who is a beachcomber. A defined route which begins on the beach as a series of fragmented workbenches wraps around the site. Views from neighbouring buildings as well as the accommodation are carved out of this route. A structural wall houses the collection as well as the living and working spaces and connects the beach to the promenade above.

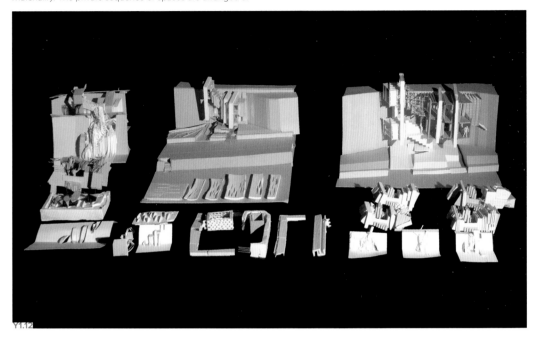

Y1.12

Y1.13

Y1.14

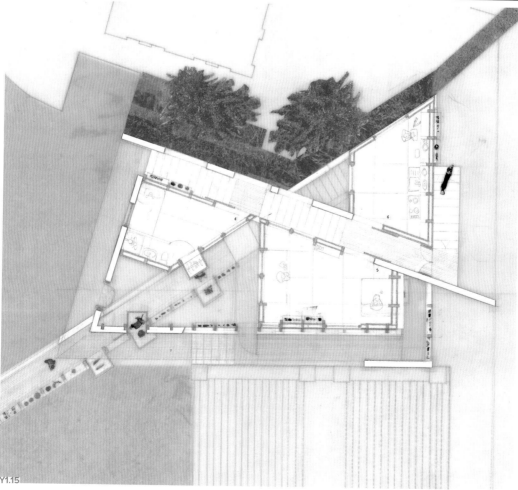

Y1.15

Fig. Y1.16 – Y1.17 **York (Nerissa) Yeung** 'The Backyard Handyman of Margate'. The design responds to the context and the relationship of the site to the surrounding context. The building is a house and a workshop for a handyman. The form and materiality are driven by connections to neighbouring buildings in which the handyman works as well as exploring how to store objects and tools within the walls of the house. The project creates a series of visual and physical connections to it's ultimate and wider context. **Fig. Y1.18 Sophie Percival** 'A House for a Cleaner and a Landscape for the Beach Visitor'. The project explores the notion of how bamboo can naturally clean dirty water which regularly floods the site at high tide. The building is nestled within three walls of concrete and bamboo. The private accommodation braces between the walls while the ground floor provides a series of lockers, paddling pools and showers for the visitors of the beach. These spaces are carved out of the walls and the newly created landscape on the ground floor.

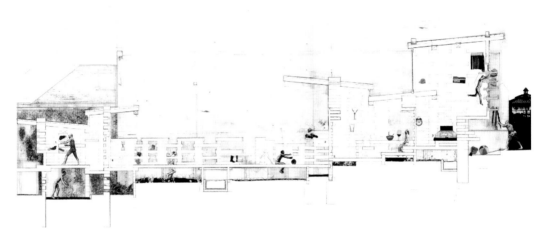

Y1.16

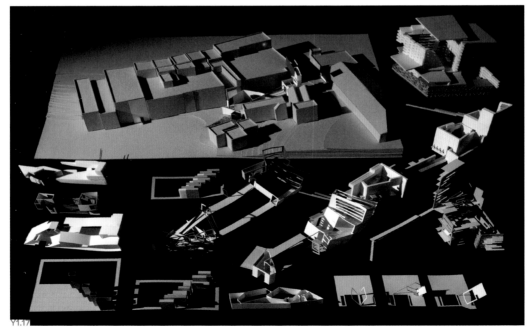

Y1.17

1.

2.

3.

4.

5.

6.

7.

Unit O

Movement London

Murray Fraser, Justin C.K. Lau

Year 2
Francis Hardy, Douglas
Kakuda Croll, Ka Yi Kwan,
Yi Ki Liong, Zi (Kevin) Meng

Year 3
Rufus Edmondson,
Alexandra Edwards,
Christian Georcelin,
Konrad Holtsmark,
Suhee Kim, Tomiris
Kupzhassarova, Julia
Rutkoska, Jack Sardeson,
Benedict Tay, Henrietta
Watkins, Zisheng (Andrew)
Yap, Park Hin Yeung

Term 1 Workshop tutors:
Nicholas Szczepaniak,
Guan Lee, Ifigeneia Liangi

Technical tutors: Aran
Chadwick, Laura Guerrini,
Ewa Hazla, Richard Townend,
Bill Watts

Thanks to our guest critics:
Francisco Alcazar, Laura
Allen, Peter Besley, Matthew
Butcher, Jason Chan, Mollie
Claypool, Ben Cowd, James
Curtis, Pierre D'Avoine,
Reenie Elliott, William
Firebrace, Jon Goodbun,
Jeong Hye, Damjan Iliev,
Arthur Kay, Yoonjin Kim, Ben
Kirk, Julian Krüger, Chee-Kit
Lai, Ifigeneia Liangi, CJ Lim,
Guan Lee, Claudio Leoni,
Ian Lomas, Samar Maqusi,
Jane McAllister, Tony Monk,
Jack Newton, Emily Pavlatou,
Frosso Pimenides, Rodolfo
Rodriguez, Jack Sargent,
Sara Shafiei, Yara Sharif,
Helen Sisley, Sarah Stevens,
Nicholas Szczepaniak,
Ben Stringer, Chris Wilkinson

We are grateful to our
supporters and partners
Make, Bean Buro, Guan Lee
and Grymsdyke Farm

The Bartlett School of Architecture 2014

Unit 0's main aim is for students to learn how to carry out intensive research – into contemporary architectural ideas, urban conditions, cultural relations, practices of everyday life – and then use their findings to propose innovative forms of architecture. Students are asked to grasp the unique speculative space offered by academic study and combine this with a commitment to social engagement, as if their projects were actually going to be built. A clear understanding of technological, environmental and developmental issues is seen as vital.

———In order to develop their design proposals, students are expected to capitalise on the full range of methods of investigation and representation: physical models, digital fabrication, photography, drawings, computer models, renderings, animations and films. In their approach, students should allow for intuitive and spontaneous design-based responses. After all, strong design ideas produced by speculative or lateral thinking can stimulate specific theoretical investigations just as much as the other way around.

———Our theme for this year's design investigation is 'movement' in the city. It can be related to the movement of people within the urban environment. Or it can be about the movement of vehicles, birds or of more ephemeral elements like the wind, rain, light and sound. By looking at London as a 'movement economy', or in more social and aesthetic terms as a 'city in motion', we posed the question: How might this be used to trigger new architectural ideas?

———In Term 1 students took part in a workshop to make sizeable prototypical objects and spaces that encapsulated the concept and realities of movement. Students then chose their own site in London for the main project. How could their design add to the importance and exhilaration of movement in the city? Student projects explored the notion of movement to propose new kinds of building uses that could encourage and enhance urban and cultural interaction. The final designs are architectural propositions that have clear structural and environmental qualities, addressing aspects of technology, craft and the means of production.

———On our field trip to Seoul in South Korea, we explored a fascinating and highly digitised city in which pressures of the movement of people, goods and data is ever-present. We linked up with local universities and leading practices to discover what is happening there architecturally.

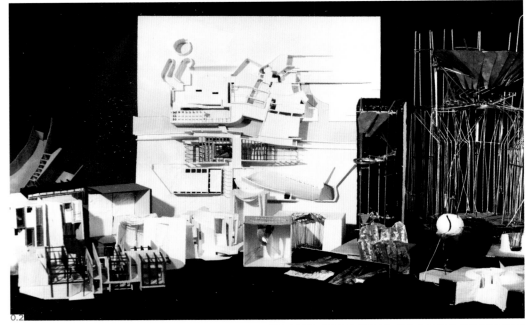

0.2

0.3

0.4

Fig. 0.1 **Konrad Holtsmark** Y3, 'Sunken Space for Contemplation', Regent's Park, London NW1, physical model. Those who might be seeking solace can retreat to these sunken hollows set within the park, and whenever there are enough believers gathered together and standing on the floor-plate, the resulting weight triggers the unexpected opening of the roof 'petal' segments overhead – immediately transforming one's experience of these internal spaces.

Fig. 0.2 – 0.5 **Konrad Holtsmark** Y3, 'Monastery for Gardening Monks', Regent's Park, London NW1. Collective photograph of all of the study models for the project; part-section showing the daylight lighting for the main chapel; model of the final design; digital render of the exterior. Set in a near-future scenario when government cuts have meant that the state is no longer able to afford to maintain Regent's Park, this project envisages a monastery for a set of ecologically focused monks who give up their lives to collect the plant waste in the park, process it in anaerobic digesters, and generally involve themselves in work that combines religious devotion with a real desire to improve London's green environment.

0.5

Fig. 0.6 Benadict Tay Y3, 'Water Droplet Screens', model photograph. This research project developed fine screens of fishing wire and natural resin as prototypes for an external building fabric that could collect rainfall, then release it slowly as droplets, so that it dripped for effect over a period of hours. **Fig. 0.7 Park Hin Yeung** Y3, 'Self-Growing Restaurant', Kings Cross Goodsyard, WC1, interior render. This scheme imagines that the Kings Cross redevelopment area next to incoming Eurostar trains will be transformed into a self-sufficient growing zone where hydroponic tubes and terraced planters are mixed with vegetarian restaurants where visitors brush up against a new breed of urban farmers. **Fig. 0.8 Douglas Kakuda Croll** Y2, 'Auto-Instrument', physical model. This prosthetic, worn under one's jacket, and played and strummed when passing through

the city, creates a different aural experience of London.
Fig. 0.9 Jack Sardeson Y3, 'New-Wave Health Clinic', Farringdon Road, EC1, exploded isometric. In a future where bacteria have become resistant to current antibiotics, this project suggests an innovative form of health clinic where patients can be fully isolated and hence escape fear of hospital super-bugs. It also revives the past history of the now-buried Fleet River, turning it into a passageway leading to the new Crossrail station, and harking back to the Fleet's medieval reputation as a spa with healing waters.

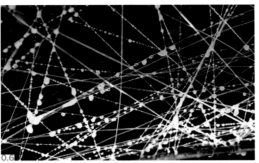

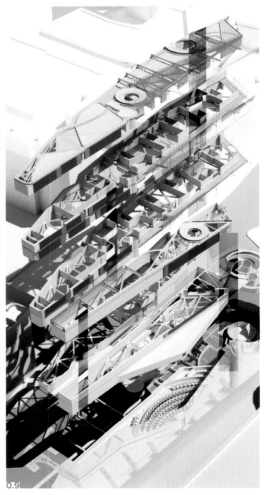

44

Fig. 0.10 **Yi Ki Liong** Y2, 'Carving and Casting', Hampstead Road, NW1, CADCAM model. Using cut-and-fill landscaping to mirror the nearby sunken mainline railway into Euston Station, this scheme for a local housing estate proposes a layered landscape with play spaces for all ages. **Fig. 0.11 Ka Yi Kwan** Y2, 'Fringe Theatre', Torbat Street, NW1, night-time render. Using an interlocking timber junction system from Japanese precedent, this is a small loose-fit theatre just off the Camden hipster drag, where audience and performers mix easily.
Fig. 0.12 **Zisheng (Andrew) Yap** Y3, 'Organically Grown Market and Restaurant', Oxford Street, W1. Borrowing from Hackney's organic restaurants that grow their own food, this project is for a food market and hydroponic growing centre at the east end of Oxford Street, set above an entrance to the Crossrail station.

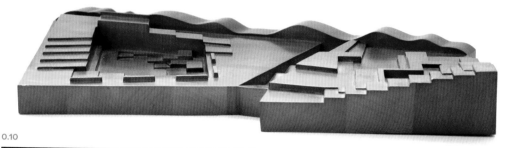

0.10

0.11

0.12

Fig. 0.13 Julia Rutkoska Y3, 'Prisoners' Rehabilitation Workshop', Bloomfontein Road, W12. Model photograph. Given the high number of prisoners that re-offend, here is a workshop facility in west London where offenders can produce furniture and other items to sell to members of the local population using the neighbourhood park in which it is situated. **Fig. 0.14 Rufus Edmondson** Y3, 'Flutter'. Rendered image of illuminated fluttering object. The project comprised an investigation into a number of fascinating and beautiful lightweight objects, each of them held in place by a minimal tensegrity structure. Here is shown a study for an illuminated lit lantern which forms part of the glimmering aesthetic of the lightweight suspended structure at night. **Fig. 0.15 – 0.16 Zi (Kevin) Meng** Y2, 'Kensal Green Crematorium', Harrow Road,

W10. Rendered interior images. This new-look crematorium, set within a beautiful existing cemetery, includes a variety of exquisite contemplative spaces that are closely linked to the painful processes of cremation and memory. **Fig. 0.17 Jack Sardeson** Y3, 'Water-Activated Light Fitting', Fleet River Tunnel, Farringdon Road, EC1, technical section of light fitting. In a scheme to reclaim the culverted and buried Fleet River, which is now no longer a passageway for London's sewage, but which still suffers from flooding, this investigatory produced a full-scale prototype of an installed device that would automatically open up and light the Fleet River Tunnel whenever there was no water present and yet which would be triggered and closed whenever the tunnel started to become inundated with water.

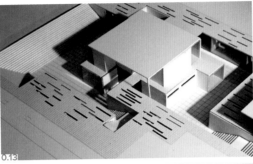

0.13

0.14

0.15

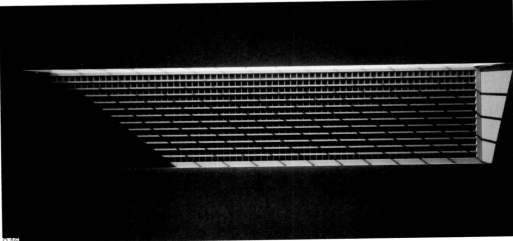

0.16

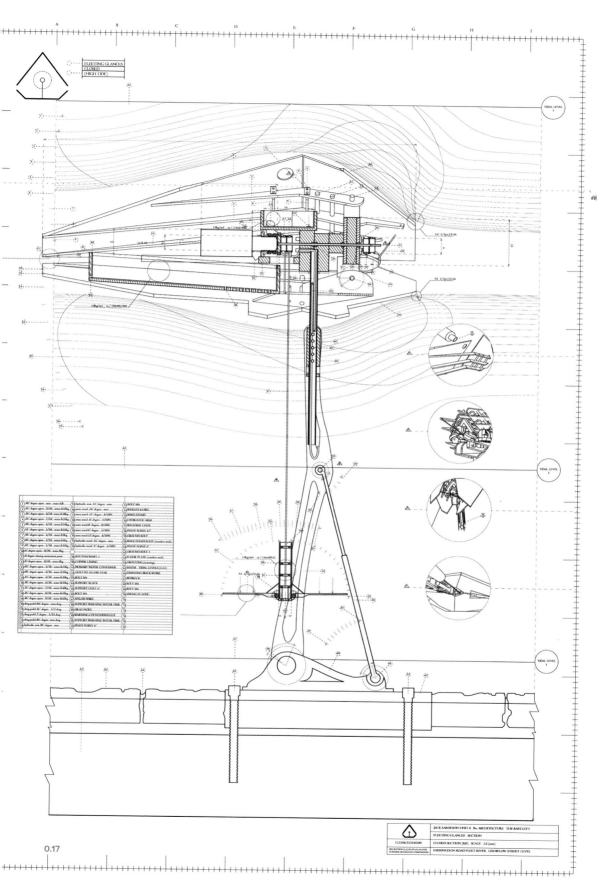

Fig. 0.18 – 0.19 **Alexandra Edwards** Y3, 'Folding Screen Studies for London Bus Stops and for Health Rehabilitation Centre', Hampstead Heath environs, NW3, rendered sometic and photos of physical model. Using a colourful illuminated palette of materials and lighting effects for an initial project to design far livelier and attractive bus stops for London's dreary streets, here a similar line of investigation went into how one might subtly alter the daylight levels inside treatment rooms and courtyard spaces for a new health building where patients can undergo special treatment and/or physiotherapy for problems with joint movements in their arms and legs. **Fig. 0.20 Christian Georcelin** Y3, 'Superbike', rendered image. This research project imagined a new superbike in which 30 or so cyclists could combine to provide a collective transport service that would only strengthen their hand in London, showing would-be critics also the wider health and energy-generation benefits of using mass cycle-power as a major alternative power source for the capital. This premise was then incorporated into a theme for a major project to design a cyclists' social/leisure hub located close to Old Street roundabout.

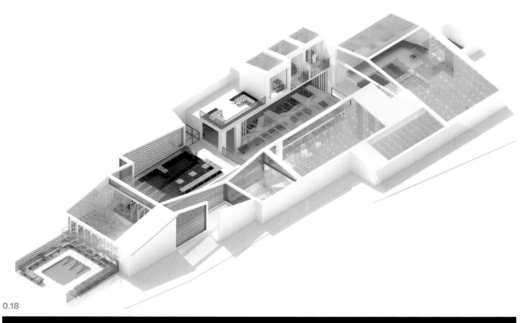

0.18

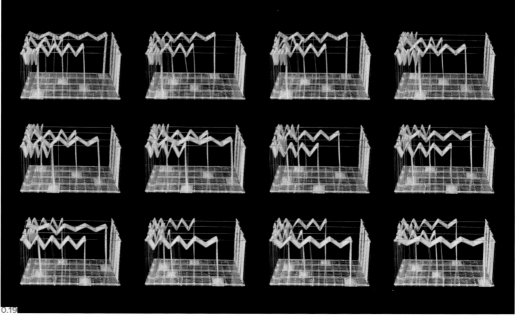

0.19

Unit 1

Civic Spectacular

Holly Lewis, Sabine Storp

Year 2
Florence Bassa, Nicola Chan, Pui Quan Choi, Christopher Dembinski, Mouna Kalla-Sacranie, Alan Ma, Tobias Petyt, Cara Williams

Year 3
Alexandria Anderson, Jessica Clements, Jamie Hignett, Aiko Nakada, Emily Priest, Claire Seager, Joe Travers-Jones, Timmy Whitehouse

Special thanks to Samson Adjei and to our sponsors, Pho, Once Milano Linen and Viaduct Furniture

Thanks to our consultants and critics: Nicola Antaki, Kyle Buchanan, Margaret Bursa, Mollie Claypool, Rebecca Fode, Oliver Goodhall, Caroline Newton, Luke Royffe, Peg Rawes, Patrick Weber, Jonas Zukauskas

Thanks to our hosts in Hanoi: National University of Civil Engineering, Vietnam Urban Planning and Development Association, Vo Trong Nghia Architects, Tran Yen The and The Son Nguyen

Unit 1 is interested in architecture as a force for collective good in the city. Our projects intend to provoke discourse and thought through social endeavour and spectacular interventions.

————We began the year by investigating London's designated 'Opportunity and Intensification Areas'. These are places of financial growth and numerous development opportunities, but also of displacement and infrastructural pressure. Our design proposals for these sites sought to reinvigorate forgotten spaces and realise the latent civic potential of underused sites. Throughout the project we produced a series of publications in order to communicate our ideas to wider, non-professional audiences.

————Whilst rapid, the pace of urban change in London is still vastly outmatched by that of Asia's large cities. For our second project, we focused on the impacts of such change on the inhabitants of Hanoi, Vietnam's capital city. Rapid urban growth and increasing development pressure is leading to greater competition for land use in Hanoi. In particular this threatens urban agriculture, which in Hanoi currently meets nearly 75% of the city's food demand. Conversion to non-agricultural urban uses presents a dilemma to Hanoi's inhabitants: balancing food security and affordability against profit. This rapid population expansion also puts pressure on the city's infrastructure, open spaces and cultural heritage.

————Our projects make proposals to address these issues by making creative responses to the economic, cultural and social dynamics of the city. The outcomes combine low cost, small-scale projects, dexterous medium-scale architectural interventions and ambitious large-scale visions for the future of Hanoi.

Fig. 1.1 **Jamie Hignett** Y3, 'Non_Civic Centre'. Provides essential services for non-registered citizens such as clean water and biogas produced from the waste of the nearby wholesale market, and social services such as access to microfinance, the Internet and meeting spaces for local grassroots democracy groups. Fig. 1.2 **Florence Bassa** Y2, 'Red River Community Building'. A nursery and workspace for the community, with floating emergency towers providing clean water, food and medicine in preparation for floods. The rooftops are cultivated and a natural filtering system cleans water, creating a marshy landscape around the nursery. Fig. 1.3 **Pui Quan Choi** Y2, 'Diabetes Medical Centre'. Rapid urbanisation has caused changes in Vietnamese lifestyle and diet which has in part has led to a rise in Type 2 Diabetes.

The design of the building was inspired by the Cu Da noodle village where sheets of noodles are hung all around the village, influencing the idea of a layered façade and thin structural columns. Fig. 1.4 **Nicola Chan** Y2, 'Street Vendor's Retirement Home'. A retirement home for Hanoi's street vendors; the building provides a safe haven for this banned community where the architecture is informed by the livelihoods and methodologies of Vietnamese street vending. Fig. 1.5 – 1.7 **Alexandria Anderson** Y3, 'The Hanoi Institute of Utilities'. The institute presents a model for sustainable and exciting development, proposing a research and experimental playground for modular, rotationally moulded systems which aim to facilitate architecture and infrastructure; building on sustainability and the potential of Hanoi's future growth.

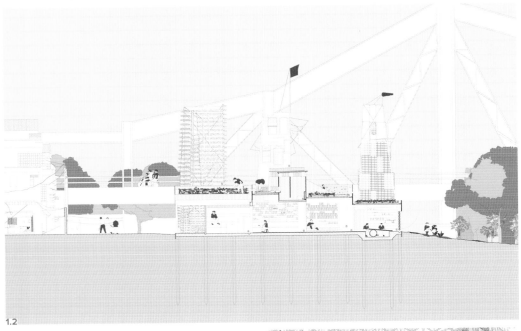

1.2

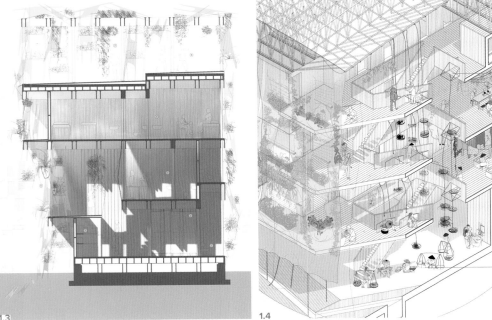

1.3

1.4

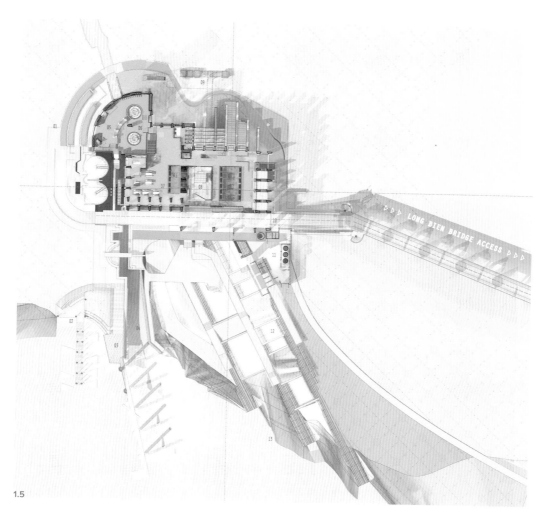

1.5

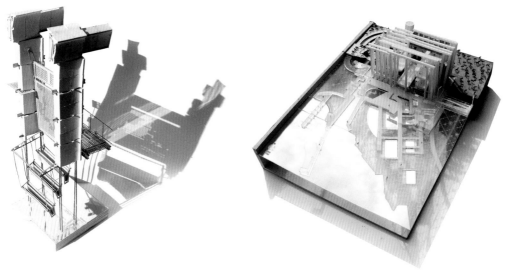

1.6

1.7

Fig. 1.8 **Alan Ma** Y2, 'Community Garden in Homerton Park', model. The main canopy acts as a central hub with movable units that can be transferred to Homerton University Hospital for patients and staff, and also as a learning activity for children. The back of the garden will be turned into a lavender field bring a piece of the countryside into the city. **Fig. 1.9 Cara Williams** Y2, 'Honesty Jam Factory', Ridley Road Market, Dalston, model. The building collects leftover fruit and vegetables. During the day jam is produced and stallholders are given free tea and breakfast. **Fig. 1.10 Aiko Nakada** Y3, 'The Wedding Tent Construction School'. Teaching students the craft of building temporary bamboo pavilions for wedding events, as well as treating bamboo in the traditional Vietnamese fashion. The building allows flooding to replenish the groundscape for the new season of weddings. Burning old wedding tents breathes life into new bamboo during the smoking process. **Fig. 1.11 Jessica Clements** Y3, 'Communal House for Lost Communities'. A modern version of a Vietnamese communal house, which serves political, economic and social functions. An overgrown green cafe structure seeks to provide not only a solar and acoustic barrier but also to connect the inhabitants with their rural heritage. **Fig. 1.12 – 1.13 Timmy Whitehouse** Y3, 'Village on Long Bien Bridge', drawings. Repurposing the Long Bien Bridge to create an elevated village for the floating migrant communities of the Red River. The project fosters the ideas of user initiated development and is implemented though an adaptable kit of parts, consisting mainly of bamboo elements.

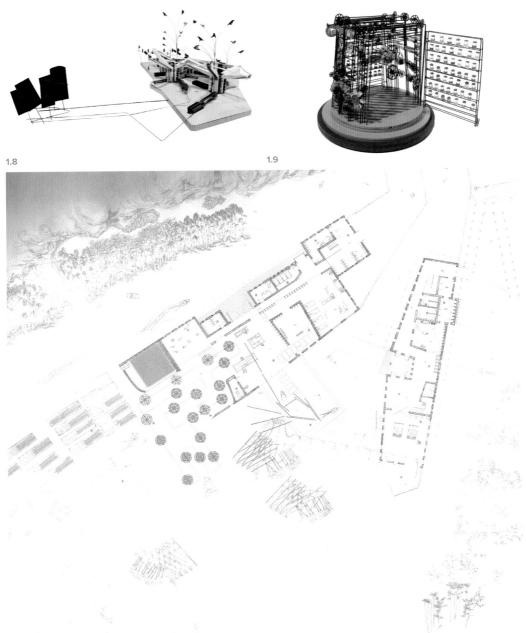

1.8

1.9

1.10

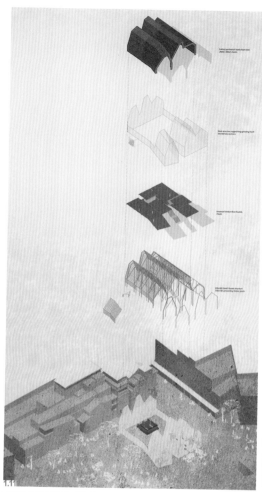

1.11

1.12

1.13

Fig. 1.14 **Christophe Dembinski** Y2, 'Hanoi Physio Centre', drawing. In response to growing problems of air pollution, constant excessive noise, a lack of green spaces and a culture of health and exercise, the proposal attempts to create a safe haven for physical therapy, using locally sourced materials to create a comfortable environment that will be a significant asset to the underserviced community who mainly work very physical jobs. Fig. 1.15 **Joseph Travers-Jones** Y3, 'Exemplary Urban Farm', drawing. The building tests the existing farming conditions on the floodplain of the Red River. The project operates as a site of agrotourism and aims to utilise the rise in floodwater to irrigate farmland with filtered river throught the building favruc and plants. The building showcases the process of filtering to the Vietnamese population and the travelling tourist also demonstrating how poisonous water can be used to drink and grow edible, healthy food within modern urban cities. Fig. 1.16 – 1.17 **Claire Seager** Y3, 'The Coffee Street Rehousing Project', drawings. The scheme is an alternative housing prototype which relocates Hang Hahn or Coffee Street into a high rise social housing scheme that promotes community, tradition and the street identity. The scheme allows for growth as the number of residents increases, this is done at a personal household scale through the architectural upgrade of the home using prefabricated coffee plastic as a building material. Expansion also occurs at a larger scale, through the addition of extra housing units. The building is a housing prototype for relocating former residents in the de-densification of the old quarter of Hanoi.

1.14

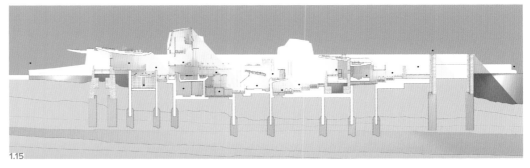

1.15

1.16

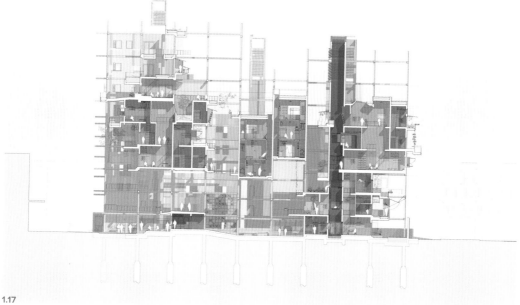

1.17

Fig. 1.18 **Emily Priest** Y3, 'Child Islands', model and construction drawings for the 'colour tower'. Prior to the implementation of a play street, the colour tower can be constructed by neighboring parents and children in order for it to become the heart of each temporary street party. The tower's main structure is reassembled at each festival, whilst its cladding remains personal to each potential child island school. Once completed, the tower becomes central to the new playground, distributing bunting, paint and streamers; reclaiming the child's right to play.

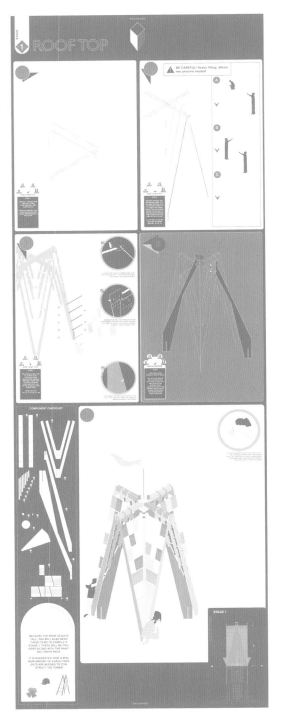

1.18

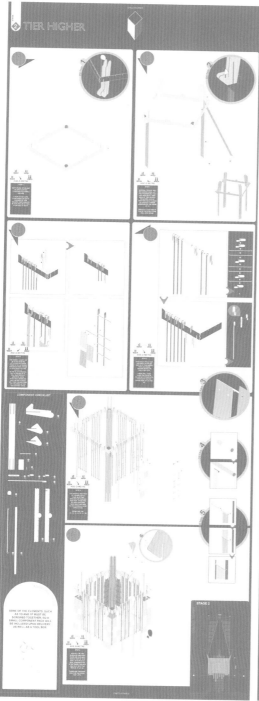

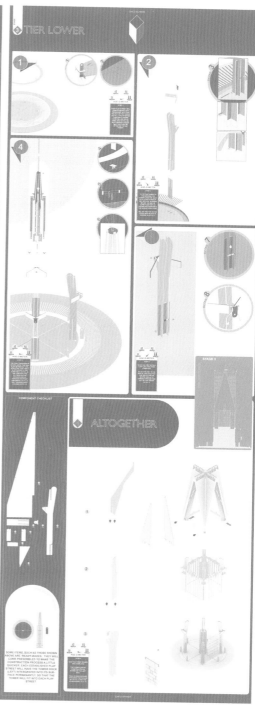

Unit 2

Interstitial Ecologies

Damjan Iliev, Julian Krüger

Year 2
Samual Coulton, Ren Zhi
Goh, Cheng Guo, Jun Wing
(Michelle) Ho, Cheung (Ivan)
Hung, Nikolas Kourtis,
Ka Wing (Clarence) Ku,
Masahiro Nakamura,
Shi Qi (Kiki) Tu

Year 3
Quiling Guan, Linghze
(Frances) Lu, Cheol-Young
(Nick) Park, Bethany
Penman, Cassidy Reid,
Saijel Taank, Marie
Walker-Smith, Jessica Wang

Unit 2 would like to thank
Oliver Wilton (Technology
Consultant), and our guest
critics for their wit and
wisdom: Bihter Almaç,
Matthew Butcher, Mollie
Claypool, William Firebrace,
Rob Howarth, Jack Newton,
Yael Reisner. We would like
to extend particular thanks
on behalf of the students
to Barry Wark for his
extraordinary support,
design input and
organisation of workshops
throughout the year

www.unit-2.com

In light of present global crises such as population expansion, natural resource depletion and environmental disasters, there is an urgent need to align urban development and architecture with nature. This year we addressed the issue of sustainability by focusing on 'Urban Ecology', an interdisciplinary field concerned with the relationship between living organisms and their urban environments. In the past few decades, Urban Ecology has offered great insights into how cities can become places where artificial and natural ecosystems coexist in harmony, considering both built and natural environments as equal habitats for biodiversity and cities as multifaceted, interstitial products in the discourse of human-nature interaction.

———Term 1 focused on the notion of thresholds and their ability to mediate between nature and architecture. Students were asked to design a site-specific, small-scale, inhabitable structure as an integral part of a larger whole in the area around Camden Market. The main aim was to rethink architecture's role as a mediator between habitat and immediate surroundings for the benefit of a more ecologically balanced urban environment.

———In December we visited Istanbul, a city that has undergone a fascinating transformative period, from an ancient settlement situated within the Bosphorus bay area to a massive urban agglomeration. Home to one of the largest urban populations in the world, Istanbul is also a city of the small, the intimate and the specific. It is saturated with intricate passageways, makeshift structures, vibrant communities and unique experiences. However, fast paced urban development, population growth, infrastructure failure and transforming economic realities postulate an ever-changing landscape. The city lacks green spaces and its connectivity to nature is fragile. There is a need to rethink traditional urban patterns and environmental responsiveness as a bottom-up approach from an architectural, interstitial scale.

———Informed by the first project and subsequent field trip investigations, students were required to synthesise the overall brief agenda into a complete building proposal. The design process started with a series of speculative spatial analyses derived from specific sites within the city centre. These analyses evolved through the appropriation of various environmental and infrastructural problems that are characteristic of the site, its immediate surroundings and wider urban context. Developing an element of environmental responsiveness through the fusion of space, structure and surface was of particular importance as it informed an ecologically sound and interstitial relationship between inside/building and outside/nature. Students were expected to further their research into various social and cultural influences that translated directly into complex internal programmes and spatial organisations. The project culminated in fully functioning architectural propositions that are well integrated into the urban, social and natural environment.

Fig. 2.1 **Cassidy Reid** Y3, 'Marine Biology Faculty'. Situated next to the historic Galata Bridge, the project is an environmental facility focused on improving aquatic ecology. The masterplan addresses problems with contaminated surface runoff polluting the Golden Horn. Water caustics inspire the aquarium design and exaggerate the aquatic experience when inside the building. Fig. 2.2 **Shi Qi (Kiki) Tu** Y2, 'Camden Mushroom Restaurant'. The façade of this restaurant specialising in mushroom dishes, is used to grow glowing mushrooms. The natural glow creates a unique atmosphere inside and outside the building. Fig. 2.3 **Marie Walker-Smith** Y3, 'Camden Birdwatching Retreat'. This small building is attached to an existing office block and offers a retreat for birdwatchers and nesting opportunities for wild bird on its

green roof. Fig. 2.4 **Cheung (Ivan) Hung** Y2, 'Camden Market Barber Shop'. A double-layered façade absorbs sound from the busy street and generates complex light patterns inside the building to create relaxing and calm atmospheres. Fig. 2.5 **Masahiro Nakamura** Y2, 'Floating Allotments', Union Canal. A shelter for two people and a number of growing platforms for hydroponic gardening. All parts are designed in a to be connected, to create larger water-based communities. Fig. 2.6 **Ren Zhi Goh** Y2, 'Biophilic School', Kabatas, Istanbul. The school adopts a striated landscape, where the floors and platforms are at varying levels to allow the building to become more permeable to natural light. The atmospheric and tactile qualities of the vegetation and natural elements surround the children and create natural learning environments.

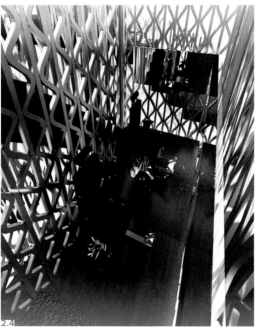

Fig. 2.7 Jun Wing (Michelle) Ho Y2, 'Horticultural Madrasa', Istanbul. Located next to an old Mosque, this building and its surrounding gardens serve the community as a religious school and distillery of fine herbal oils used for religious ceremonies. Fig. 2.8 Bethany Penman Y3, 'Molecular Gastronomy Culinary School and Restaurant'. The project proposes a building where modern practices can be as celebrated as the rich culinary practices rooted in Istanbul's daily life. She approached this much like a molecular chef creating a new gastronomic recipe: by breaking it down into its molecules, arranging these and assembling the final product. The culinary school, restaurant and research aspects are these individual components that work together to form the cohesive building. Through experimenting with sugar, Bethany wished to

capture spaces where a multi-sensory eating experience could be enjoyed. The public walking past the entrance façade experience a flavoured taste mist humidified into the air, while smelling the sweet scent of a syrup being clarified. Fig. 2.9 Samuel Coulton Y2, 'Carpet Restoration and Natural Dye Workshop', Istanbul. By literally weaving into its immediate context, the project aims to restore a historic courtyard steeped in Turkish textile history, reproducing its concentric nature on macro and micro scales. The proposal also responds to two adjacent mosques by aligning its primary grid structure towards Mecca, creating a landscaped prayer garden at its centre, shaded by the open façade. This would, in time, create a new network of green spaces in similar derelict squares, all of which would contribute to the natural dyeing process.

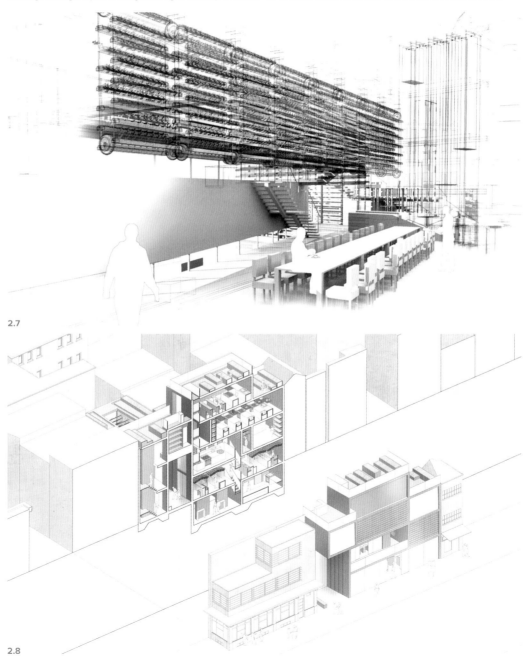

2.7

2.8

Fig. 2.10 Quiling Guan Y3, 'Tulip Hammam', Istanbul.
Fig. 2.11 Ka Wing (Clarence) Ku Y2, 'Shadow Theatre and
Coffee House', Istanbul. **Fig. 2.12 Nikolas Kourtis** Y2, 'Taksim
Democracy Forum', Istanbul. The building acts as a meeting
place for democratic exchange by providing debating theatres,
galleries, meeting spaces and radio station. Hidden inside is a
secondary circulation route to protect activists in the event of
government lockdown and police raid. **Fig. 2.13 Saijel Taank**
Y3, 'Earthquake Monitoring Centre'. **Fig. 2.14 Jessica Wang** Y3,
'Istanbul Waterfront Spa'. The spa building uses its large roof
structure to purify water which is then used in the building.
A small lab produces beauty products from algae which are
grown onsite. **Fig. 2.15 Lingzhe (Frances) Lu** Y3, 'Istanbul
Greening Nursery'. The project takes inspiration from wheeled

Ottoman miniature gardens to explore the possibility of
improving greening coverage for modern Istanbul. By
exporting gardens, the design ambition is to relieve the
pressure between city expansion and ecology. **Fig. 2.16
Cassidy Reid** Y3, 'Marine Biology Faculty'.

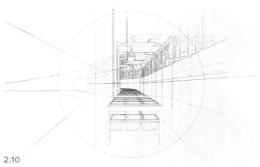

2.10

2.11

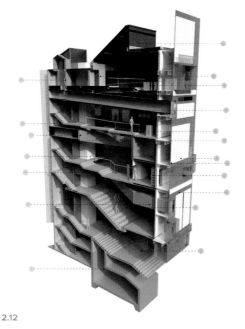

2.12

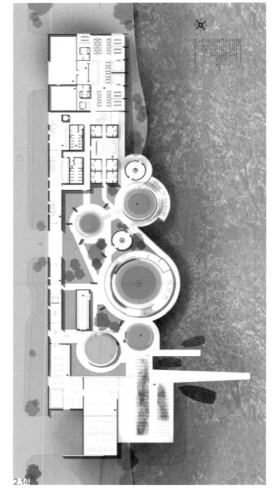

2.14

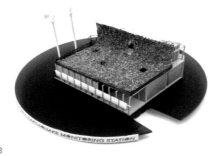

2.13

66

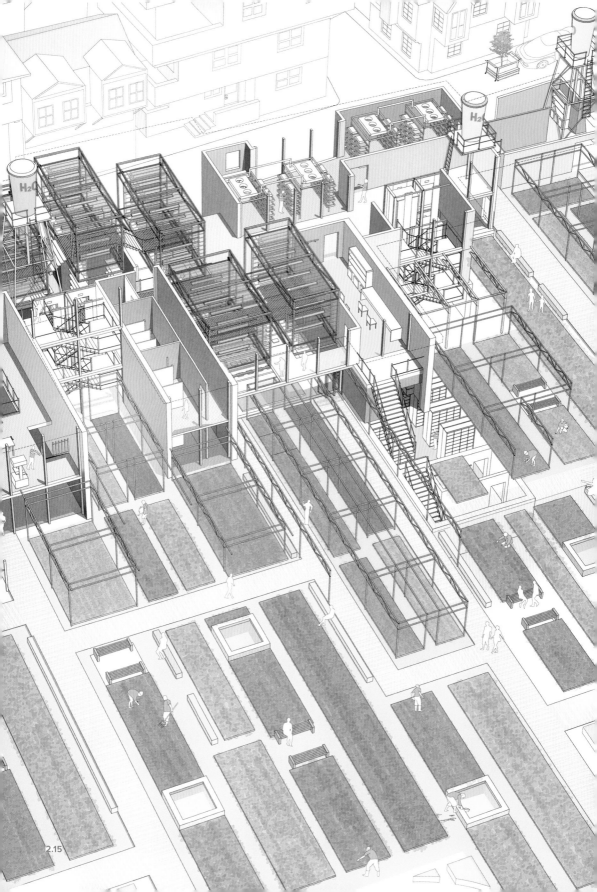

2.16

Unit 3

Off Grid: The Mojave Desert and the Inhabitance of Evasion

David A. Garcia, Jan Kattein

Year 2
William Bellamy, Flavian Berar, Patrick Dobson Perez, Alice Hardy, Jessica Hodgson, Lubna Ibrahim, Kim Jaemin, Lee Kelemen, Subin Koo, Palaan Lakhani, Matei-Alexandru Mitrache, Oliver Parkinson, Emilio Sullivan, Sophie Tait, Astrid Von Heideken

Year 3
Himwai Lai, Songyang Zhou

Thanks to our consultants and critics: Abi Abdolwahabi, Jake Attwood-Harris, Matthew Butcher, Richard Collings, Elizabeth Dow, William Hodgson, Luke Jones, Heini Philipp, Isabelle Priest, Sophia Psarra, James Santer, Julian Siravo

Even today, the call of the wild echoes across the barren landscape, tempting eccentric scientists, adventurers, fortune seekers, alternative communities and felons to venture into the unknown. Part of the eternal imaginary of the escapist, the Mojave Desert has collected for over a century, societies and individuals in search for autonomy, isolation or a new beginning – a social *tabula rasa*. Ironically, the power structures that they have often fled from have themselves exploited this territory to unfold initiatives at the fringes of the acceptable. Both of these realities, often living side-by-side – the fugitive and the regulator – end up as partners in crime, connected more by texture than by content, capitalising on the scale of the desert as a mechanism of disappearance. The offshoot is that more often than not, these initiatives have generated their own logic, a new architecture defined by the parameters of the desert landscape.

———The seditious urge to tinker at the boundary of what we thought possible has scratched a chronicle of abandoned missions, questionable experiments and risky undertakings into the dusty desert soil. David Lynch's 1984 film *Dune* puts it into words: inhospitable living conditions appear to provide a fertile ground for technological, social and political innovation. A lack of accountability can inspire novel methods and actions.

———The site for this year's Unit 3 quest was the Mojave Desert, 64,750 sq. km of disconsolate landscape at the boundary of the three states: Nevada, Arizona and New Mexico. A land of infinite possibilities, layered with histories from the gold rush to the cold war, from the ancient Hopi culture to the age of environmental technologies. Along the old Route 66, past dried salt lakes, site of the robot races, Area 51, the gigantic Hoover Dam, the utopian commune run by grassroots eco-eccentrics, past ghost towns, abandoned silver mines and Joshua tree groves. Decay occurs in slow motion, hardly altered by the force of nature, preserved for an eternity.

———During Term 1 students staked the territory. Working at 1:1, they devised, prototyped, designed and built constructs that allowed them to survey, chart, investigate and even alter the sites during the expedition. At night, and through a transformation of their devices, they functioned as shelters for the low temperature conditions. This first-hand investigation, allowed the students to define an architectural brief and choose a site, through a proactive relationship with the context.

———Term 2 focused on design investigations framed by the brief, which manifested themselves in a large array of media, discussions, prototypes and narratives, in order to transform the investigations into a built environment. All in accordance with the many discoveries, social requirements and environmental challenges experienced and studied through the first semester.

Fig. 3.1 **Alice Hardy** Y2, 'Cyclical Community Shelter', plastic film, rip-stop fabric, electric motor, fan and PV cells. The Mojave Desert is the home of diverse communities. For over a century, societies and individuals in search for autonomy, isolation or a new beginning have gravitated to this barren landscape. The inflatable acts as a temporary abode, an ad-hoc communal structure that can be set up in an instant, wherever and whenever appropriate. The bulbous form culminates in a beacon, which is marked by a signal colour that can be seen across long distances, advertising the shelter across the desert landscape. A series of portable photovoltaics charge a 12v battery during the day, which in turn powers a fan that maintains the structure at constant pressure even when there is no sunlight. Its extreme lightness means that the

structure is susceptible to the wind. Internal tethers connected to a specially tailored suit allow the envelope to constantly re-configure through simple body movements. **Fig. 3.2 William Bellamy** Y2, 'Biosphere'. The ambition of the design is to allow weight created by water and plants to inform the space within the cube-shaped shelter. Experiments with the elasticity of fabric help to create a space that evolves with the plants, as they are collected. **Fig. 3.3 Subin Koo** Y2, 'Cacti Lab Shelter'. Like the Barrel cactus, the shelter expands for night-time accommodation. When it is being unfolded, the inner supports push out the spine that becomes the umbrella shape, mimicking the cactus' night flower as well as adding another outer layer for insulation. With the inner fabric attached, at night the shelter has three layers of protection from the cold

3.2

3.3

3.4

3.5

desert night. **Fig. 3.4 Alice Hardy** Y2, 'Cyclical Community Shelter'. **Fig. 3.5 Lubna Ibrahim** Y2, 'Micro-Mining Shelter'. The purpose of the device is to explore the mining landscape and the residues left over from heavy mining chemicals and machinery in the abandoned mines of the Mojave Desert. Using the device in different topographies from Death Valley to Salt Lake City, it digs through the surface of the ground and filters though the soil to collect minerals that are then stored in the shelter. **Fig. 3.6 Songyang Zhou** Y3, 'Bio-Algae Suit' Advancing desertification and the increasing proportion of carbon dioxide in our atmosphere poses risks to the survival of mankind. The bio-suit establishes a symbiosis between nature and the human body. A sealed personal environment provides oxygen supply to the human body which in turn provides

carbon dioxide that feeds the algae contained in a network of clear capillaries. Exhaled breath goes into the back container and is mixed within the algae-liquid which is then pumped through the capillaries to photosynthesise. At the front of the system oxygen is harvested and the algae once again infused with carbon dioxide from exhaled breath. Surplus algae can be extracted from the system to serve as a food source.

3.6

Fig. 3.7 Flavian Berar Y2, 'Geodesic-Tumbleweed'. This device has the primary objective of drawing a section through the desert with the aid of the wind. Its inspiration is taken from the wind's ability to carry sand grains long enough to refine them, an important factor in the production of the singing sand of the Kelso Dunes. In order to rotate across the landscape, the spherical geodesic structure resembles that of tumbleweed, while the fabric skin wraps around giving it structural strength and the qualities of a shelter. The exterior structural layer serves as support for additional sails that can either be attached or taken down whenever trying to catch the wind under changing conditions. **Fig. 3.8 Sophie Tait** Y2, 'Story-Projection Shelter'. From lost native tribes to lone backpackers to new urban settlements; despite its harsh conditions, the Mojave Desert has been home to many different communities. Due to the transient nature of desert life, these people's stories and experiences often are lost over time. For this project, Sophie became a collector of narratives; of people, landscapes and events within the Mojave Desert. A suitcase contained a built-in camera, an inhabitable projection screen and a portable projector. Deploying the structure during the dark desert nights turned the site into an ad-hoc outdoor cinema, allowing the audience to relive the memories of the landscapes experienced the previous day. **Fig. 3.9 Patrick Dobson Pérez** Y2, 'Seismometry in the Mojave Desert' The device consists of two seismometers to be operated at separate times, one during dusk and one at night. The first is a rotating vertical seismometer which communicates the seismic

3.7

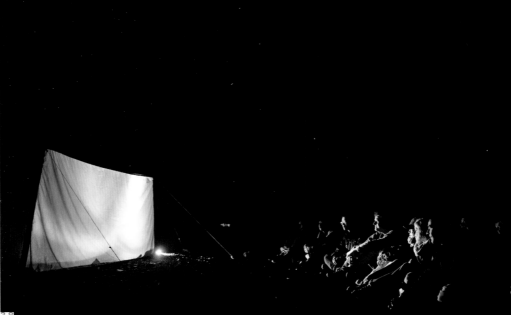

3.8

74

activity of its surroundings by imprinting different diameter circles into the responsive dewy sand at dusk, slowly drawing them around the base of the device. The sizes of these circular imprints indicate the magnitude of each particular reading. This is the macro-seismic function of the device. This mechanism and frame can be converted swiftly into a simple shelter which in turn houses the secondary seismometer and the occupant. The device is a smaller horizontal seismometer which projects its reading of the occupant's movement during sleep onto a roll of photo sensitive paper attached to a 1-hour egg-timer using an embedded laser pen. This is the device's micro-seismic function. **Fig. 3.10 Matei-Alexandru Mitrache** Y2, 'Portable Solar Heater'. In order to tackle the debate about the scale of solar power plants, the Attachable Solar Cooker

functions as a personal source of energy. A parabolic dish focuses sunlight on a specific point where more than one device can be installed – a concentrated photovoltaic cell, a water vessel or a frying pan. The mirror is adjustable and allows movement regardless of the sun's position. An identical dish doubles the amount of generated power and enables the formation of an inhabitable space.

3.9

3.10

Fig. 3.11 Lee Kelemen Y2, 'The Therapeutic Mafia Centre'. In this centre for pathological gamblers, from the school of thought of a game called Mafia, the idea of roleplay is used in order to rehabilitate the users and clean up the city's image. They dress and act as if they were the mob men who established casinos in Las Vegas. **Fig. 3.12 Jessica Hodgson** Y2, 'Metro-Market'. Los Angeles is a city built around cars, with over crowded freeways and an underused Metro system. This train station aims to increase the Metro use in Los Angeles by playing off the city's second greatest obsession, health. The station doubles up as a growing space for organic fruit and vegetables, which are then sold on the station or distributed across the city using the trains on the Metro line. In this way the metro becomes an attraction, but also a convenience,

and the commuter can purchase their groceries literally on their way home. **Fig. 3.13 William Bellamy** Y2, 'Death Valley Hostel'. This hostel is located in Death Valley – one of the most hostile climates of the world. This project looks to deal with this environment by learning from the local tribe – the Timbisha Shoshone – who have lived in Death Valley for centuries in tensile structures during the summer and adobe shelters during the winter. The hostel applied this principle of creating multiple conditions with architecture, to help occupants to cope with the extreme change in temperature that occurs between day and night. A kinetic tensile roof has both a biomicral cycle where at sunrise it lifts up and collects condensation. **Fig. 3.14 Paalan Lakhani** Y2, 'Badwater Basin Visitor Centre'. Home to the hottest, driest environment of the

3.11

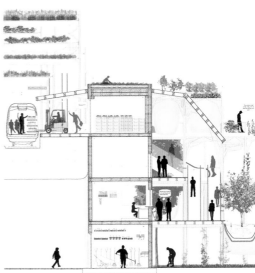

3.12

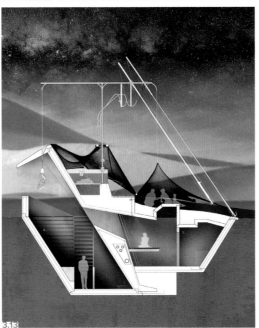

3.13

3.14

USA and the lowest point in North America stays hidden Badwater Basin – a salt-encrusted landscape which remains a natural phenomenon through the evaporation of Lake Manly, leaving behind a self-enriching landscape of salt. The proposal aims for a visitor centre to welcome the tourists by providing shelter, facilities and education about the salt landscape – all of which are lacking currently at the site. This allows for a self-sufficient building celebrating the natural existence of the salt where the building thrives and survives from the salt landscape itself, testing salt as a building material growing its own shading from the saline pools of Badwater. **Fig. 3.15 Alice Hardy** Y2, ' Cyclical Community Sprawl'. A community-led interference project to establish a subtle infrastructure within a community adverse to society itself. Slab City is a

collection of individuals with a growing population due to the current housing crisis. Using a contrasting relationship between the neighbouring military infrastructure the proposal uses completely reclaimed materials to establish a prototype for a new way of building.

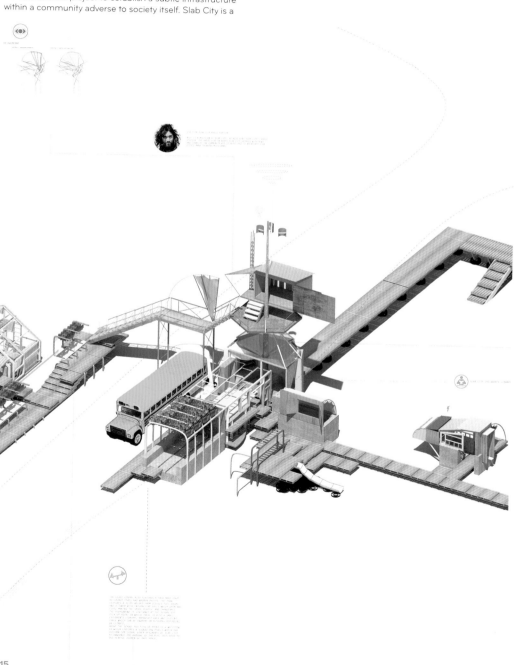

Fig. 3.16 Patrick Dobson Pérez Y2, 'Hoover Dam 2021'. The overall project is a reclamation of the Hoover Dam after the year 2021, when it is predicted that water levels of Lake Mead will drop to an elevation where the dam is unable to continue producing any power. Terraces and floating allotments will produce food which will be collected and prepared in a central floating communal structure. Throughout the course of each day there will be an 'agricultural spectacle' – participated in by tourists – in which the allotments are rowed into a geometric dance across the water and fog harvesting nets are lifted by bespoke hot air balloons in order to irrigate the terraces. The legacy of the project would be to extend outwards and down the terraces as the lake's water levels decrease until a fertile valley is left sitting behind the looming ghost of a once-mighty construction. **Fig. 3.17 Emilio Sullivan** Y2, 'Still Lives From Mobile Homes'. In a city dominated by the car and pockets of America's most rich and famous, Los Angeles often neglects its most vulnerable. The project parasites from 'The Stack Interchange' in Downtown LA and provides housing and views that would otherwise be inaccessible in the motorised labyrinth of roads. Taking the much maligned and mundane in the Los Angeles cityscape, the project creates a new hub for the area and slows down the car-centric Los Angelenos to the possibilities of new vistas and interaction with a micron of the largest homeless population in the United States. **Fig. 3.18 Oliver Parkinson** Y2, 'Mojave Air Space Port Drive-Through Museum'. The project is a reconfiguration of existing airport facilities, centered on an air/spacecraft manufacturing

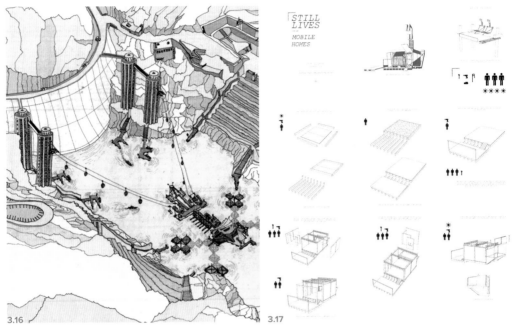

3.16

3.17

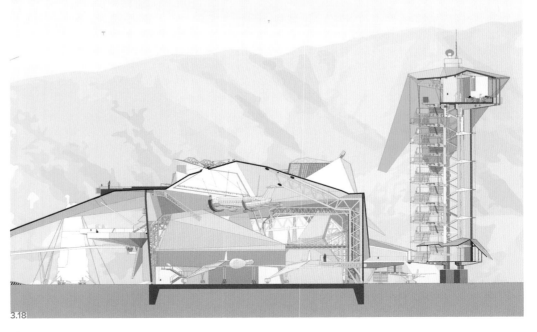

3.18

company. Visitors to the site pass through a suspended driveway that is inserted into the workshop space. Above hang earlier record-breaking craft that were once designed, built and tested by Scaled Composites. The viewing deck above provides views down into the exhibited planes and the workshop space below. Both the cladding and the walkways hang from an internal frame, mirroring that of aircraft construction. The iconic Voyager Café and Flyers Lounge are incorporated into this driven experience, forming a single conglomerate along the runway interchange. The aim is to recognise the rich history associated with this iconic airport whilst allowing for an adaptable testbed for future commercial space travel. **Fig. 3.19 Himwai Lai** Y3, 'Mojave Airship Port'. The Mojave Desert has been a major testing area for prototype aircraft since the Second World War, contributing much to the abundance and dominance of heavier-than-air technology in aviation. Airships however, have taken a backseat since the Hindenburg disaster and have never really played the role of the dominant aircraft type ever since. Enter the Aeroscraft, a next-generation dirigible with precision thrust vectoring, the ability to independently take off, hover and land anywhere, as well as carry over 60 tons of freight. With ever rising gas prices, the need for fuel-efficient airships like the Aeroscraft will be increasingly in demand and thus a new airport typology could be designed to better suit the needs of these floating behemoths, as well as to enhance the experience of flying with these vehicles.

3.19

5/F HANGAR FLOOR ELEVATION

Unit 4

Datum Shifters

Ana Monrabal-Cook, Luke Pearson

Year 2
Annecy Atlee, Uday Berry, Niki-Marie Jansson, Sonia Magdziarz, Douglas Miller, Sarah Stone

Year 3
Laurence Blackwell-Thale, Max Butler, Xi Yao (Joyce) Chen, John Cruwys, David Flook, Olivia Hornby, Gregorios Kythreotis, Maggie Lan, Lisa McDanell, Ellie Sampson, Elin Söderberg

We would like to thank Gavin Hutchison for his support in his role as technology tutor and regular critic for the Unit. We would also like to thank our critics this year for their invaluable feedback: Ben Addy, Abigail Ashton, Matthew Butcher, Kristijan Cebzan, Rhys Cannon, Stylianos Giamarelos, Penelope Haralambidou, Colin Herperger, Gavin Hutchison, Will Jefferies, Diony Kypraiou, Adrian Lahoud, CJ Lim, Alan Penn

Unit 4 continues its explorations into architectures of public delight, antipathy or bemusement by examining the role of clarity, resolution and imagery in communicating and propagating spaces and events. Our modern systems for reading, traversing and positioning ourselves within space are mediated by constant flows of data. But these structures are based on correlation to the real world – fixed points, levels – the 'Datum' within a city.

————What if a key Datum could change? How would this skew the city and open up new possibilities for novel types of space and public occupation? What are the new forms of architecture that will emerge from these fluid situations? To synthesise these new architectural typologies, we challenge ourselves to pull such conditions apart and become 'Datum Shifters'.

What is a Datum Shifter?

We investigate the notion of Datum in the context of the physical and virtual city. We consider Datum Shifters to be those who have pushed and probed technology, theories and ideas to allow us to see the city and its architecture in new terms.

————Chicago is the home of the American Datum Shifters. The city has had its ground level raised block by block in an unprecedented act of civil engineering overcoming nature. As its ground shifted and its buildings crept skyward the city became a landscape of datums in flux and flexible territories.

————When William Le Baron Jenney completed the first skyscraper, he changed the datum of architectural proportion and scale forever, creating the catalyst for Chicago's growth into a landscape of tectonic and monolithic structures that challenge bodily scale. In a world increasingly compressed or stretched by communication tools, Chicago represents the original template of a city formed by technology, where architecture has outgrown human magnitudes.

We are Datum Shifters!

Unit 4 takes a critical position in relation to the creation of architecture and its communication through representation. What are the new forms of architecture that will emerge from the rupture between the physical and the digital? How is hand drawing being augmented or redefined by new technologies and interfaces?

————Datums invisible to the human eye can be seen and acted upon by other devices for viewing and recording. Cities are no longer purely physical entities, but multi-scalar sites for events and information overloads. Datum Shifters propose buildings that play with these reference points, and respond to the context of the city as a combination of physical, cultural and ephemeral conditions.

————We propose that the architectural datums of Chicago – its proportions, ornamentations, technologies and notorieties, can be deformed and reformatted into architectures that enmesh technological developments within the latent historic and cultural conditions of this 'ur-American city'.

Fig. 4.1 Douglas Miller Y2, 'The Machining of Chicago'. A CTA maintenance facility in the Chicago Loop serves as a blue-collar symbol against the increasing marginalisation of Chicago's rail workforce. The project proposes an architecture of infrastructural materiality and industrial heft that re-emphasises the layered spaces of Chicago created by the city's relationship to technology. **Fig. 4.2 Niki-Marie Jansson** Y2, 'The Fermilab Interface: People Collider'. An outreach centre for the publicly funded Fermilab particle physics centre, located in Chicago's Millenium Park – resembling the huge hadron collider machines of Fermilab. **Fig. 4.3 Sarah Stone** Y2, 'Pharma Laboratory'. A space for advanced chemical reactions sited in Chicago's medical district, the architecture is defined through a series of interlocking testing rigs and biosafety zones for conducting experiments, and steam-cleans itself periodically. **Fig. 4.4 – 4.5 Lisa McDanell** Y3, 'CPD Internal Affairs Station'. Responding to recent examples of the Chicago Police's corruption, the project proposes the intertwining of Police Station spaces with those of the Internal Affairs creating a landscape of duality, where the thicknesses of materials, and extents of space are in a perpetual flux. **Fig. 4.6 Max Butler** Y3, 'The Synthetic Slaughterhouse'. Coined the 'frankenburger', many are repulsed by lab grown in-vitro meat. The building presents the process to the carnivorous American public, but in an altogether different light. Constructed from 'grown' materials such as bacterial brick and microbial cellulose, the building expounds the delights, possibilities and advantages of synthetic biology.

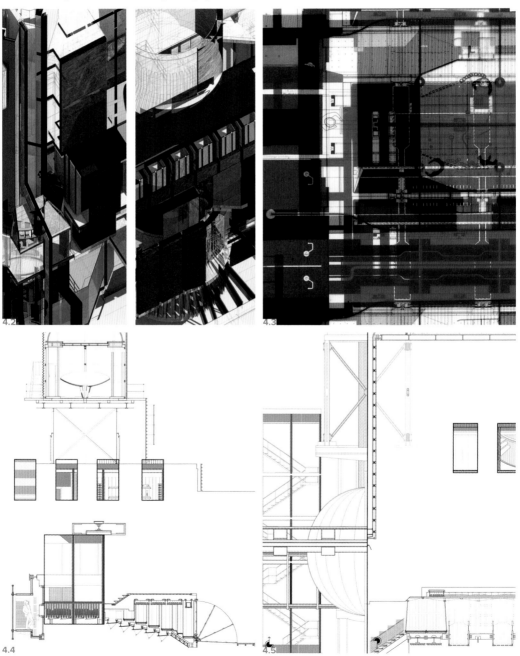

4.2

4.3

4.4

4.5

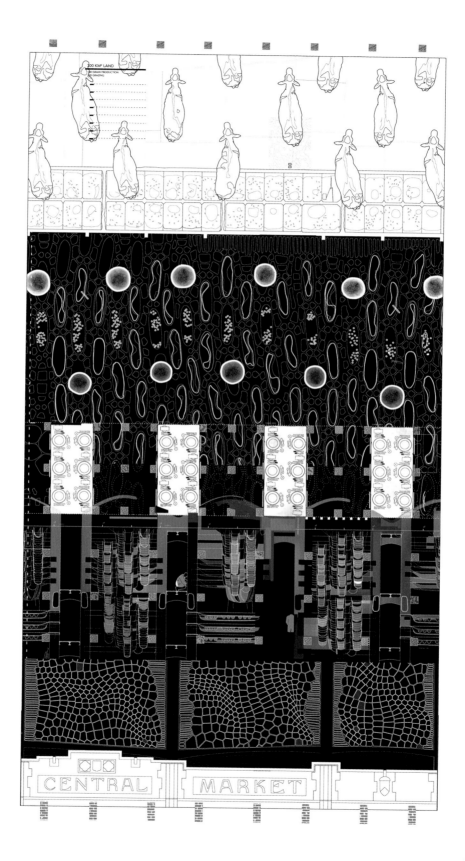

4.6

Fig. 4.7 – 4.8 **Laurence Blackwell-Thale** Y3, 'The Heliolithic Community Centre'. After a researching the impact of digital devices on human physiology, the project examines architecture as an interface. Through an articulated roofscape, the surrounding light conditions of Chicago are manipulated through lenses, materials and filters, to create zones of circadian rhythm within the building. The building provides a number of different amenities, all attuned to a particular wavelength of light, and the reactions this causes in a person's physical and emotional reaction fosters a new sense of community at the block scale of the city. **Fig. 4.9 – 4.11 David Flook** Y3, 'Home Building 2035' + 'Village MC-1'. Home Building 2035 speculates on the spatial implications for suburbia that arise from highly referential and restrictive

aesthetic architectural codes meeting the modernity of the manufacturing techniques with which they are mass produced, and proposes a new framework for changing the public appetite. Village MC-1 is inspired by the quasi-suburban prairie lands of Fermilab, where cutting edge research is conducted in cottages. The result is an architecture that materialises in the form of a cultivated Mid-Western Prairie that doubles as scientific test ground. This fabricated landscape attempts to provide an environment suitably 'precise' for Fermilab's ongoing experimentation yet 'imprecise' to allow for the processes of burning that propogate the Prairie landscape. This new architecture defines the parameters of an experiment that explores the manufacturing of myth, the sociology of science and formation of fact.

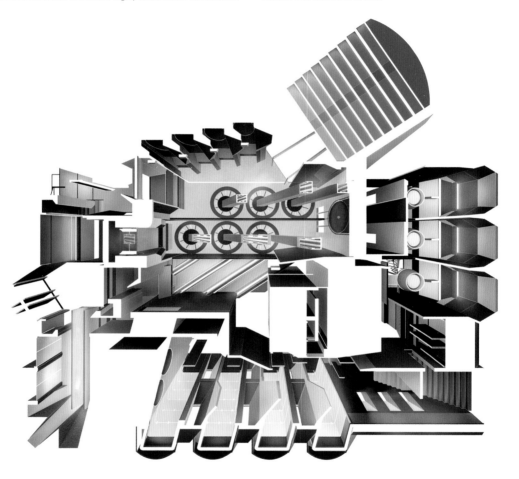

4.7

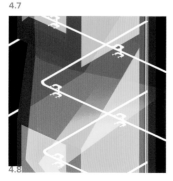

4.8

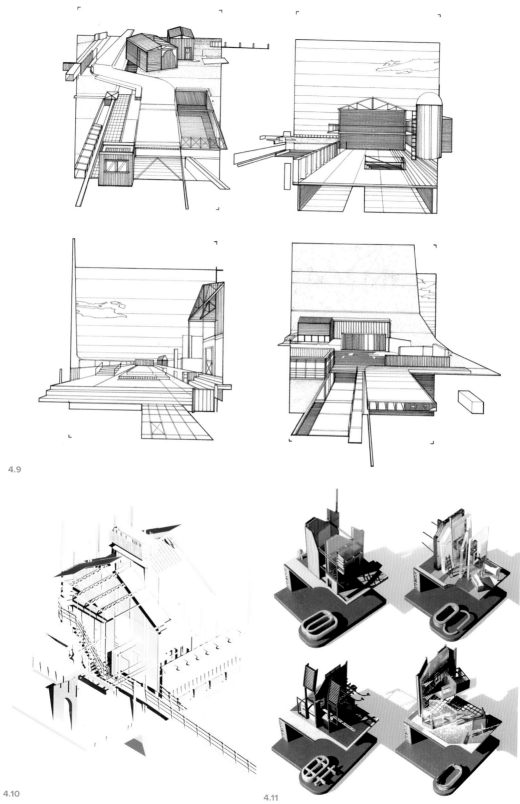

4.9

4.10

4.11

Fig. 4.12 **Xi Yao (Joyce) Chen** Y3, 'The Lakeshore Disclosure Hotel'. The project deals with Chicago's huge heat changes across the year by developing a strategy that sees the building as a giant 'wall' with many smaller heat zones intertwining within. The building plays with disruptions of an idealised elevation, and utilises versions of the famous Chicago Window, a central viewing pane flanked by two ventilating windows. By peeling apart the laminations of the wall, the hotel maintains spaces classified into climatic zones such as tent, cabin or cave. Sitting on the shore of Lake Michigan, the hotel not only provides framed views back across the skyline of the city, but takes advantage of the lake's particular nature – at once a beachside resort, then an ice-locked retreat. Fig. 4.13 **John Cruwys** Y3, 'Route 66 Museum'. The Route 66 Museum is proposed as part of a combined effort including groups such as the National Parks Service, to preserve the memory and history of the famous highway. The result is a technological landscape built around the diverting of the South Branch of the Chicago River in order to create a water computer. Through the careful use of fluid dynamics, water flows can be manipulated through ceramic logic gates, effectively turning these flows into binary decisions, and turning the flow of the Chicago River into a landscape-scale computation device. This computer performs 'glacial speed' calculations in order to grow and germinate a series of landscapes across the site that correspond to the states that form the route of the 66. Appearing as a yearly cycle, these three dimensional pixels contain traces of roadside architecture and of the indigenous

4.12

plants of each of the region states. Alongside a series of archival buildings collecting ephemera from the route, the landscape thus becomes a new form of hybridised national park, encapsulated within its site near the start of the famous route. **Fig. 4.14 Sonia Magdziarz** Y2, 'Pop-Up Cinema'. As part of Rahm Emmanuel's drive to regenerate Chicago's Uptown areas through their historical relationship to music, and the number of old music halls and cinemas that lie decaying in such areas, the project proposes new forms of pop-up architectures that can be inserted into these old spaces. By creating these new architectures to focus on the ornamentation and detailing of the existing space, these picture palaces can find a new life. **Fig. 4.15 Annecy Atlee** Y2, 'The Kinzie Cabin Collective'. The project proposes an

architecture that sits as the driver for a new collective approach to the homeless community around Kinzie Street in Chicago. The creation of living units and market stalls not only provides skills in tradesmanships for the local residents, but also starts to build a new collective community around the elevated tracks of the L train – turning the 'launching' of each pod into a public event.

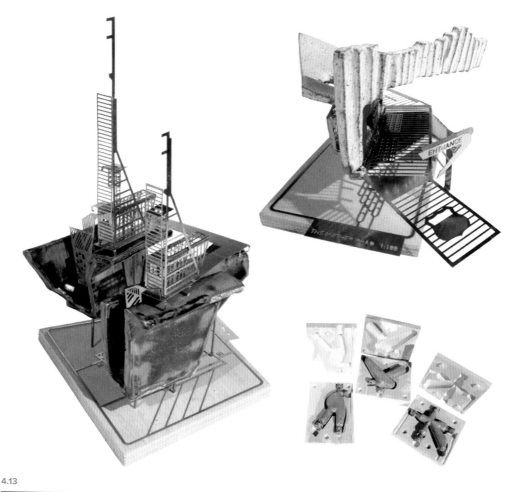

4.13

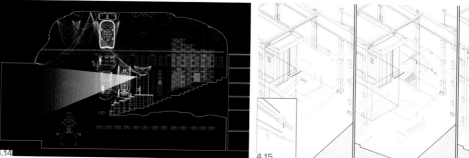

4.14

4.15

Fig. 4.16 **Uday Berry** Y2, 'Goose Island Brewery'. A brewery and tourist centre for the Goose Island Brewery, using huge concrete weights to cantilever an elevated 'dive bar'. Fig. 4.17 **Maggie Lan** Y3, 'Augmented Histories'. Examining the monumental nature of Chicago's architecture as a *tabula rasa* for the application of new forms of ornamentation through augmented reality technologies. Fig. 4.18 **Gregorius Kythreotis** Y3, 'Place-hacking the Pedway'. The project examines Chicago's Pedway, a series of non-contiguous pedestrian access tunnels secreted across the city. Inspired by the 2D/3D slippage present in the mechanics of videogames such as Fez and Monument Valley, and the ways in which such games can define architectural experiences, the project proposes territories brought into and out of alignment through animated,

spinning drawings. Fig. 4.19 – 4.22 **Ellie Sampson** Y3, 'Bucktown Housing Court'. Honoring the memory of Richard Nickel, a Chicagoan famous for his heroic rescues of Louis Sullivan ornamentation destined for the wrecking ball, the Housing Court draws from the diverse architectural context of Bucktown to create an architecture that becomes a field of symbolic objects and spaces. By overlaying this onto a site with three postal addresses, yet subservient to the procedures and regiments of the courthouse, the project examines the role of threshold in the function and symbolism of the court, allowing for sound to seep out to and from the surrounding rumbles of the L-train. The project suggests a new architecture for Chicago, where memory, symbol, technology, scale and composition all combine into new typologies of building.

4.16

4.17

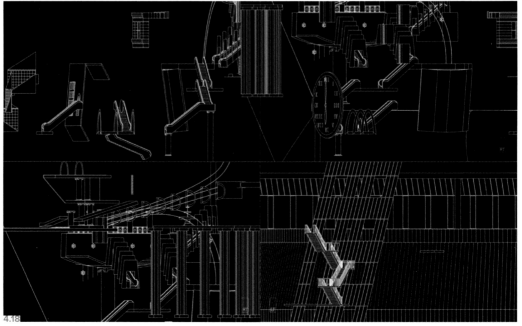

4.18

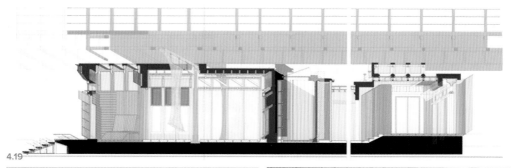

4.19

4.20

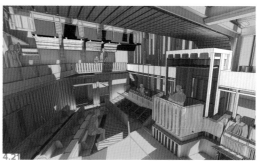

4.21

4.22

Unit 5

The Super-Specific: Las Vegas, Las Vegan

Pascal Bronner, Thomas Hillier

Year 2
Kamola Askarova, Boon Yik Chung, Grace Fletcher, Patrick Horne, Jonah Luswata, Francesca Savvides, Valerie Vyvial, Allegra Willder, Max Worrell

Year 3
Matthew Bovingdon-Downe, Clare Dallimore, Isobel Parnell, Rose Shaw, Chris Straessle, Carolyn Tam, Hei Man (Belle) Tung, Simon Wimble

We would like to thank our technical tutor, Giles Bruce, and our critics throughout the year: Yota Adilenidou, Matthew Butcher, Barry Cho, Ming Chung, Max Dewdney, Pedro Font Alba, Stephen Gage, Polly Gould, Christine Hawley, CJ Lim, Shaun Murray, Frosso Pimenides, Nicholas Szczepaniak, Tania Sengupta, Martin Tang, Nick Tyson, Paolo Zaide

The Bartlett School of Architecture 2014

In this time of modern globalisation it is crucial to remember the importance of the bespoke, specific and the tailor-made in architecture. Each reflect upon the customs and culture of a given place, time and programme. Unit 5 believe that it has never been so important to push for a place-specific approach to design. The Unit is an imaginarium for built futures where narrative is used to explore, discover and invent unique realities within which these super-specific architectures are sited.

————This specificity is explored through rigorously crafting drawings to a point at which the drawing itself may come to life and be thought of as an actual architecture. A drawing can become an extreme force, a manmade wonder, and a spectacular fantasy of human imagination. Like real buildings, drawings need to be maintained, if required they need to be revised and extended, refurbished and restored, customised and modified, demolished and redrawn. Similarly to the way a house or a city gets adapted and modified over time, a drawing needs to grow and develop into something that goes beyond mere representation. We are 'drawing-board travellers' who treat drawings, models and collages as real places that are used to explore spatial narratives and speculate on future building typologies.

Las Vegas

This year, the major project was sited in Las Vegas. Before we ventured onto the compacted desert sand of Nevada State the Unit spent the first part of the year investigating Las Vegas from afar in an attempt to understand its history, its masterplan, its neighbourhoods and most importantly its inhabitants. Through this research the students created their own visual manifestos in preparation for the field trip. Inspired by real tales and Las Vegan fables these speculations aided them in developing specific programmes and sites that were then explored across the year.

Las Vegan

Undoubtedly a one-off city, Las Vegas is built out of super-specific circumstances, its desert climate, economy, 24-hour lifecycle, reliance on tourism, constant exchange of people, relaxed laws, salacious nightlife, urban sprawl and heroic self-aggrandising monuments all affect how Las Vegans live in or around this unique metropolis. It appears the domestic architecture currently available to Las Vegans hasn't kept up with the pace of the city. With dreary and dull suburban neighbourhoods having been the answer for the century gone, we see a need for an alternative, super-specific architecture for future Las Vegans. We posed the question: How will a Las Vegan live, and more importantly how will he or she live in the future in a city that is little over a century old?

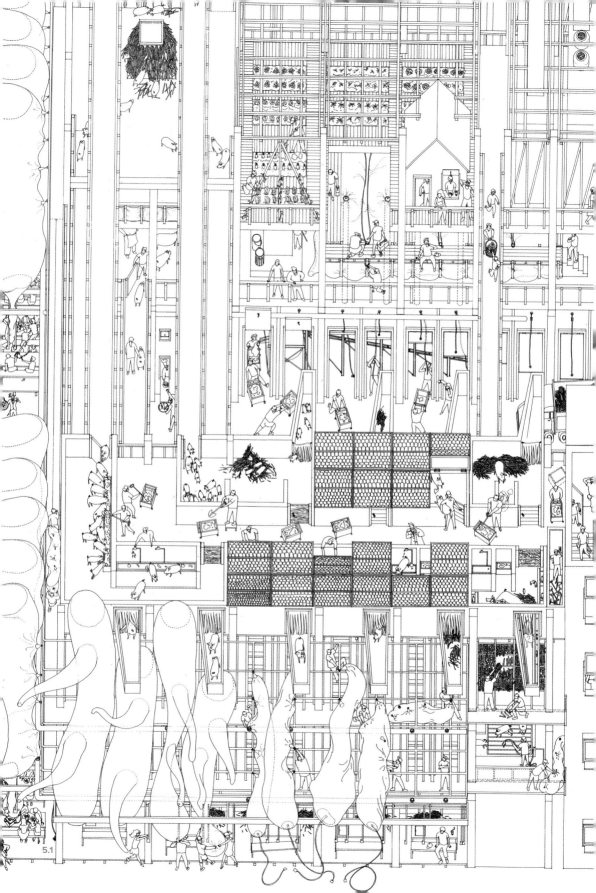

5.1

Fig. 5.1 Boon Yik Chung Y2, 'The Las Vegas Happy Pigs Pig Farm'. This self-sustaining free-range farm tackles the city's over-reliance on imported food. Leftover buffet food is converted into feed for pigs, whose manure is collected to produce biogas that fuels the farm and connected BBQ restaurant. An ever-changing facade of biogas balloons becomes both a fuel for cooking and a new addition to the Downtown street experience. **Fig. 5.2 Valerie Vyvial** Y2, 'Neon Boneyard Cathedral'. This ever growing, lightbulb-clad Cathedral maintains and stores redundant neon signs within its deep, open walls, turning the building into a spectacle in its own right. **Fig. 5.3 Allegra Willder** Y2, 'The Shrimp Wing at Planet Hollywood'. Sited to address the redundant rear façade that backs onto a derelict and desolate desert landscape, this

hotel wing offers luxury 'Hollywood' themed rooms with the promise of Vegas-style shrimp cocktail whose ingredients are grown on-site. **Fig. 5.4 Max Worrell** Y2, 'Paradise Soap Factory and Bath House'. Far from the glamour of the nearby Strip sits Paradise, a run-down suburban home to thousands of the Strip's hotel cleaners. The soap factory recycles the discarded soap from these nearby hotels which is then sold back to the Strip as new. This in turn offers local residents the opportunity to raise funds for projects to clean up Paradise. **Fig. 5.5 Francesca Savvides** Y2, 'Cragin & Pike's Unbiased Insurance Company'. Surprisingly, in this city of great risk, very few Las Vegans are insured. To address this, the proposal turns insurance into a commodity that can be gambled for in exchange for market research.

5.2

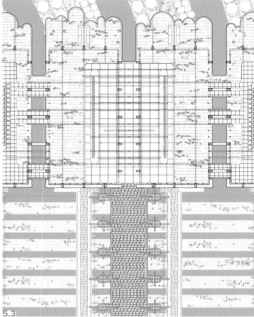

5.3

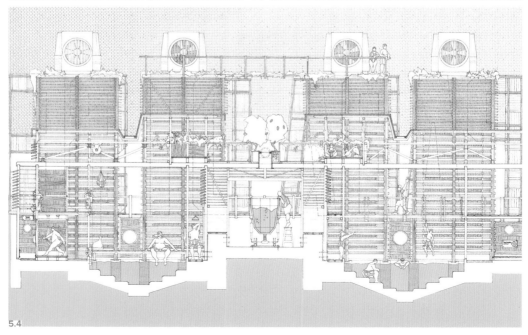

5.4

5.5

Fig. 5.6 **Grace Fletcher** Y2, 'Las Vegas, Las Vegas, Las Vegas'. Every hotel casino along the Strip assimilates a different, distinct part of the world creating a unique theme matched by no other. The pyramids of Egypt become the Luxor Hotel whilst the Paris hotel has it own, half-scale Eiffel Tower. Sunk into the desert sand, Las Vegas, Las Vegas, Las Vegas is a hotel casino that imitates Las Vegas itself, creating a copy of a copy. Fig. 5.7 **Kamola Askarova** Y2, 'Temple of Secrets'. As the saying goes "What happens in Vegas, stays in Vegas." But what do you do with the physical secrets from the night before? The Temple of Secrets offers a secure haven where one can deposit fresh secrets, remove existing secrets, destroy secrets or even purchase strangers secrets at the Temple Auction House. Fig. 5.8 **Isabelle Tung** Y3, 'The Las Vegas Sand Retreat'.

In the very near future, Las Vegas' water supply is going to run desperately low. Located in a derelict sand quarry, the Las Vegas Sand Retreat uses solidified sand to create a unique landscape of perfume infused hot sand baths, providing a lavish experience for tourists whilst creating an alternative to water based spa treatments. Fig. 5.9 **Patrick Horne** Y2, 'Las Vegas Storm Drain Maintenance HQ'. A considerable proportion of Las Vegas' homeless population has sought refuge in its extensive network of underground storm drain tunnels. This government-funded initiative is a recycling facility which utilises the tunnel occupants' navigational expertise, spatial adaptations and collective ingenuity to keep the drains clean and therefore protect the ecosystem around Lake Mead, the floodwater's final destination.

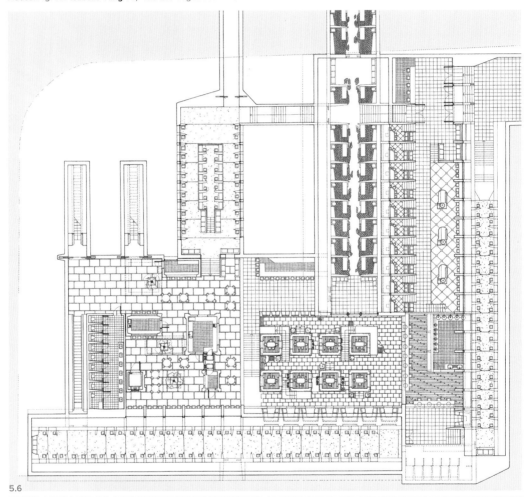

5.6

5.7

5.8

Fig. 5.10 Matthew Bovingdon-Downe Y3, 'International Dark Sky Association HQ'. The IDAHQ is a scotopic architecture that seeks to reacquaint people with darkness. The building has no artificial light of its own, instead it taps off the haze from the many hotel casinos that surround it. During the day the building attenuates incident atmospheric light, providing amateur astronomers with the requisite conditions for optimum dark adaptation, preparing them for appraising the night sky. Fig. 5.11 Clare Dallimore Y3, 'Demolition Landscape'. The proposal translates the 12 steps of gambling addiction recovery into a series of spaces for rehabilitation. Using the rubble from exploded casinos as a construction aggregate the building and surrounding landscape is sculpted by a series of water-based interventions that create a haven away from the addictions of Las Vegas. Fig. 5.12 Chris Straessle Y3, 'Signs of Growth HQ and Nursery.' Famous casino signage is re-interpreted and manufactured as arable signs. These signs are planted with a combination of plants, flowers and vegetables, all of which are grown aeroponically on the buildings rooftop before being installed across the Strip. Fig. 5.13 Jonah Luswata Y2, 'The Las Vegas Gun Amnesty and Peace Retreat'. Situated within a shooting range, the Gun Amnesty seeks to deconstruct this heterotopic space though a reversal of its previous program, to one where the gun is demystified, degraded and disassembled. The Peace Retreat offers redemption through the tactile reworking of the resultant recycled material and a reacquaintance with the surrounding landscape.

5.10

5.11

5.12

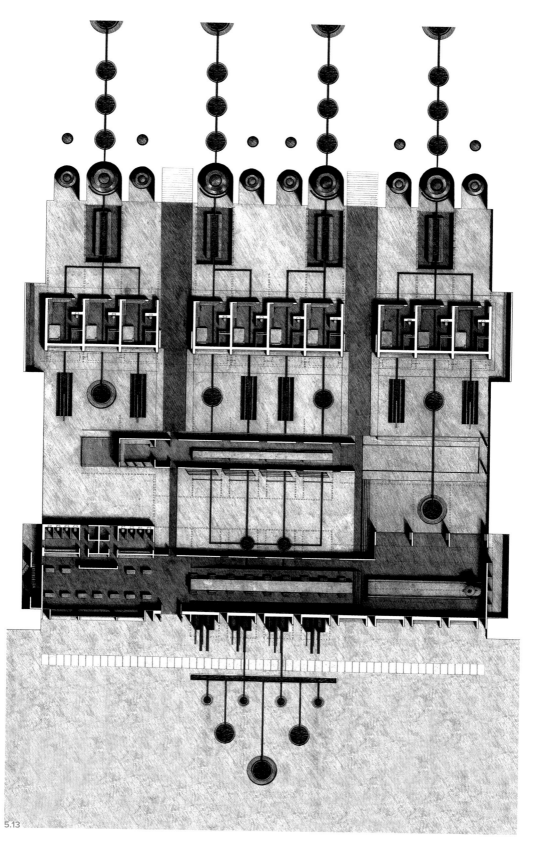

5.13

Fig. 5.14 Carolyn Tam Y3, 'The Hoover Dam Cactus Cooperative'. Research suggests that, as early as 2035, the water level feeding the Hoover Dam will be too low to sustain Las Vegas' thirst for hydroelectric power. Speculating on both future energy creation and the future redundant infrastructure of the Hoover Dam the HDCC investigates the use of cacti as a credible power source. Accommodation, laboratories and fields of cacti transform this concrete monolith into a reservoir of organic electricity production. **Fig. 5.15 – 5.17 Rose Shaw** Y3, 'Dashboard Confectionery'. Las Vegas has the highest rate of road accidents caused by drink driving in the US. Sited alongside a motorway ramp exiting the city, the proposal is a drive-thru service station that exports healthy bodies and minds. Influenced by American consumer culture and

designed completely around the car, the building consists of a series of architectural interventions intended to sober up drivers before leaving Las Vegas. **Fig. 5.18 Simon Wimble** Y3, 'The Golden Wedding Chapel'. Hovering above a derelict gold mine that contains five million pounds worth of unrefined gold dust, the Golden Wedding Chapel offers an alternative ceremony to the impulsive, superficial and synthetic culture of the shotgun wedding. Influenced by the notion that the wedding ring is a symbol of eternity, the resident goldsmith extracts raw material from the deposits below to craft wedding bands for each couple that arrive. This process defines the architecture; excess rock from the extracted gold is used to create the building blocks that make up the chapel walls, creating a building ingrained with a sense of time.

5.14

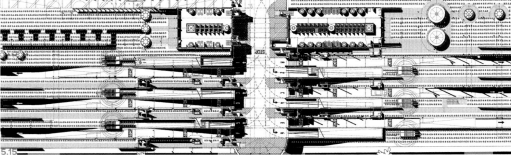

5.15

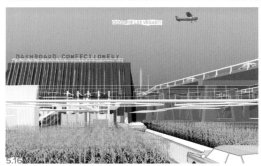

5.16

5.17

5.18

Unit 6

Edge: Fragile Landscapes

Christine Hawley, Paolo Zaide

Year 2
Oliver Colman, Thomas Cubitt, Ye Lone (Jarrell) Goh, Katja Hasenauer, Niema Jafari, Robert Newcombe, Sylwia Poltorak, Laszlo von Dohnanyi

Year 3
Supichaya (Susan) Chaisiriroj, George Courtauld, Georgina Halabi, Yu-Me Kashino, Samuel Tan, Yiren (Aviva) Wang, Anqi (Angel) Yu

Unit 6 would like to thank our technical advisor Matt Springett and our critics: Abigail Ashton, Peter Bishop, Izaskun Chinchilla, Nick Elias, Naomi Gibson, Jens Kongstad, CJ Lim, Tim Lucas, Farlie Reynolds, Yeoryia Manalopoulou, Tim Norman and Oliver Wilton

A special thank you to the Santander Foundation for their generous support

The Bartlett School of Architecture 2014

As the prospect of environmental stability slips away and we experience a climate that becomes increasingly volatile, the challenge will be to understand how to provide shelter in this environment. The scenario is fifty years in the future, which if the climate pundits are correct, will be a time characterised by increasing storms, drought and rising sea levels. Within this context, Unit 6 considers the organisation of communities and how this would affect not only the design of housing but also the infrastructure that supports them. With the influence of research, analyses and speculation the Unit questions models of living and developed infrastructural proposals tested within fragile edge conditions.

———The early nineteenth century Quaker philanthropists such as Cadbury and Rowntree understood that working communities needed far more than merely housing to lead a secure and productive life. Bournville and New Earswick were the influential forerunners of the garden city movement that developed models of mixed development that were conceptually radical yet rooted in ideas about humanity. Similarly, the brief for this year demanded a radical approach where housing and infrastructural plans are not referenced by the status quo but an imaginative vision of life at the midpoint of the twenty-first century. Not only did the students consider the social consequences of design but also the technical challenges of changing weather patterns on fragile landscapes.

———The Unit explored sites at the mouth of the Thames Estuary. Cliffe Marshes and Gravesend both share a geographic characteristic in that they are on the edge of water and particularly vulnerable to the forces of the weather. The first site is a fragile ecological site, historically the site for brick and cement making and latterly a RAF base in the second-world war, more recently it was part of the hotly disputed site for the third London airport. Today, the marshland contains strange archaeological relics, traces of its historic past, a tangled network of watercourses and marshland that supports an important diversity of wildlife. Gravesend was a naval and shipbuilding town and still supports industries that are water-based, it is also a commuter town for those that work at Tilbury docks. Each site provided different challenges, one that had to address all the responsibilities of delicate ecology and the second the dual responsibility of considering the context of the town and the water's edge.

6.1

Fig 6.1 Unit 6 Group Model, Initial site research of Thames Estuary 50 years into the future. Fig. 6.2 – 6.3 Anqi (Angel) Yu Y3, 'Gravesend Residential Tower'. In response to pressures of increasing housing demand and loss of green spaces due to flooding, the typology of a residential tower hybridises these issues. A series of interlocking housing units connect to a number of different gardens ranging from communal spaces to private vertical green balconies. Fig. 6.4 Supichaya (Susan) Chaisiriroj Y3, 'The Cliffe Wetlands Visitor Centre'. A regional marshland visitor and education facility for the study of the fragile environment and biodiversity of the Thames Estuary landscape. The building plays on the abundance of water reeds which can be processed into thatch as a building material and takes opportunities to develop moments of the building which blend into the surrounding landscape. Fig. 6.5 Samuel Tan Y3, 'Cliffe Marshes Gateway to London 2064'. Due to the expansion of river transportation and mobile technology advancements, people will live a more transient life. The project acts as a hybrid work-home travel nodal point, whilst ecologically enhancing the sensitive marshscape where it is sited. The combined ferry terminal with accommodation caters to a future where our lifestyles have become increasingly decentralised from notions of home or work.

6.2

6.3

6.4

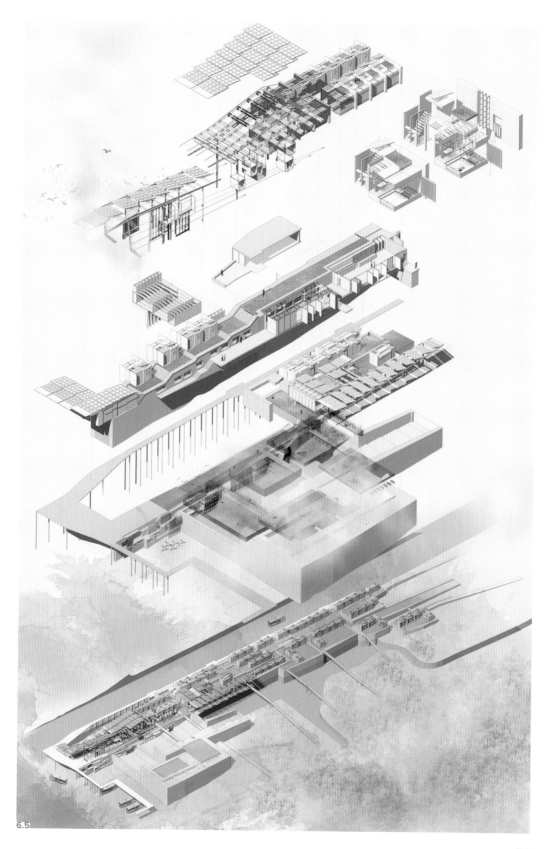

6.5

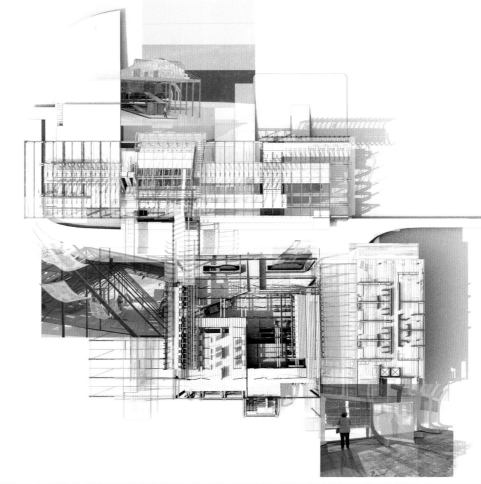

6.6

6.7

6.8

Fig. 6.6 **Yiren (Aviva) Wang** Y3, 'Twilight of Life Centre'. A community centre for the Active Third Age in Gravesend functions to preserve oral history and to act as an active archive for the town. Set into existing factories and shipyards of Gravesend, this building forms a physical and social reservoir of memories of Gravesend's prosperous past. Fig. 6.7 – 6.8 **Laszlo von Dohnanyi** Y2, 'Observatory'. Sited in one of the least light-polluted locations in the UK, the hands-on teaching astronomical observatory provides research and education facilities. It allows visitors to retreat into the ground and connect back to the night sky, acting as a celestial retreat for stargazers. Fig. 6.9 – 6.12 **George Courtauld** Y3, 'Managed Retreat'. An oyster farm and processing plant to respond to protein shortages and alternative food sources in the future. The project plays on the language of the Victorian vernacular and adapts to different seasons and cycles; processing spaces are temporarily repurposed as retreat accommodation and the building responds to the fluctuations of ebb and flow.

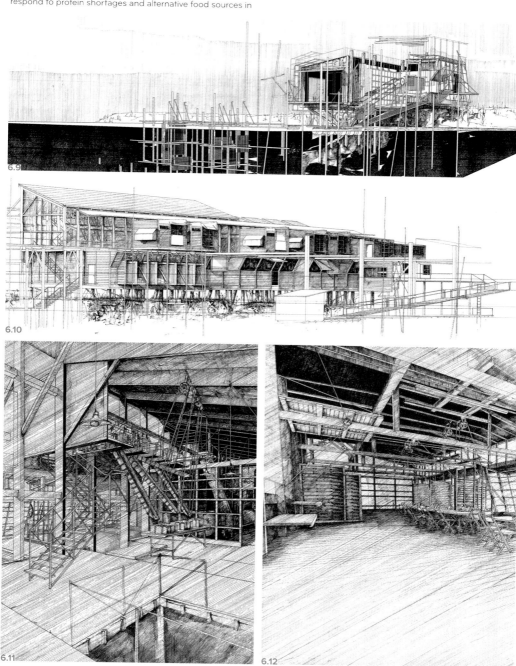

6.9

6.10

6.11

6.12

Fig. 6.13 **Niema Jafari** Y2, 'Super Earthed Lido'. Thames Water is upgrading their Victorian sewage system to a super sewer, allowing an increase in river water purity. The lido utilises the water from the Thames at high tide and is planned around two WWII decoy buildings. Dredged material discarded in Cliffe forms the Lido intrinsically linked to the dynamics of the area. Fig. 6.14 **Georgina Halabi** Y3, 'Cliffe Bread and Breakfast'. A retreat and public waterscape which makes use of the tidal changes to power waterwheels that propel private cabins to retreat or plug in to the main building. A main waterwheel is used for making bread for the retreat guests and the Higham town residents. Fig. 6.15 **Sylwia Poltorak** Y2, 'Aromatherapy Gardens'. A garden retreat for the city of London set into the particular wind and light conditions of Cliffe Marshes. The main building contains an interior garden that creates a miniature landscape of walking paths, terraces and flower beds of lavender. Fig. 6.16 **Oliver Colman** Y2, 'Flood Displacement Campus'. Forecasting a 2m rise in sea level by 2064, large numbers of people will be displaced from their homes due to extreme flooding along coastal waterways. The campus will temporarily accommodate these people for a month, creating a sense of community with public spaces within the central hub and the collective accommodation blocks. Fig. 6.17 **Katja Hasenauer** Y2, 'Cliffe Marshes Nature Retreat'. The retreat, balancing delicately on the remains of Shornemead Fort, creates a connection between old and new. Located adjacent to the River Thames within a vast nature reserve, the retreat focuses on the surrounding views of existing natural beauty.

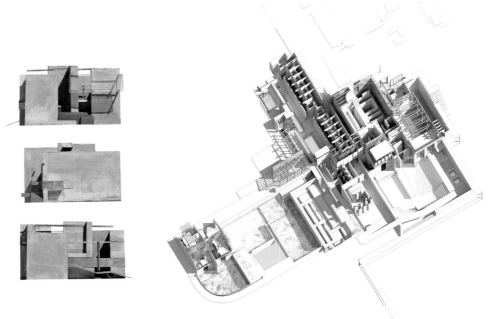

6.13

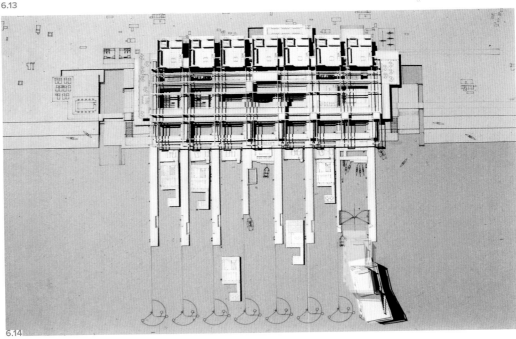

6.14

106

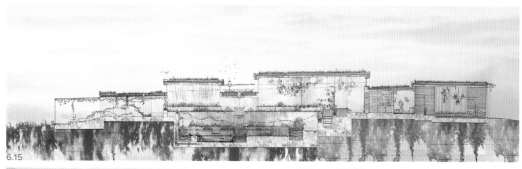

6.15

6.16

6.17

Fig. 6.18 Robert Newcombe Y2, 'Gravesend Horticulture Centre'. The Gravesend Horticulture Centre set in 2064 is a porous walled garden, sheltering and propagating an oasis of nature at the centre of the historic gateway to London, whilst re-activating a decaying post-industrial context. **Fig. 6.19 Ye Lone (Jarrell) Goh** Y2, 'The Seafort Fish Farm'. The derelict offshore Redsands Fort has been repurposed into a modernised salmon farm. New infrastructure meets with the rusting shells of the steel towers, and visitors can spend a day fishing and dining while being surrounded by fragments of a wartime relic. **Fig. 6.20 Thomas Cubitt** Y2, 'Shornemead Garden City'. A housing development placed adjacent to the Thames Estuary. In response to the rise in sea level, the project acts as an example of a village that could co-exist with the

flood zone, harvesting the tide in order to generate energy. The development is suspended above a series of water gardens which absorb tidal surges and mitigate flooding on a larger scale.

6.18

6.19

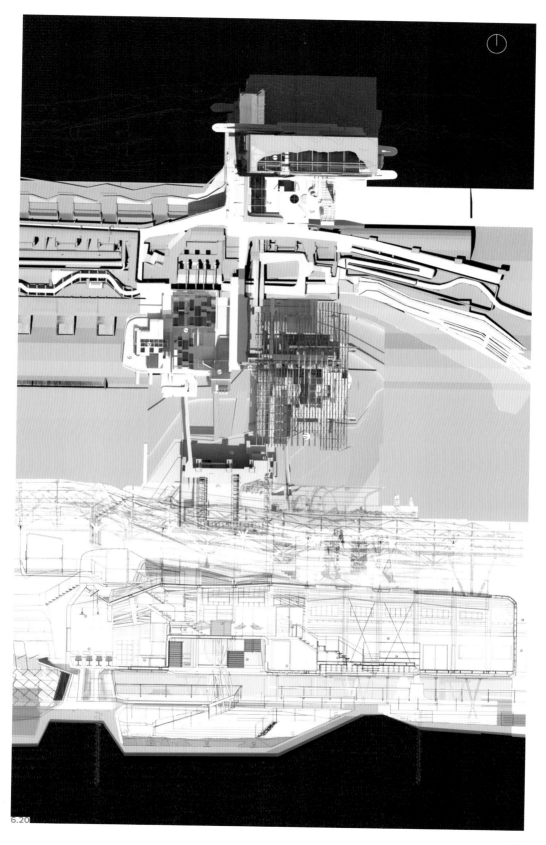

6.20

Unit 7

Short Stay

Ming Chung, Nick Tyson

Year 2
Katherine Feltwell, Lucca
Ferrarese, Wang Chun
(Vincent) Fung, William
Kirkby, Daniel Little,
Kin Lam (Glynnis) Lui

Year 3
Daryll Brown, Muzhi Chen,
Shirley Lee Mei Ying,
Wenhao (Perry) Li, Smiti
Mittal, Huynh Nguyen,
Carina Tran, Panagiotis
Tzannetakis, Zhanshi Xiao

Special thanks to our
critics, guests and friends:
Abi Abdolwahabi, Adam
Atraktzi, Bim Burton,
Matthew Butcher, David
Briggs, Mollie Claypool,
Kate Davies, Inigo Dodd,
Nick Dunn, David Miller,
Luis Fernandez, Richard
Grimes, Edgardo De Lara,
Chris Matthews, Wes Rosen,
Bob Sheil, Lauren Shevills,
Paul Smoothy, Timmy Tae-In
Yoon, Emmanuel Vercruysse,
Nick Westby

The Bartlett School of Architecture 2014

Unit 7 continues to embrace the workshop as a place to learn, experiment and cultivate new ideas in order to develop a practice that relies upon a tactile understanding of materials as a fundamental part of the design process. We are interested in making as an approach that is experimental and open-ended, leading to new and unexpected architectural possibilities.

————This year we explored proposals for an anticipatory architecture that combined material modularity with programmes for transitional inhabitation. We are inspired by the utopian vision of the Metabolists who pioneered the concepts of adaptive architectural infrastructures combined with a meticulous organisation of component parts. Spatial prototypes were developed through direct engagement with real materials and associated processes of fabrication in The Bartlett workshops. These material prototypes became a springboard to test ideas of modularisation and sought to offer alternative ways to embed a new architecture within the Manhattan grid.

Project 1: Capsule

Capsule is a micro-space for urban environments and explores material characteristics at human scale. Minimal dwelling typologies were explored that balanced material economies with qualities of inhabitation. This initial design project was principally developed through large-scale models and experimental one-to-one scale prototypes that simultaneously addressed material detail and the ergonomics of capsule design.

————Our field trip to New York offered a rich cultural platform to support design activities for our second project, Short Stay. We visited the vertical galleries of the New Museum by SANAA, the linear elevated landscapes of the High Line by Diller Scofidio, the 'permanent installation' home studio at 101 Spring Street by Donald Judd and the fabrication workshop of Situ Studio. The Bowery, one of the oldest thoroughfares on the Lower East Side of Manhattan was the focus of our research. In the late 1800's it was a neglected area filled with heap hotels, theatres and bars. The removal of the elevated train track in the 1950's transformed the neighbourhood into a frenetic mix of commercial establishments, and high-end cultural institutions.

Project 2: Short Stay

Short Stay invited students to define transitional urban programmes, to investigate new ideas for inhabitation alongside time-based public activities in the Bowery. Where Capsule investigated the single unit at human scale, Short Stay introduced collective inhabitation and infrastructural interventions that mediated with urban infill sites within the city grain of Manhattan. Proposals ranged from adaptable micro-architecture for seasonal cultural events to adaptive macro-vertical systems for migratory populations.

————The projects aim to capture design intent: somewhere between ideas and material processes, for an architecture that can remain nimble and responsive to the continually evolving fabric of the city.

Fig. 7.1 Muzhi Chen Y3, 'Prototype Flat Pack Shelter'. Laser perforated stressed skin plywood. **Fig. 7.2 – 7.3 Kin Lam (Glynnis) Lui** Y2, 'Reading Capsule'. Ergonomic activity composite and assembly sequence for deployable reinforced fabric shell. **Fig. 7.4 Daniel Little** Y2, 'Temporary Urban Shelter'. Rib jointed recycled paper segments forming monocoque shell. **Fig. 7.5 Muzhi Chen** Y3, Tailor Shop House, New York. Universal prefabricated cross laminated timber units are wrapped in a perforated user adapted façade which mediates local daylight conditions with rituals of living and working. **Fig. 7.6 Shirley Lee Mei Ying** Y3, 'Poetry Capsule'. Laser cut tessellated interlocking plywood skin. **Fig. 7.7 Katherine Feltwell** Y2, 'Capsule Coat'. Velcro fastened waxed fabric insulated kernels.

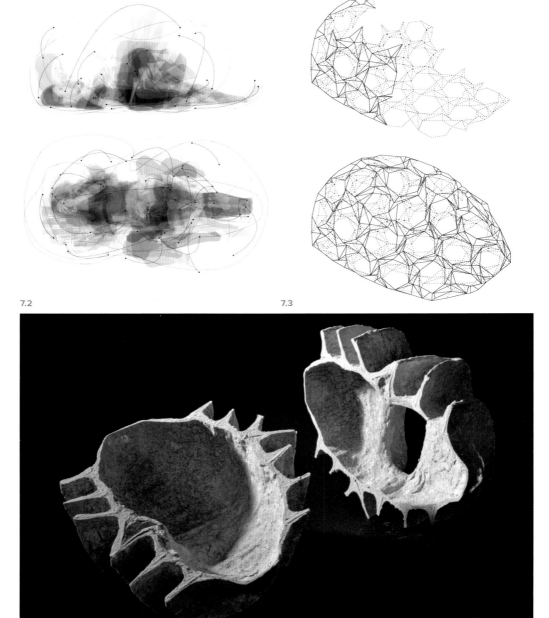

7.2

7.3

7.4

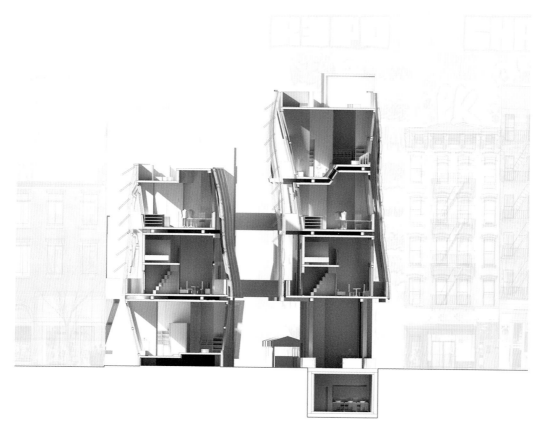

7.5

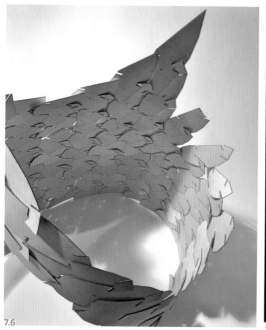

7.6

7.7

Figs. **7.8 – 7.9 Daryll Brown** Y3, 'Vertical Market', New York. Orchard Street market is encouraged to expand vertically into small-scale loft space galleries. Section through composite steel and fabric cast superstructure. Study models, brass rod and phenol coated plywood. Figs. **7.10 – 7.12 Wenhao (Perry) Li** Y3, 'Seafood Market and Restaurant'. Schematic for prefabricated components and vertical transportation rooms. View from New York yellow cab. Section of streetlevel live seafood market, hotel accommodation capsules and rooftop restaurant connected by transit dining rooms.

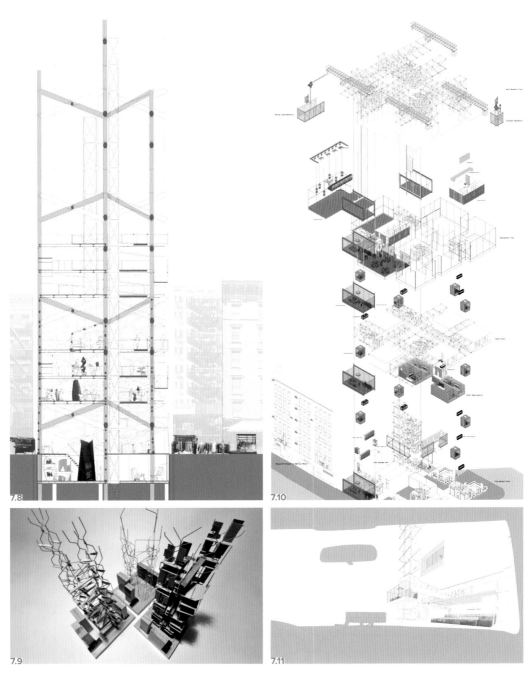

7.8

7.9

7.10

7.11

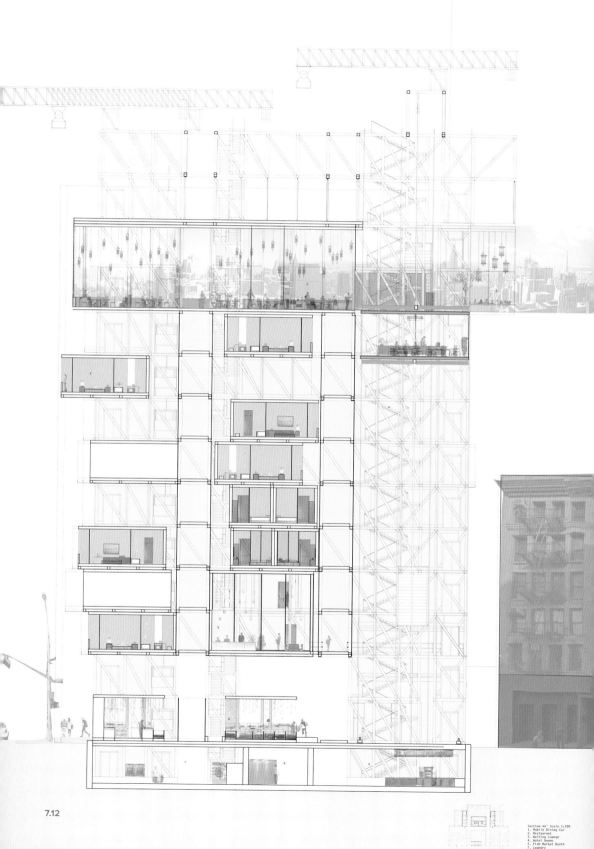

7.12

Section AA' Scale 1:100
1. Mobile Dining Car
2. Restaurant
3. Waiting Lounge
4. Hotel Rooms
5. Fish Market Booth
6. Fish Market Booth
7. Laundry
8. Staff Changing Room
9. Kitchen

Fig. 7.13 & 7.15 **Huynh Nguyen** Y3, 'Workshop for Transitional Living', New York. Schematic of component assembly – street level workshop, communal, social and educational facilities with adaptable dwelling clusters. Capsules located in the upper levels of the block interior share a system of gantries with the self build production line sequences. Capsule Prototype with interlocking CNC milled plywood structure Fig. 7.14 & 7.16 **Smiti Mittal** Y3, 'Yoga Capsule.' 3D printed study models exploring hexagonal ground matrix, dodecahedron structure and hybrid systems. Diamond Guild, New York. Light basket structures are designed to filter daylight through the residential school and workshops and intensify light conditions through a series of lenses to the street level public space.

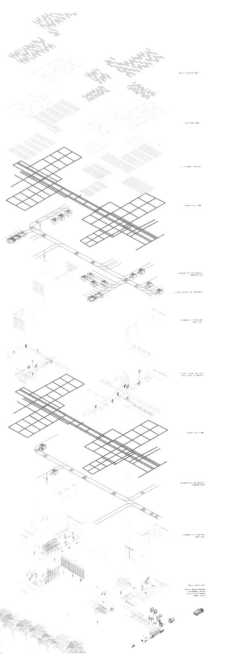

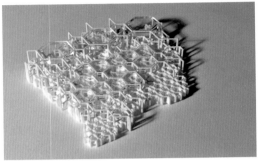

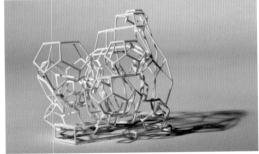

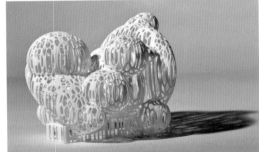

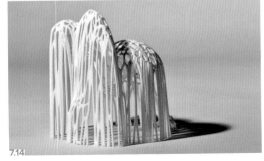

7.13

7.14

7.15

7.16

Fig. 7.17 – 7.20 **Carina Tran** Y3, 'Prototype Bivouac and Seasonal Performance Rig, New York'. Sequence of adaptive suspended reinforced fabric cells. Study model and test rig for prototype system. Section drawing through existing gap site, courtyard and rooftop with space frame performance rig. The Rig facilitates a changing timetable of events ranging from roof top music performances, poetry readings to cinema club, enveloped by a series of adaptive fabric membranes that moderate light, temperature and acoustics.

Figs. 7.1, 7.4, 7.6, 7.8, 7.10, 7.13, 7.14, 7.16 photographed by Paul Smoothy.

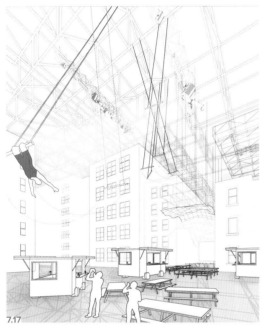

7.17

7.18

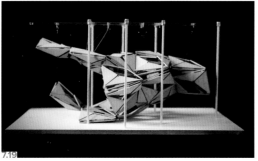

7.19

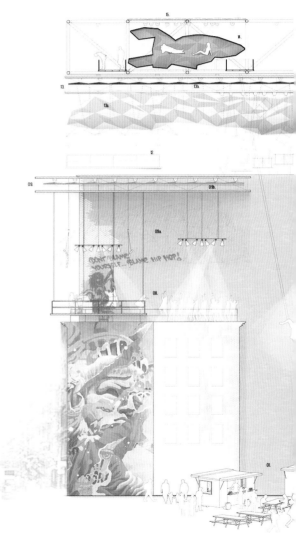

7.20

Unit 8

Details and Misbehaviors

Rhys Cannon, Colin Herperger

Year 2
Naomi De Barr, Kelly Frank, Egmontas Geras, Aqsa Iftikhar, Rikard Kahn, Wenya Liu, Priscilla Wong

Year 3
Charlotte Archer, Thomas Budd, Tik Chun (Zion) Chan, Emma Colthurst, Kar Tung (Karen) Ko, Ian Ng, Joshua Stevenson-Brown, Joshua Toh Kai Heng, Eleanor Daisy Ursell, Hoi Yiu (Carolyn) Wong

Thanks to our critics: Abi Abdolwahabi, Ben Addy, Laura Allen, Alessandro Ayuso, Nat Chard, Sarah Custance, Bernadette Devilat, Richard Grimes, Phillip Hall-Patch, Jonathan Hill, Diony Kypraiou, Adrian Lahoud, Felipe Lanuza Rilling, Jack Newton, Alan Penn, Frosso Pimenides, Franco Pisani, Hugo Sands, Peter Scully, Matt Springett, Tomas Stokke, Natalija Subotincic, Mark West, and Fiona Zisch

Special thanks to Scott Batty for his dedicated work as Year 3 Technical Tutor and also to Ness Lafoy, Steven Pippin and Marcus Stockton for sharing their works with the studio

We are grateful to our sponsors Moxon Architects and Prandina

The Bartlett School of Architecture 2014

We are interested in the beauty of the almost correct

The Unit sets out to establish the importance of finding more within the world than that which is obvious. Intuition leads to invention but also demands risk taking. It is an uncertain area where the answers are not generally known. A sort of misbehaviour exists within the process of making that allows a character to emerge, somehow even richer.

————Architecture, and the development of any idea, frequently reveals these glitches or gremlins. If nurtured, these moments can give lead to a degree of character or personality, anthropomorphism even. The very fabric of a building can come alive and it can begin to exert an unexpected influence upon those that occupy and interact with it. The Unit considers such character by proposing architectures as players within a wider landscape and that 'contextuality' is the term for the interplay and conversation between them.

————The last few years have seen a proliferation of computer generated imagery and usage of digital techniques within student work. We seek to re-invigorate the use of handcrafted fabrication in parallel to this and better understand the application and transition to digital techniques within the design and production process. Physical models and objects have for centuries, represented one of the most engaging means to describe and declare architectural intention.

————Venice and northern Italy was our focal point of study and invention for the second term. Errors, mistakes and abnormalities were encouraged and these unexpected attributes of the making process of the first term's work became the foundation of the building proposals. We paid homage to the craftsmanship and attention to detail within the works of Carlo Scarpa, the passion and precision engineering of Italian high-performance cars, and the sculptural concrete forms of Giovanni Michelucci's churches.

————Examples of the Unit's ambition are realised through a range of projects including: Joshua Toh's 'Cathedral of Craft' which explores the extremes of cast concrete and fabric formwork with its performance and ability to be both monumental and delicate; Karen Ko's 'Venetto Town Hall' examines the development and manipulation of traditional Venetian architecture and Josh Stevenson-Brown's 'Construction School', an intimate examination of Venice stripped back to basics; as well as the careful observations, attention to detail, anomalies and quirks of culture found within Daisy Ursell's 'Venetian Film Studios' and Tom Budd's unexpected night in 'Hotel Coletti'.

Fig. 8.1 Joshua Toh Kai Heng Y3, '1:10 Test Model of Tailored Classical Fabric Cast Doorway'. The final model in a series of study models tailoring a classical fabric architecture. Centering around the study of the technique of fabric formwork; casting into it; exploring the design potential of a fabric architecture introducing concepts of the body and the act of undressing. **Fig. 8.2 Joshua Toh Kai Heng** Y3, 'Short Section of The Venice Cathedral of Craft'. The Venice Cathedral of Craft was a proposal for a dramatic building by the Rialto Bridge in Venice housing an atelier for the Italian fashion house of Valentino. The building was a culmination of a year long study into the design potential of a tailored fabric cast architecture. The proposal involved the selective preservation of a classical palazzo onsite and the insertion

of fabric cast elements to create a series of cathedral-like spaces celebrating the architecture and the craft of Venice. **Fig. 8.3 – 8.4 Joshua Stevenson-Brown** Y3, 'Venetian Construction School, interior views'. A site of unused buildings become occupied in phases by the school. Temporary school facilities are set up onsite, while the existing buildings are dissected by the students to learn about the revealed construction techniques used to deal with the shifting conditions of the city. Adapting, developing and experimenting with these techniques students go on to build the permanent parts of the school.

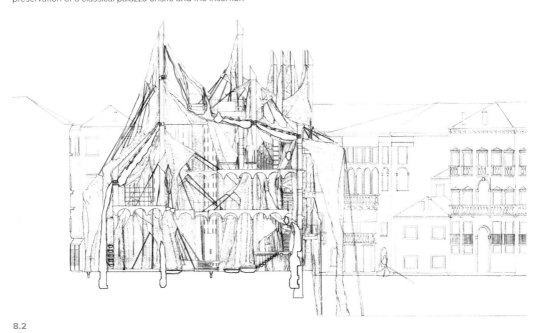

8.2

8.3

8.4

Fig. 8.5 **Ian Ng** Y3, 'Slit-Scan Test Rigs'. A series of bespoke
'slit-scan' cameras were fabricated and arranged accordingly
to capture a variety time-based decays and interactions. The
resulting imagery thus embodied an additional time-scale,
depicted within the horizontal track of the photograph.

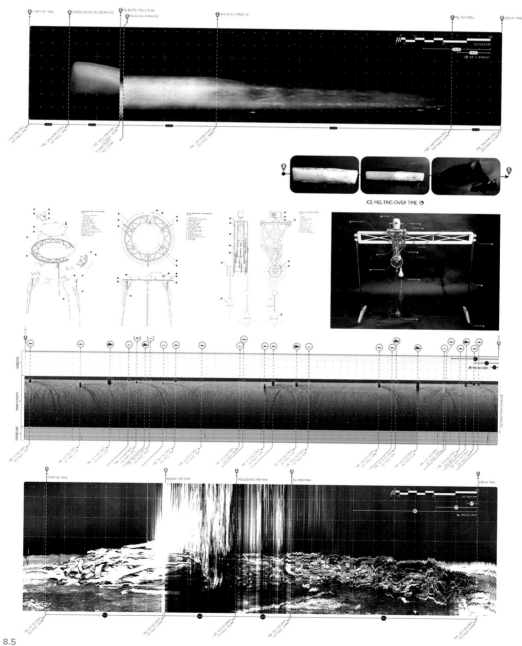

ICE MELTING OVER TIME

8.5

Fig. 8.6 – 8.7 **Rikard Khan** Y2, 'Linear Drawing of the Route taken by a Member of the Rowing Club'. The building responds to studies of navigating the city of Venice with the experiences of expanding and compressing spaces. It also responds to Venice's sensitive relationship of land and water with the fluctuating tide, the experiences of these two networks individually and how they can overlap and interweave. The floating elements are refined, controlled spaces, and make reference to Venetian boat-building tradition. The two building elements adapt to different tides, reconfiguring routes within the building. **Fig. 8.8 Hoi Yiu (Carolyn) Wong** Y3, 'The New Mercato del Pesce'. Built on the site of the existing fish market, it uses an intricate woven system of brass sunpipes to bring light from the sun-soaked rooftops to the darker alleyways

below. Steam from the kitchen and mist from the freezer room collide to create a suspended body of vapour within specific spaces, giving volume to the light intersecting it. The circulation of guests is choreographed to inhabit and interact with this volumetric light, transforming the functional into the spectacular. **Fig. 8.9 Egmontas Geras** Y2, 'A House and Delicatessen', Venice. A chef and his family inhabit a concrete house on the edge of a residential piazza. The house is comprised of concrete elements that are moulded to become an animated infrastructure of activities inside and outside its boundaries. The walls are abundant with rainwater and seagulls as much as hams and bread as the family struggles to inhabit a concrete which attempts to support a medley of Venetian activity.

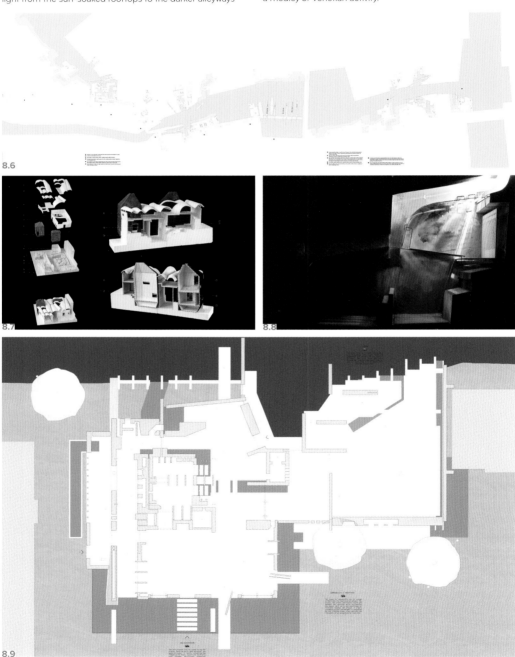

8.6

8.7

8.8

8.9

Fig. 8.10 **Naomi de Barr** Y2, 'A Map of an Imagined Surface'. Drawn using a mapping instrument consisting of: a magnifying glass; set of mirrors; additional water and a varying scale, which are used to distort a real surface to and create a site-specific map. A graphical code is produced through the positioning of each cartographic tool which aids the interpretation of the map. Fig. 8.11 **Kelly Frank** Y2, 'Star-Gazing Inn'. A clustered series of private boutique suites form a constellation of buildings to facilitate the occupants to observe the Venetian night sky. Fig. 8.12 **Charlotte Archer** Y3, 'Sound Park and Touring Musicians Residence'. The Venetian tide changes four times a day shifting the horizon and altering the way you experience the city from the water and the flooding ground, Il Parco del Suono seeks to heighten this experience.

Undulating tidal shifts dictate subtle differences between the architecture of the landscape and water levels affecting sound pockets. The sound map illustrates the uniqueness of each experience by mapping frequency ranges, sound sources, lapping water and clunking gondolas, all translating tidal shift into a true Venetian performance. Fig. 8.13 **Tik Chun (Zion) Chan** Y3, 'Urban Wetland Park', East London. Adjacent to the busiest spaghetti junction in London, the scheme aims to regenerate the natural landscape of Roding Valley, and create a mini urban oasis within the gap of surrounding heavy infrastructures by transforming the site into a wetland park. The bowl-shaped landform collects wash-off from the motorways, and purifies it using series of constructed wetlands before entering the river.

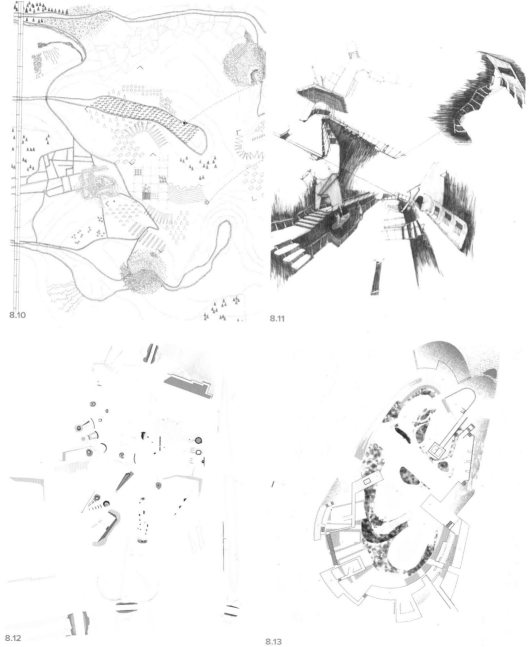

8.10

8.11

8.12

8.13

Fig. 8.14 Priscilla Wong Y2, 'Nursery and Urban Park', development model. A tectonic landscape of subtle undulating surfaces, capturing rainwater into a series of cisterns for the irrigation of the nursery and park. **Fig. 8.15 Kar Tung (Karen) Ko** Y3, 'Pinhole Camera Assembly'. The operation of the pinhole camera relies on engaging the user's curiosity. Each handle turns a different mechanism within the camera, which manifest themselves in the movement of sand filled weights below the camera. The camera records the static surrounding environment and the movements of the user, influencing the mechanisms within that further distort the image recorded by the camera to give a final result. **Fig. 8.16 Emma Colthurst** Y3, 'The Gimbal'. This reconnects the landscape of Royal Victoria Docklands, taking each piece of industrial renascence as players within the rings. Each piece sits in its own coordinate and relationship to its fellow players. As the rings turn, the spatial relationships between the pieces shift as they are juxtaposed against each other. In these brief moments of observation the Gimbal realigns the landscape, refocusing the Docklands in moments of realisation, before falling away.

8.14

8.15

8.16

Fig. 8.17 **Thomas Budd** Y3, 'An Unexpected Night in the
Hotel Coletti', short-section. A series of unique and peculiar
interactions between the various hotel guests and staff are
accentuated by an architecture interconnected by the various
mechanical; electrical and operational services of the hotel.
Fig. 8.18 **Thomas Budd** Y3, 'Instructional Re-configuration,'
drawing and photograph. A speculative drawing, modelling
and photographic exercise undertaken in the London
docklands which explores the potential for the inner workings
of a camera to reorganise and reconfigure spatial relationships.

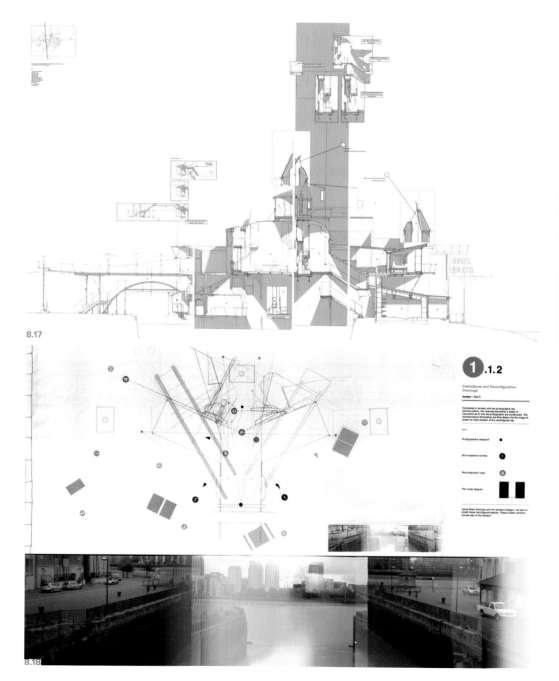

8.17

8.18

Fig. 8.19 Kar Tung (Karen) Ko Y3, 'Venetto Town Hall'. The new architecture is an attempt to find a balance between the old and the new and to exemplify the result of the experiment, in which the architect's take on the future of Venice manifests itself in the architecture. The architecture exploits the play of light and shadow to reveal what has been preserved and what has been demolished. Negative spaces are created by the demolished segments enabling new contemporary interventions. **Fig. 8.20 Aqsa Iftikhar** Y2, 'Landscape of Smell'. The drawing explores the depiction of smell as a colour and the sequence of actions undertaken by the local fisherman preparing their nets. **Fig. 8.21 Wenya Liu** Y2, 'Fish Market and Restaurant'. A building on the site of the existing Rialto fish market formed of a eries of interlocking brick arches creating inner volumes to nestle the activiites of the market and restaurant. **Fig. 8.22 Priscilla Wong** Y2, 'Nursery and Urban Park Model', short-section. The relationship with the canal, water and shifting tidal conditions is further exploited within the new addition to the Venetian urban landscape.

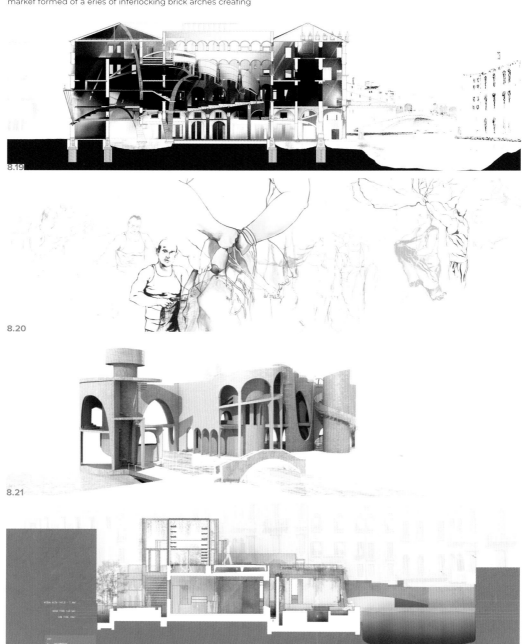

8.19

8.20

8.21

8.22

Fig. 8.23 **Eleanor Daisy Ursell** Y3, 'Venetian Film Studio', plan.
The Venicetian Film Studio is a speculative comment on
the reality of Venice behind its tired and infamous façade.
The play between fact and fiction within the architecture
allows for a 'super Venetian' backdrop of activity on camera
by creating a convincing and realistic setting. The studio
design is driven by the notion of flexibility and optimum
adaptability of the sets between films in parallel with the
creation of the preconceived views held of Venice. The site
lies within Dorsoduro in Venice, Italy.

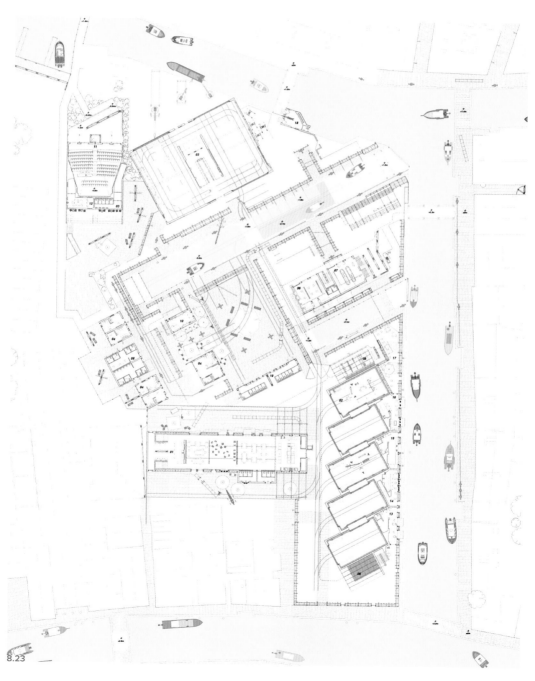

8.23

Unit 9

Performance

Max Dewdney, Chee-Kit Lai

Year 2
Tae Woo Hong, Angus Iles,
Yangyang Liu, Rosa
Prichard, Soma Sato,
Anastasia-Christina Stan,
Yu Xuan The, Ernest Zhi
Heng Wang

Year 3
Yin Fung (Jacky) Chan,
Duncan (Harry) Clover,
Marcus Cole, Ruochong
(Robin) Fu, Xiang (Robin)
Gu, Claire Haugh, Abigail
Portus, Ivo Tedbury

Unit 9 continues to work with
ongoing collaborator Arup
Associates for Year 3
Technical Dissertations.
Special thanks to James
Ward and Mick Brundle

Unit 9 also continues an
on-going collaboration
with Denis Vlieghe who
runs a Physical Computing
Workshop as part of Project 1

Special thanks to:
Abi Abdolwahabi,
Julia Backhaus, Alexander
Barretta, Peter Bishop,
Greg Blee, Iain Borden,
Alastair Browning, Mick
Brundle, Ming Chung,
Gary Edwards, Pedro
Font-Alba, Murray Fraser,
Maria Fulford, Stephen Gage,
Joshua Green, Penelope
Haralambidou, Catherine
Harrington, Carlos Jimenez
Cenamor, Constance Lau,
Holly Lewis, Jamie Lilley,
Ian Ng, Sophia Psarra,
Jane Rendell, Peg Rawes,
Sabine Storp, Ned Scott,
Gabby Shawcross, Camila
Sotomayor, Nick Tyson,
Manijeh Verghese, Denis
Vlieghe, Victoria Watson,
James Ward, Nick Westby,
Danielle Wilkins, Simon
Withers

The Bartlett School of Architecture 2014

We see space as scripted, not a tabula rasa. *Space is inherited and is always attached to geographies, histories, and policies.* [1]

We are interested in the Performance of Architecture, both as a set of scripted, artistic and cultural acts and actions as well as investigations into the 'Performance Specification' (particular properties) of buildings, assessed through their material and environmental properties. Vital to the 'Performance of Architecture' is the performance of cities, through their ecology, technology and infrastructure. The performances of cities are marked through events and actions such as protests (as seen in Rio 2013 and London Riots/Occupy 2011/2) and celebrations (World Cup 2014 and Olympics 2012/16). It is through the mediation of technology that performances between buildings and cities' are linked. The use of digital social communication networks and the high-tech industrial revolution of digital technologies are changing the way in which we fund, occupy, produce and design architecture. An understanding of both the social and the technological are vital for architects to help shape the environmental and social performance of our future cities.

Architecture is in a constant state of construction and reconstruction, co-production of the social and technical. [2]

For the last two years we have visited Brazil. This year the building proposals aim to act as new urban networks and as responsive generators for future exchange and adaptation for users' changing needs sited in Rio De Janeiro, Brazil. The specific focus of research was on the materiality of Brazilian Architecture, looking at its performance specific to both the environmental as well as social conditions. We have studied the links between a series of case study buildings, understanding their construction techniques, material expressions and social contexts as a means to inform a critical position in relation to each student's choice of building programme.

This is why I'm interested, although it's a dangerous phrase to use, in responsive architecture, that responds to appetites rather than problems. But I don't want to have to define the appetites. The architecture has to be very responsive, but rather loose... [3]

This year Unit 9 worked in collaboration with University of Columbia's Studio X in Rio De Janeiro.

1. Rachel Hann, 'Blurred Architecture: Duration and performance in the work of Diller Scofidio + Renfro', *Performance Research: A Journal of the Performing Arts*, 17:5, 2012, p.15
2. Bruno Latour, *Reassembling the Social: An Introduction to Actor Network Theory*, (Oxford: OUP, 2007)
3. Cedric Price in conversation with Richard Goodwin, *Public Life – Public Place*, Issue 1 (London: Architectural Society, 1979)

Fig. 9.1 **Ivo Tedbury** Y3, 'Ghost Landscapes of Rio'. These devices seek to communicate images of a demolished urban fabric which previously occupied the site, specifically, in what is now the 2016 Rio Olympic park. Responding to the strict public space advertising laws introduced in Brazilian cities, all that is visible to the naked eye are strips of shimmering LEDs – instead the experience is mediated by technology: when a camera is swiped over LEDs, the strip delivers the image in individual columns of pixels. Fig. 9.2 – 9.4 **Ivo Tedbury** Y3, 'Circuit Atlantica, Formula 1 Track and Pit Building', Copacabana Beach. A permanent structural intervention on the iconic site, which supports the temporary spaces that accommodate the race over the specific timeframe, but which can be stored underground during the rest of the year.

A 'canopy' of LED strips is hung over the track, allowing the viewing experience to be augmented by a motion-sensitive light display, but also generating advertising revenue through the 'panning photography' technique, specific to motor racing. This revenue in turn subsidises business start-up and community spaces which occupy spatial units along the strip for the rest of the year, forming a raised promenade which looks over the beach, linked to existing pedestrian routes using ramps across the road.

9.2

9.3

9.4

Fig. 9.5 **Duncan (Harry) Clover** Y3, 'National Music Conference Centre and Lido'. Sited on the iconic Arpourador Rock between Ipanema and Copacabana beches in Rio De Janeiro the building acts as a wave energy hydro electric power station, seasonal music performance and conference centre while providing all round lidos. The sea wall is made up of oscillating water columns which shelters the lido bathing area all year round, these pools are tiered and once drained create a festival auditorium for the Rio music conference and other national celebrations. The building has three stages and each roof articulates and opens in festival period using hydraulic wave power.

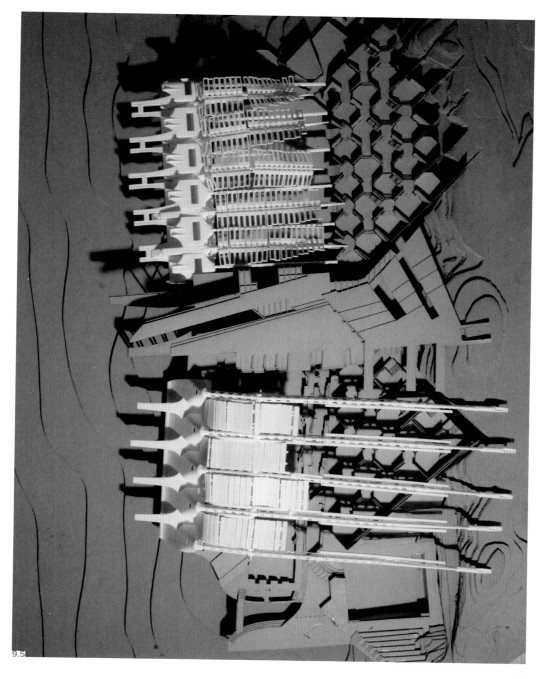

9.5

Fig. 9.6 **Ruochong Fu** Y3, 'iSportsPark', Centro, Rio de Janeiro. The sports park is for office workers and local residents located in the Centro area of Rio de Janeiro. The building's interactive façade pulsates according to athletes' heart rates, allowing spectators and pedestrians to tell the intensity of the on going events. Together with other interactive and digital technologies it creates an immersive social and sporting environment. Activities includes gaming, training, relaxing, shopping and dinning. The building is visioned as a living architecture operating 24/7 and aims to use innovative sporting experiences to attract people and bring life back to the area, while also serving as an urban intervention and bridge within otherwise uninhabited business district. **Fig. 9.7 Tae Woo Hong** Y2, 'Capoeira Performing Device'. The project looks at the key

characteristics and movements of Capoeira, a popular game and Brazilian maritial art. The key qualities of Capoeira are constant motion, balance and speed. Through a series of interactive prototypes the final device replicates the fundamental movement of Capoeira known as 'Ginga', activated through players interaction with light sensors.
Fig. 9.8 Yin Fung Chan Y3, 'Desalination Plant in Rio de Janeiro'. The building acts as an environmental model responding to two major conditions of the site: water and waste pollution in Botafogo Bay. Rubbish floating on the water surface is collected by boats for recycling and generating electricity with a Biomass boiler. The energy produced from the waste collected is then used to desalinate water from the bay providing fresh water for visitors. The systems and

9.6

9.7

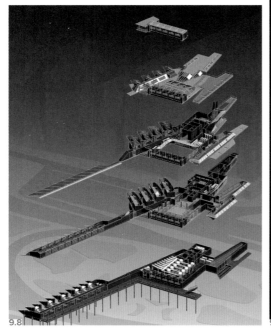

9.8

9.9

processes of recycling and purification form part of the
building's fabric and are displayed to the public. **Fig. 9.9**
Ruochong Fu Y3, 'iSportsPark', Centro, Rio de Janeiro, model.

Fig. 9.10 Xiang Gu Y3, 'Interactive Sunflower Device'. Programmed with Arduino, the interactive device responds to the movement of light within Rio De Janeiro. The components rise and fall, tilting and turning to capture the movement of the sunlight throughout the day, creating a reflective field condition and solar collection above and shadow play below. **Fig. 9.11 Claire Haugh** Y3, 'Orchidarium'. (See also Fig 9.18) **Fig. 9.12 Yu Xuan Teh** Y2, 'Institute of Rio De Janeiro Landscape and Tourist Jetty'. Rio de Janeiro's natural landscapes have been declared a World Heritage Site by UNESCO. The project is sited in one of the city's most picturesque locations. The project provides private spaces for landscape architects and UNESCO committees and researcher as a forum to discuss the preservation of Rio's

natural landscape. The building also provides a public tourist jetty with cafe and viewing platforms allowing visitors to experience the landscape beyond. **Fig. 9.13 Ernest Zhi Heng Wang** Y2, 'The Samba Rhythm Machine'. The machine's performance incorporates various elements of Samba dance and music. Like a Samba drum bateria, the Samba Rhythm Machine is controlled by a Mestre (band conductor). A Kinect reads hand movements and translates these readings into motor movements, moving the device's components and creating multiple performances akin to the carnival in Rio.

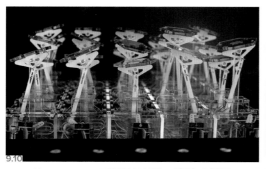
9.10

9.11

9.12

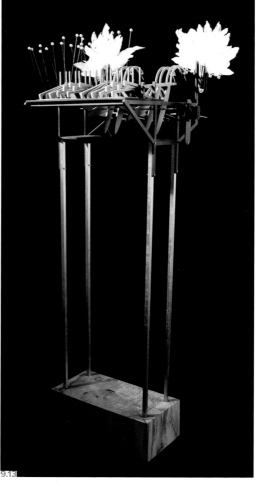
9.13

Fig. 9.14 Abigail Portus Y3, 'Performance Centre'. The building is a performance centre and social hub, nestled alongside the Lapa aquaduct which accommodates a tram stop, between the Santa Teresa favela hillside and the main city. It provides an open community space with a central paraboloid theatre that projects an optical illusion of activity in the centre up to the floor above. This provides a virtual viewing plane, so visitors can benefit from a 'secondary' performance. **Fig. 9.15 Ivo Tedbury** Y3, 'Circuit Atlantica', Formula 1 Track and Pit Building, Copacabana Beach. (See Fig 9.2) **Fig. 9.16 Rosa Prichard** Y2, 'Camdomble Church'. The Candomble ritual steps are translated into experiential spaces within the building. The two façades address contrasting neighbourhoods – one poorer and largely Candomble believers, and one wealthier and largely observers. The synthesis of these groups is achieved through shared human experience – such as music, dancing and feasting – which are irrespective of class. **Fig. 9.17 Marcus Cole** Y3, 'Reification of Data'. Taking precedence from Brazil's ambitious plans to form its own internet, the project looks into the potential of depicting the digital within the analogue through the production of shadow QR codes. The device explores the potential for individual pixel blocks to form the basis of a façade system that responds to the sun. When positioned correctly, the cast shadows align to form QR codes. The physical model also explores the realms of sciography, acting as a prototype for a moving façade system that creates a link between the digital and physical realms.

9.14

9.15

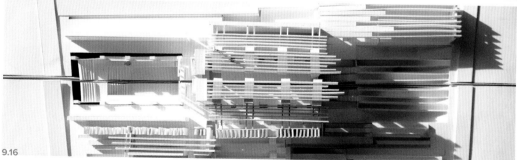

9.16

9.17

Fig. 9.18 Claire Haugh Y3, 'Orchidarium'. Woven into the grid of an old derelict hotel in the mountains outside of Rio de Janeiro's city centre is the Orchidarium. A botanical gardens for Brazil's native orchids, seed store and research facility, the project not only provides new jobs for residents within the local Canoas favela but also becomes the new outpost for the Darwin Initiative based in Kew, England. At night the building's façade is visible across the city as three dimensional images are projected onto its wires. **Fig. 9.19 Marcus Cole** Y3, 'Reification of Data'. **Fig. 9.20 Marcus Cole** Y3, 'The National Institute of Data: Analogue & Digital Archive'. The National Institute of Data forms part of a speculative government scheme providing the first steps towards a technologically independent Brazil. Its purpose is to provide a platform for the public to involve themselves in the undertakings of its government but also for the production of a data centre capable of fuelling Brazil's 'datapendency'. Thus as well as a modular data centre design, the building contains a public archive storing patents linked closely to Brazil's technological past, present and future. **Fig. 9.21 Duncan (Harry) Clover** Y3, segment of a temporary floating pontoon venue for Rio's carnival. Using the pressure exerted on the floor and waves passing underneath the fabric ceiling oscillates the jewels of mirror attached casting fragmented beams of light across the floor. Water is simultaneously pumped up to a Japanese cistern in the ceiling, which fills and tips at intervals then flowing down through tubes while vibrations from the venue's sound system reflect the conditions of the waves.

9.18

9.19

9.20

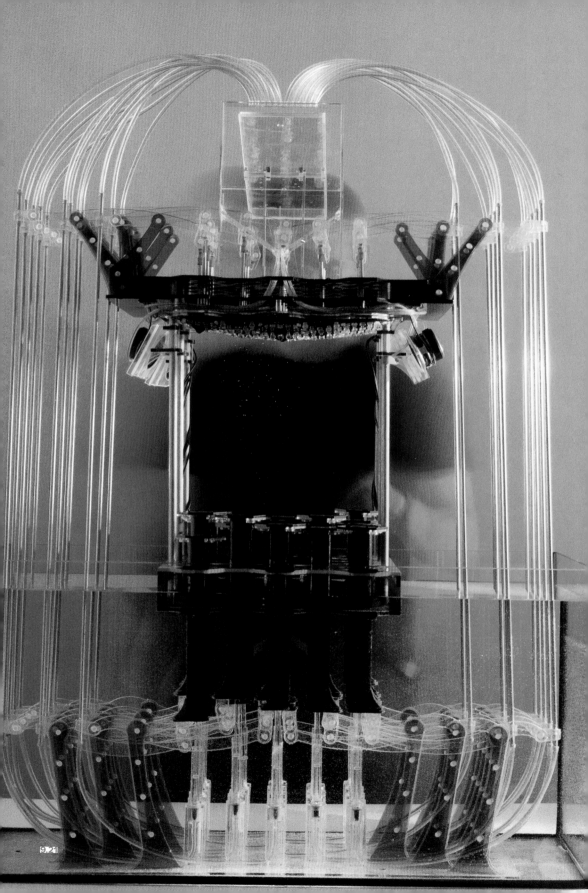

BSc Architectural & Interdisciplinary Studies

Elizabeth Dow, Barbara Penner

The Bartlett School of Architecture 2014

Architectural culture has never been the exclusive product of architects, but now, more than ever, there are many other people working in related fields (film, media, curation, design and creative practice) who shape debates and ideas around architecture in significant ways. In bringing together architectural research and design and creative practice courses, the BSc (Hons) in Architectural & Interdisciplinary Studies (AIS) aims to produce the development of independent-minded graduates who are equipped to participate in these complex debates.

————This is a unique programme that allows students to follow modules within The Bartlett as well as with modules in other UCL departments. It builds on the successful BSc Architectural Studies programme, which ran between 2002-2012 and produced over 110 graduates. Graduates have gone on to postgraduate studies and professional careers in a wide variety of fields including: journalism, landscape design, lighting design, international development, fine arts, photography, printmaking, arts education and management, events management, urban planning, law, accounting, property valuation, and construction management. They have pursued graduate studies at universities such as the Royal College of Art, Central St. Martin's, Imperial College, London School of Economics and ETH in Zurich as well as at UCL.

————The great strength of the BSc AIS programme is its interdisciplinarity: students are able to tailor their own course of study to suit their particular interests and future postgraduate and career plans. The course suits highly motivated, independent students who are interested in architecture, design, and urban studies, but who also wish to take advantage of electives on offer elsewhere in UCL. Popular choices are Art History, Management, Languages, Economics, Psychology, History, Mathematics, Anthropology, Law, Archaeology, and Geography.

————There are three specially tailored course modules for BSc AIS students within The Bartlett: Architectural Research, Dissertation, and Design and Creative Practice (Project X), samples of which are reproduced on the following pages.

The Dissertation

Barbara Penner, Brent Pilkey

Students
Nadira Amrani, Amanda Campbell, Yvonne Cheng, Stephen Henderson, Casper Horton-Kitchlew, Ysabel Kaye, Suhee Kim, Alishe Khan, Fong Yi Khoo, Qianwen Ou, Laura Skeggs, India Smith

The Dissertation in Architectural & Interdisciplinary Studies enables students to undertake an independent research project of 10,000 words. The emphasis in this course is on conducting original research and producing an investigative in-depth written piece, supported by appropriate visual and textual documentation. This module is taught through individual or small group tutorials, supplemented by occasional seminars and group meetings. The aims of the module are to enable students to conduct primary research, to think critically about issues with architectural implications, and to develop and showcase practical writing skills. This year students were also strongly encouraged to think creatively in terms of the overall design layout and composition.

Yvonne Cheng
Analysing Twentieth Century Performance Spaces

'Music is liquid architecture; Architecture is frozen music' is Goethe's famous expression that linked these two seemingly unrelated art forms and disciplines through our perception and experience of them. Iannis Xenakis (1922-2001), a Greek composer, who worked as an engineering assistant with architect Le Corbusier (1887-1965) and studied music with composer Olivier Messiaen (1908-1992) in the 1940s and 1950s, invented an unprecedented musical style, which he calls 'stochastic' composition, through the combination of architectural and musical processes. As a result, Xenakis's works have materialised Goethe's abstract quote. His music complicates traditional norms of interaction between stage and auditorium; music that is performed and the space which music flows through. Our experiences of both artforms are transformed anew.

————Post-war public concert halls in the Western world, which continue to dominate the performance art scene today, were designed to provide a setting for professional performances with emphasis on the cultivation of music. However, throughout Western music history, there are countless examples of musical creations that destabilised this relationship. From as early as the sixteenth century, organ music has been used to enhance the magnificence of the interior of cathedrals, reversing the roles of the centrepiece and its accompaniment. For Xenakis, this relationship is taken a step further – his compositions produce architecture and music simultaneously, deliberately contesting the fundamental differences between these two disciplines and allowing the audience's perception to oscillate between their inner and outer senses; their auditory and visual experiences.

————In this dissertation I investigate both performance spaces as musical form and the idea of architectural membranes in Xenakis's compositions. By comparing Xenakis's music and ideas with a performance space in London – the Southbank Centre's Queen Elizabeth Hall (QEH) – I draw a connection between hearing music and inhabiting performance spaces. The organisation of public and private realms in the auditorium is ambiguous, both complementing and contesting the perception of music that is composed 'spatially'.

————While traditionally, auditorium designers searched for ideal acoustic environments to alter and refine the volume and character of music, Xenakis was interested in controlling the act of listening by the all-encompassing experience of perceiving music inside his architecture. In 'Architecture and listening to music' (1983), Xenakis pointed out that orientation of a performance space is an important criterion of listening to music. Inside the QEH's auditorium, layers of materials surround the audience, including timber, exposed concrete, metallic surfaces and leather coverings. The effect is a sense of intimacy. As a result, although musicians and their instruments are constrained on the stage at a specific distance from the audience, a sensation of comfort is created in this public space by the weight and temperature of surfaces all around the structure of the auditorium to soften frontal perspective indirectly, giving way to the perceptions of vision, hearing, and touch all at once.

Stephen Henderson
Tactics, Theatrics, and Urban Scenography

In Henri Lefebvre's highly influential *The Production of Space* (1974), he explains that 'to change life … we must first change space.' For Lefebvre, to engage in 'a total revolution — material, economic, social, political, psychic, cultural, erotic, etc.' requires the changing of space. Space, he says, contains the potential to allow other kinds of life to exist, but the form it takes in allowing our current life to exist necessarily leads only to the life we have. This is not to say that our current setup renders other kinds of life entirely impossible, but that space must change to facilitate these other kinds if they are to flourish. The changing of space, as the key to changing life, therefore, relies on different concepts of space being understood by the entire society that engages with it.
————The dissertation produces a manifesto for the design of scenography (spatial, theatrical design) which aims to change the conceptions of space held by the audience prior to their experience of a performance. The essay draws on political theatre of the twentieth century (particularly the works of *The Caucasian Chalk Circle* by Bertolt Brecht, *Oh What a Lovely War* by Theatre Workshop, and Punchdrunk's *The Drowned Man: A Hollywood Fable*, a more recent piece of immersive theatre) and the adoption of theatrical techniques in political demonstration. Occupy London and protests that occurred in Minsk in 2011 are taken as examples of the alternative conceptions of space people can have within strategic spaces. Michel de Certeau's ideas about 'strategies' and 'tactics' are drawn upon to show how we might come to new conceptions of space by subverting prescribed interactions with space.
————The format of the essay presents the reader with both strategy and the capacity to subvert. Each chapter of the essay exists on its own as a separate entity (both in textual and physical form), and it is designed to be read in any order that the reader wishes, though a strategy is manifested in the cover images of the chapters and in the page numbering system, which both provide clues to a suggested reading order. Images are presented away from the text as plates with conventional figure references in place, so that readers can draw their own parallels between text and image beyond figure references, or in multiple locations, as the reader sees fit. Finally, a single appendix is presented to be read at any time so that the reader may see where the argument is heading (or has headed). This appendix is the culmination of the dissertation: a manifesto, whose tenets are defined throughout the final chapter. The intention of such a physical design embodies the principles of the manifesto, and can be thought of as a kind of textual scenography, in which interaction and aesthetic have been designed spatially.

Project X: Design and Creative Practice 1, 2 and 3

Elizabeth Dow, Kevin Green, Chee-Kit Lai, Freddy Tuppen

Year 1
Florence Chester, Yufan Jin, Edoardo Lomi, Madeleine Valcour, Robyn Vey Thomas Visscher, Velvet Young

Year 2
Caitlin Abbott, Laura Scudder, Saskia Selwood, Alex Vine, Angus Whitehead

Year 3
Nadira Amrani, Amanda Campbell, Stephen Henderson, Fong Yi (Emmanuelle) Khoo Casper Horton-Kitchlew, Ysabel Kaye, Laura Skeggs, India Smith

Thanks to our consultants and critics: Abi Abdolwahabi, Katy Beinart, Ina Baumeister. Polly Gould, Kevin Green, Jan Kattein, Rebecca Lane, Barbara Penner, Jane Rendell, Catrina Stewart, Mark Sustr

Project X: Design and Creative Practice aims to help students build a creative and reflective practice of their own. It enables them to undertake a mode of working that particularly interests them and an independent practice-based project in which they can research and pursue a subject of their preference. Students are asked to think of architecture in interdisciplinary ways, explore alternative approaches to design and situate their work within a broader cultural context. The work is developed in conjunction with a short written piece. Key questions confront students at different stages of the year concerning the nature of their practice, the contribution of their work to the broader field of architecture, the originality of their project, and the selection of appropriate media for the ideas pursued.

———For our Year 1 Project X students we ran three short projects: 'Home', 'The Endless Loop' and 'A Cabinet of Curiosities'. The projects allowed the students to work at different scales, both in groups and individually, and with a wide variety of media.

———For our Year 2 and 3 Project X students the year started with Project 1 'Occupation Occupation' and we asked the students to occupy a confined space within The Bartlett, appropriating the language and sensibilities of a specific occupation e.g. filmmaker, illusionist. This was followed by the project 'Border' in which students identified an existing border condition and then proposed, designed and constructed an intervention within the border.

———In Term 1 we travelled to Berlin for a field trip, which inspired and influenced each student's individual projects and research paths. In Terms 1 and 2 we were very pleased to have Professor Jane Rendell lead two writing workshops. Jane asked the students to develop and reconsider their design work through writing, drawing upon the themes of her own 'site-writing' work. We also ran a bookbinding workshop that allowed students to consider how the presentation and subsequent binding of their work could inform and be informed by their individual design projects.

———Each student has followed a research path that initially stemmed from projects 1 and 2, but soon developed into a unique and personal direction. The resulting projects are speculative and diverse, as is the use of differing media, ranging from animation, electronics, pop-up books, scale model-making, set design, scriptwriting, joinery, film projection, casting, community consultation, documentary film, curating and material testing, to name just a few.

Fig. X.1 Stephen Henderson Y3, 'Reminiscence and Murder,' model: laser-cut acrylic, plywood, MDF, LEDs, Arduino, and video projection. An interactive model for an interactive stage set of two stories adapted from Oliver Sacks' *The Man Who Mistook His Wife For A Hat*. The model responds to user 'movement' through the space with fragments of narrative. Fig. X.2 Florence Chester Y1, 'Endless Loop'. Stills from a film that explored the constant motion, sense of excitement and shifts in perspective experienced in Primark. Fig. X.3 Stephen Henderson Y3, 'Reminiscence and Murder'. The model contains a series of push-buttons which trigger video projections of imagined theatrical space at 1:1. The intention is to make the model user consider the implications of their choices about how they interact with and produce space, both in the model and in the everyday. Fig. X.4 Stephen Henderson Y3, preparatory sketch to resolve the systems in place to allow the model to work. A laptop, Arduino and pico projector were concealed in the base of the model, along with all the wiring for the LEDs. Projections occur on the model itself, asking questions about the scale of the viewer.

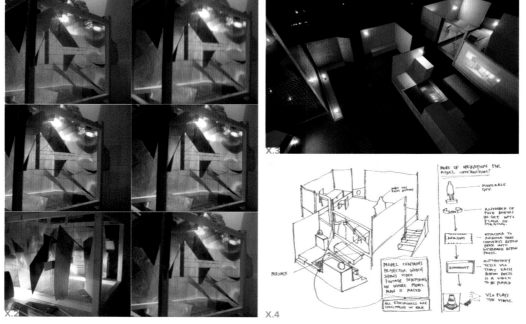

X.1

X.2

X.3

X.4

Fig. X.5 **Casper Horton-Kitchlew** Y3, 'Transported Desert Cave'. Flame fired clay, dried leaf and packing crate host, the appropriation of everyday objects, materials, scents and sounds the elements and housed in a basic packing crate. The aim is to transport the viewer, fleetingly, into another very different world. Fig. X.6 **Casper Horton-Kitchlew** Y3, 'Transported Rainforest'. three species of moss culture, two-way mirror and packing crate host.

Fig. X.7 **Caitlin Abbott** Y2, 'They'll Have us Hanging Around 'til we're Dead'. 1:25 models set up for filming, Act 2 of a backlit shadow stage production of Tom Stoppard's play 'Rosencrantz and Guildenstern Are Dead'. **Fig. X.8 Ysabel Kaye** Y3, 'Hansel and Gretel', a proposal for a modern day setting of the fairy tale 'Hansel and Gretel' set within The Royal Exchange Theatre, Manchester. The play and set have two parts, the original story and a contemporary story, which are intertwined into one performance. A section through a model, showing the set within the context of the theatre, depicting three potential lighting techniques. **Fig. X.9 Ysabel Kaye** Y3, 'Hansel and Gretel', a laser cut out book benignly depicts the scene when the children overhear the parents discussing their intention to abandon them in the forest, for lack of food.

Fig. X.10 **Ysabel Kaye** Y3, 'Hansel and Gretel', a laser cut book depicting the forest in the play. The charring of the laser cutting conveys the foreboding atmosphere of the scene.

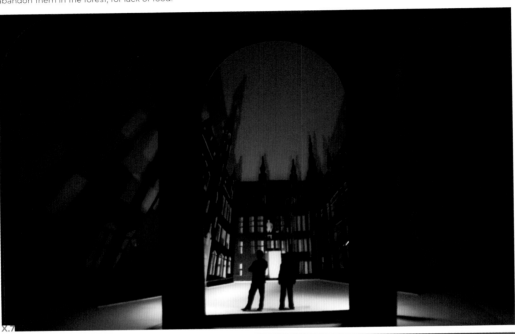

X.7

X.8

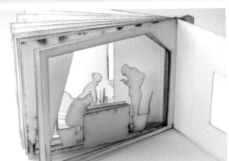

X.9

X.10

Fig. X.11 **Caitlin Abbott** Y2, 'We do Onstage the things that are Supposed to be done Off'. Equipment and models for filming. Fig. X.12 **Nadira Amrani** Y3, 'Occupation'. A film that explores how the lobby space in Wates House is used, by occupying the space for a period of two hours, the subject can seemingly predict and speculate upon the mundane activity behind her. Fig. X.13 **Casper Horton-Kitchlew** Y3, 'Origami Gate', a collage photograph of paper model. An initial project exploring the microscopic structures of protein channels at a macroscopic scale, within a 1:1 context. Fig. X.14 **Nadira Amrani** Y3, 'Architectural Perspectives'. A film projection installation, using four simultaneously projected films, three stories are told, the three perspectives and use of space is explored through a fourth space. The site of the projection installation unites three distinct architectural sites which are viewed through the perspective of the un-planned-for users; the skateboarders and the parkour and graffiti artists.

X.11

X.13

X.12

X.14

Fig. X.15 **Thomas Visscher** Y1, 'Home'. Handcrafted miniature homes, considering themes of the everyday vernacular we associate with the home, alongside some stranger more personal architectural vernacular. **Fig. X.16 Robyn Vey** Y1, 'Leather Bag', leather bag, photographs, newspaper cuttings and memories. A story – part fact and part fiction – of a young girl who travelled to London in the 'Kindertransport' from Germany in WWII. The contents of the bag are the girl's from 1939 and those of her adult granddaughter who is travelling across London in 2014 to deliver the contents to the Imperial War Museum. **Fig. X.17 Edoardo Lomi** Y1, 'Mineralised Culture'. Clay, cement, film (plastic), aluminium and coal, elements from our recent history form this collection, we see them as a mineralisation (a fossilisation) of our present contemporary culture – as discovered, interpreted and misinterpreted by future archaeologists. **Fig. X.18 Angus Whitehead** Y2, 'B-R-A-I-N'. A set of handcrafted wooden cogs and gears, operated by remote controls, slowly and eventually operates a switch. They carry out everyday tasks with great effort to humorous effect. **Fig. X.19 Angus Whitehead** Y2, 'B-R-A-I-N'. A micro-controller measures the amount of moisture in the plant's soil, switching on the water pump when it is too low.

X.15

X.16

X.17

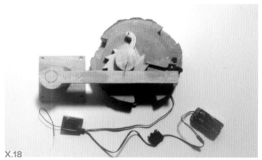

X.18

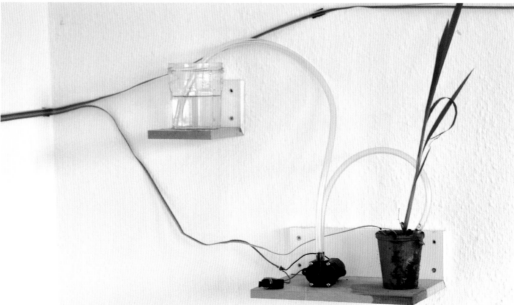

X.19

Fig. X.20 Fong Yi (Emmanuelle) Khoo Y3, 'Preserving Studio 331B'. Cardboard, the Architectural Studies studio, room 331b preserved as a boxed scale replica. Fig. X.21 Fong Yi (Emmanuelle) Khoo Y3, 'Peepshow of the Ground Floor Corridor'. Cardboard, a boxed scale replica of the ground floor corridor seen through a peephole. Fig. X.22 Fong Yi (Emmanuelle) Khoo Y3, 'Toilet in a Cup', cardboard. A Wates House toilet cubicle preserved in a generic coffee cup.
Fig. X.23 Fong Yi (Emmanuelle) Khoo Y3, 'Generic Shelf in The Bartlett – An Archive,' metal spur shelving, MDF shelf, brown manila folders, box file and boxed models. A photographic and model archive of The Bartlett that encourages the viewer to investigate by opening up files, looking through peepholes and peering into the various items.

The collection is enigmatic and playful but also a nostalgic reflection of a building that is soon to be demolished. Fig. X.24 Laura Skudder Y2, 'That Golden Stain of Time', film still and installation photograph. The project is a one-take stop motion animation of a continuous architectural drawing. It explores the theme of architecture as a silent witness to humanity and the lives of the residents who lived in the Blue Plaque Gower Street houses.

X.20

X.21

X.22

X.23

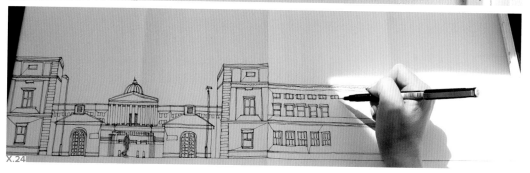
X.24

Unit 21 field trip to Ordrupgaard Museum, Copenhagen, Denmark

MArch Architecture
ARB/RIBA Part 2
152

Unit 10

Fauna City

Bernd Felsinger, CJ Lim

Year 4
Ran Chen, Marcin Chmura,
Lauren Fresle, Manuel
Gonzalez-Nogueira,
Alfie Hope, Kagen Lam,
Ashwin Patel

Year 5
Nick Elias, Siyu (Frank) Fan,
Ryan Edward Hakimian, Anja
Leigh Kempa, Woojong Kim,
Jason Lamb, Chun Yin
(Samson) Lau

Unit 10 would like to thank
Simon Dickens for his
teaching of the Design
Realisation module

The March Hare and the Hatter were having tea, a Dormouse was sitting between them, fast asleep... the table was a large one, but the three were all crowded together at one corner of it. 'No room! No room!' they cried out when they saw Alice coming. 'There's plenty of room!' said Alice indignantly, and sat down in a large armchair at the end of the table. [1]

Whether pest, pet or livestock, the relationship between humans and fauna has always been fundamental to the urban, cultural and economic consequences of communities in cities. On a visit to New York City in 1842, Charles Dickens noted that on Broadway, the well-to-do ladies in bright clothes and parasols were mixing with portly sows and hogs. Many urban centres have historically been places of animal cultivation, processing and trade. In London, before the arrival of modern food transportation, it was reckoned that each cow lost about 20 pounds in weight on every 100-mile walk to Smithfield Market.

————Regardless of our dwindling appreciation of fauna in cities, our dependency on them is ever increasing. Oysters once covered much of the east coast of the USA. The impact of the seemingly small actions of individual oysters carving out reefs is so huge that it has been attributed to tempering the wave action in the area; so much so that Shell Oil Company has even invested US$1 million in an oyster shell recycling scheme to reinvigorate the oyster populations around the coast. The oysters are also integral to the ecosystem, creating habitable conditions for many other species.

————In his 'animal farm', George Orwell elevated animals to positions of governance. What appearance will a city take and what kind of social spaces will result in such a scenario? The discourse of the Unit often takes the notion 'What if...' as its starting point. Interests in technical exposition and environmental science to stimulate programmes and spatial innovation strengthen the use of poetics and fictional narrative in projects. In Project 1 'Learning from Nature', we speculated and invented alternative realities by 'adopting' a member of the fauna, and in the process took lessons of sustainability from the ecological system. Project 2 'The City', was informed by individual studies and critical thinking to establish an urban design proposal with a complex narrative and programme. We invited students, as with Alice, to posit a divergent status quo on the city of the twenty-first century, taking speculative and sometimes impossible ideas into visionary wonderlands.

1. Lewis Carroll, *Alice's Adventures in Wonderland*, (London: Macmillan, 1865)

10.2

Fig. 10.1 **Nick Elias** Y5, 'PoohTown'. 1920s Slough, introducing Winnie the Pooh as the protagonist, to exploit 'happiness' as an alternative industry. Pooh re-evaluates covert responses to socio-political exclusion by prescribing idealised happy architecture in a nostalgic make-believe pilgrimage around Slough, ultimately for financial gain. Fig. 10.2 **Woojong Kim** Y5, 'The City of Sleep'. Located in the Bristol Channel, the City of Sleep investigates the spatial and symbolic potential of cathedrals. The floating infrastructure facilitates a community of the third age in deep sleep through cryogenics, while providing a safe haven for local sea birds. Fig. 10.3 **Anja Leigh Kempa** Y5, 'Remembering Spring in Tokyo'. Climate change threatens Japan's iconic emblem of Spring, the cherry blossom. Remembering Spring integrates an urban garden

infrastructure, revitalising native symbolism and traditions to inform a sustainable energy initiative through the recreation of spring. Fig. 10.4 – 10.5 **Chun Yin (Samson) Lau** Y5, 'The European Seat of Climate, Confidence and Credibility'. The ECCC is an investigation into the urban consequences of a carbon sequestration backed monetary system in the EU. Through five key architectural characters, the carbon-negative capital comments and tackles the financial hubris, political incompetence and environmental ignorance of the post-2008 financial crisis European Union.

10.4

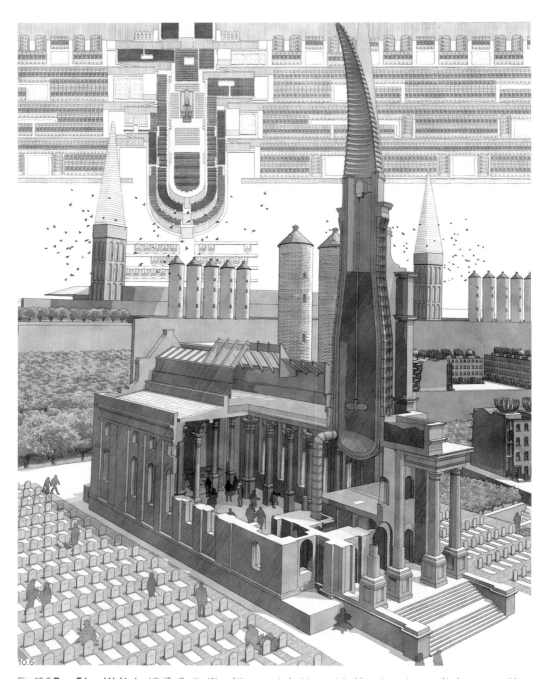

10.6

Fig. 10.6 **Ryan Edward Hakimian** Y5, 'To Go the Way of the Dodo'. The archaic views and ideologies of Prince Charles are applied to re-imagine London's Tower Hamlets. Is looking backward the best way to step forward? Fig. 10.7 **Siyu (Frank) Fan** Y5, 'Obama's Ark'. An architectural placebo, Obama's Ark is a disaster relief center located in Cape Disappointment. The masterplan employs the construction of an artificial moon as a piece of political propaganda to recapture the faith and confidence of Americans towards their federal government. Fig. 10.8 – 10.9 **Jason Lamb** Y5, 'Frackpool: The Legacy of Hydraulic Fracturing'. Chinese investment prompts the transitory integration of hydraulic fracturing in Blackpool for the exploitation of shale gas. The hydraulic fracturing instigates urban regeneration and provides a framework for new industries, sustainable water systems and induces renewable methods of energy production.

Unit 11

Ground Control

Laura Allen, Kyle Buchanan, Mark Smout

Year 4
Andrew Barrington, Nicholas
James Blomstrand, Katie
Browne, Harry Grocott, Wei
Zeng (Lucas) Ler, Gareth
Marriott, Ka Yee (Tracey)
Shum, Marcus Stockton

Year 5
William Armstrong, Jennifer
Dyne, Daniel Felgendreher,
Mara-Sophia Kanthak,
Rachel King, Daniel Lane,
David McGowan, Joseph
Paxton, Sandra Youkhana

Thank you to our
consultants: Dan Cash,
Stephen Foster, John Lyall

Thanks also to our critics:
Shumi Bose, Margaret Bursa,
Pedro Font Alba, Bill
Hodgson, Will Hunter, Johan
Hybschmann, Alan Penn,
Zofia Trafas, Patrick Weber,
Finn Williams, Oliver Wilton

"La suisse n'existe pas" (Switzerland does not exist) – in this one key sentence Switzerland introduced itself at the World Exposition in Seville in 1992. This was because it is not uniformity, but variety in a small space that defines Switzerland. [1]

Unit 11 pursues an interest in the intersection between architecture, landscape, science and technology, the natural and the synthetic – a form of environmental architecture where the landscape is both the site and the source of inspiration and invention. This year Unit 11 travelled to Switzerland where the fusion of territorial, technical, political and social forces combine to produce a distinct cultural and physical landscape that has provided the touchstone for our work.

Landlocked Islands
Switzerland has been described as a landlocked island, a result of physical isolation imposed by geological circumstance. In a country with four national languages and 26 semi-autonomous self-governed Cantons, it is perhaps no surprise that Switzerland does not consider itself to exist in the terms of monolithic statehood understood by its European neighbours.
———Swiss isolationism is perhaps most dramatically expressed in the Swiss National Redoubt, a defensive plan developed in the 1880s and only recently downscaled, which augments the natural alpine fortress with an extensive safety net of manmade booby traps laced into key infrastructure, combined with carefully located and disguised trompe l'oeil fortifications. Today this Swiss national 'resistance' is increasingly at odds with the ongoing urbanisation and internationalism of the region. Cultural and physical flexibility challenges the old topographic order and rustic sentimentality with which the Swiss conceal their modernity.
———Historically the landscape has attracted enthusiasts, artists, architects and engineers alike, however the awesome dominance of its sublime and elemental mountains belies a culture of modernity and innovation. The mountains provide an environment for scientific research in the form of instrumented field sites (which investigate environmental events such as avalanche control and ecosystem monitoring), and the mammoth technical landscape of the Large Hadron Collider at CERN housed in a 27-kilometer tunnel 100m underground.

Lie of the Land
Our work this year has focused on technological strategies, geographical environments, science facts, science fictions, cultural myths and emerging realties. Real and hypothetical problems have been posed and scrutinised in our studio-cum-laboratory environment. We have explored the conditions, incentives and results of cultural resistance and change, and interrogated the paradoxes, dualities and antithetical relationships inherent in the Swiss landscape and culture.

1. Ben Vautier

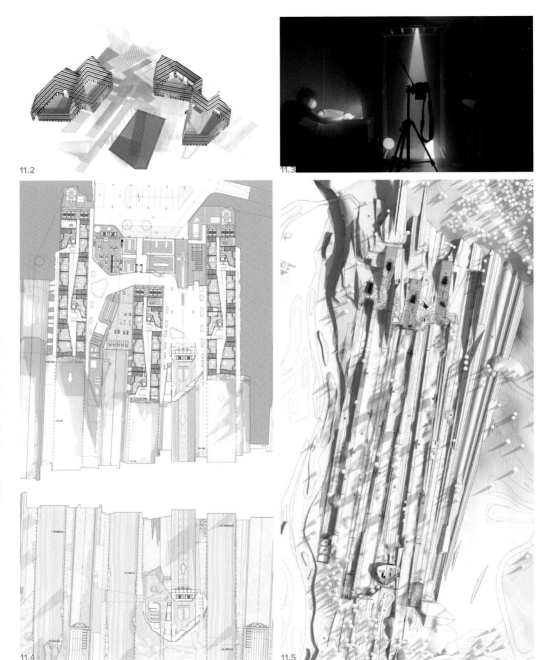

11.2

11.3

11.4

11.5

Fig. 11.1 **Daniel Lane** Y5, 'The Old Bern Snow Mountain Paradise', site plan. Draped over the rooftops of Bern, the Snow Mountain compounds the urban and alpine landscapes, redefining the ski empire of Switzerland in a warmer future where snow is scarce. **Fig. 11.2 Lucas Ler** Y4, 'Projecting Light onto Cloudscapes'. The atmospheric quality created by the microclimate in the room can be further enhanced by projecting light on to the cloudscape. Inspired by Anthony McCall's works, an ephemeral enclosure can be created by just using light and moisture in the air. **Fig. 11.3 Nicholas Blomstrand** Y4, 'Syrian Refuge in Bern'. Residential courtyards borrow heavily from the traditional Syrian vernacular and are, in essence, the refugees' front rooms – spaces for meeting and socialising. These intensely decorated spaces maintain a connection to the heavens through large glazed areas of the roof and lead out onto balconies overlooking the centre of the Swiss capital. **Fig. 11.4 – 11.5 William Armstrong** Y5. Using the compositional principles of the picturesque movement the Gletscherschlucht Seasonal Hotel, Switzerland, shifts seasonally, creating a composite landscape where the instability of the alpine geology and the stability of the picturesque ideal are jointly visible, shifted and celebrated. **Fig. 11.6 Marcus Stockton** Y4, 'SÄNTIS:MET/GEOstn'. A user deployed off-grid habitation scheme designed to overcome the issues posed by inhabiting remote locations. The core building elements (sledges) are designed to enable users to transport supplies over difficult terrain and to make sure everything taken to site has a purpose.

11.7

11.8

11.9

11.10

Fig. 11.7 Andrew Barrington Y4, using ice to create a 'negative' of an existing building in the centre of Berne, Switzerland. Voids become solids and solids become voids. The new terrain creates a unique surface on which to move over, but one that still responds to the original formwork underneath. The building can now be read through the eyes of a climber as roof ledges become cornices and arcades become ice caves. **Fig. 11.8 Tracey Shum** Y4, 'Mapping the Swiss Crevasse'. The body of the model describes the dense, dynamic environment of a crevasse with wire articulations portraying the different heights and curvatures of the space. They are connected in a way that accentuates the fluidity of the environment. The vertical brass poles are turned and controlled by muscle wire devices, creating environments that gradually enclose and

open up with the references marked on them emphasising a sense of progression. **Fig. 11.9 Daniel Felgendreher** Y5, 'Terminal Lead Repository', Thun. Speculating on a post-military time, the obsolete garrison is redeveloped into a recycling site for the contaminated soil of 6000 abandoned Swiss shooting ranges. The project deals with both the sociocultural legacy of Swiss shooting traditions and its toxic materialisation by proposing a soil phytoremediation process on Indian mustard fields. **Fig. 11.10 Rachel King** Y5, the 'New Lausanne Transhumance Valley' recontextualises essential elements of rural Swiss farm life into the urbanscape. This works as a radical means to reconnect local residents with a diminished traditional dairy landscape, injecting a direct visual abundance of cows, pastures and farmers back into the heart

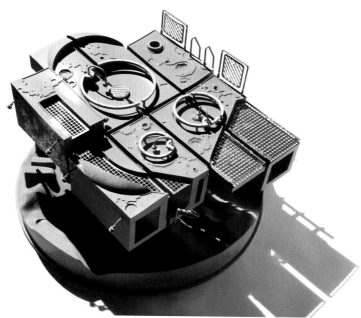

11.11

11.12

of the city. **Fig. 11.11 Harry Grocott** Y4, 'Bern White Water Centre', sectional model (pontoon). Milled high-density composite, acid-etched steel and 3D printed components. The pontoon is designed to rise and fall with fluctuations in the level of the glacially sourced river Aare, while the conditions required to enable white water kayaking, surfing and bathing are generated and balanced by the systems of the building itself. **Fig. 11.12 David McGowan** Y5, 'Little Switzerland' explores how the re-appropriation of the sense of place can be asserted onto the site of Matlock Bath, which is commonly known as the 'Switzerland of Britain' through a series of prescribed vantage points and experiences that aim to enhance this existing relationship.

11.13

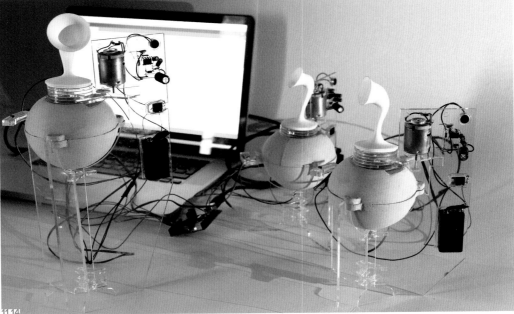

11.14

Fig. 11.13 **Jennifer Dyne** Y5, 'Strangelet Defenchalets'. Could a strangelet from the Large Hadron Collider threaten the landscape of Switzerland's defence strategy? The Defenscape, a zone in the heart of the Alps, protects the country's population from perceived attack. Luxurious holiday lodges transform into dense survival mode, creating a Swisslet community complete with mini Matterhorn and numerous Swiss imitations, concealments and dualities – the Swiss Army Knife of bunkers. Fig. 11.14 **Gareth Marriot** Y4, 'Trans-Alpine Network Instrument'. A series of responsive terrain instruments that interact with their surroundings and with each other. The 'terrain' has been refined into slip cast reverberation chambers; tones are then amplified through 'alphorn' structures: with echoes performed based on the level of the initial interaction.

Passers-by behave as the 'Alps' as they block the sounds between. Fig. 11.15 **Joe Paxton** Y5, 'Field Research Community'. Taking advantage of Switzerland's vast water resource, new lakes and ice reserves augment the Alpine landscape providing a more resilient store of water and energy for the future of Switzerland and its European neighbours. Synthesising these two new elements of the landscape, the Field Research Community takes on a new role of monitoring and preserving ice in its many states, whilst simultaneously benefiting from this new resource. Regulated melt water feeds into the wider Super-River network across Switzerland which aids flood mitigation, water buffering, energy buffering, and freshwater storage.

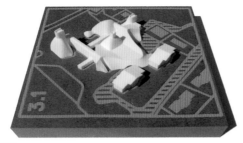

11.16

11.17

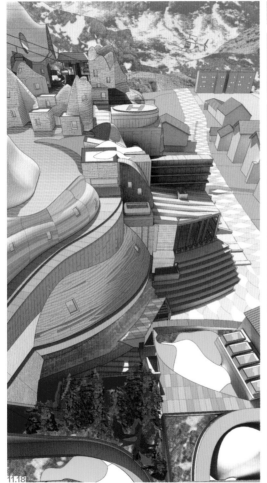

11.18

11.19

Fig. 11.16 – 11.17 Sandra Youkhana Y5, 'Media Planning'. An architecture clobbered by actions of engagement with the media of planning, speculating on new morphologies that not only apply, but emphasise the latent possibilities offered by regulation. Andermatt's Building Code states, 'Angled and detached buildings are vertically projected onto the lengthening of the corresponding façade'. This projection of angles onto corresponding façades continues the language of existing buildings onto those yet to be designed. The growth of one approved angle to a body of another carves out parts of the building that respond to neighbouring roof pitches. Baugespann poles applied to Swiss landscape indicate the volume of a forthcoming building or structure at 1:1. Standing as a planning medium that facilitates for the relationship

between consented structures and the physical landscape, they are read as a low-resolution form of visual verification. **Fig. 11.18 – 11.19 Sandra Youkhana** Y5, 'Andermatt, Swiss Alps'. Combined with the application of reinterprative planning strategies that reveal the design potential held by Andermatt's Zoning Plan and Building Code, the proposal seeks to gain an understanding of the commune and its role in the development of Switzerland, re-emphasising the country's unique relationship to its landscape through a reshaping of the Alpine vernacular. In contrast to existing structures in the area, it is an example of a new typology offered through coercion. The scheme examines the Swiss tendency to inhabit indeterminate types of terrain, communicating an inversion of the valley within the flatness of the commune.

11.20

Fig. 11.20 Mara-Sophia Kanthak Y5, *Si le Soleil ne Revenait pas* – after C.F. Ramuz's novel from 1937 – recounts the story of Grengiols' inhabitants and their fear that the sun won't return after one long winter in which the village, located in the Rhône valley and overshadowed by the highest Swiss mountains, does not receive direct sunlight – a condition the villagers call 'schattenhalb'. The dystopian scenario of the disappearing sun incites the villagers to devise architectures and infrastructures of preparation in different scales that stage and cherish shadow, darkness and the diminished light: a 350 metre high tower, reaching over the shadow into the sunlight; light saunas; dark zones for eye adaptation; mirrored light sharing tunnels between the neighbour's and the own house to utilise the artificial interior illumination most efficiently; and an installation framing the village church that employs fibreoptic cables to redirect the sunlight gathered by the tower into the building. As such, the church interior turns into a permanent celebration of light.

Unit 12

The Shock of the Old and the Shock of the New

Matthew Butcher, Elizabeth Dow, Jonathan Hill

Year 4
Akhil Bakhda, Samiyah Bawamia, Larisa Cosmina Bulibasa, Alex Cotterill, Ben Ferns, Helena Howard, Tereza Kacerova, Joseph Reilly, Adam Shapland

Year 5
Rodolfo Acevedo Rodriguez, Amy Sullivan Bodiam, Emma Clinton, Jason Coe, Leon Fenster, Alastair King, Samuel Rackham, Louis Sullivan, Daniel Wilkinson, Xuhong Zheng

Thank you to James Hampton, our Design Realisation Practice Tutor and Ben Godber, our Design Realisation Structural Consultant

Thanks also to our critics: Ross Exo Adams, Fulvio de Bastiani, Shumi Bose, David Buck, Ben Campkin, Emma Cheatle, Mollie Claypool, Nigel Coates, Tom Coward, Tina Di Carlo, Stewart Dodd, Adrian Forty, Daisy Froud, Ben Godber, James Hampton, Penelope Haralambidou, Colin Herperger, Charles Holland, Catherine Ince, Moira Lascelles, Marina Lathouri, Constance Lau, John Macarthur, Igor Marjanovic, Luke Pearson, Barbara Penner, Chris Pierce, Rahesh Ram, Peg Rawes, David Roberts, Michiko Sumi, Tania Sengupta, Liam Young, Alessandro Zambelli and Fiona Zisch

The Bartlett School of Architecture 2014

A Twenty-first Century Grand Tour

Eighteenth century architects spent at least three years in Italy, collecting ideas, principles, experiences and artefacts to transfer home, from south to north. Their purpose was not to copy what they had seen but to translate it to a new context and climate, thus inventing a new architecture and a new landscape. The Grand Tour continued into the twentieth century. Commissioned to design a house when he was 20 years old, Ludwig Mies van der Rohe's first client paid for his tour of Italy, while Rome inspired Louis Kahn in 1950 and Roma Interrotta defined postmodernism in 1978. This year, we travelled to Florence, Mantua, Venice, Verona and Vicenza on a twenty-first century Grand Tour. The most creative architects have always looked to the past to imagine a future, studying an earlier architecture not to replicate it but to understand and transform it, revealing its relevance to the present and future. Twenty-first century architects should appreciate the shock of the old as well as the shock of the new.

Designs on History

In 1969 Vincent Scully concluded that the architect will 'always be dealing with historical problems – with the past and, a function of the past, with the future. So the architect should be regarded as a kind of physical historian … the architect builds visible history'. Like a history, a design is a reinterpretation of the past that is meaningful to the present, transforming both. Equally, a design is equivalent to a novel, convincing the user to suspend disbelief. We expect a history or a novel to be written in words, but they can also be cast in concrete or seeded in soil. The architect is a 'physical historian' and a 'physical novelist'.

What is a New City Today?

Our site is Stewartby, a 1920s model town built to serve the world's largest brickworks. The London Brick Company commissioned neo-classical public buildings and housing by Sir Albert Richardson, The Bartlett Professor of Architecture, who lived nearby. Today, the brickworks is abandoned and the town is empty, but just an hour from London.

———To imagine a new city, each student has designed its first civic building, which is a microcosm of the city and a catalyst for its growth. A hybrid of architecture, infrastructure and landscape, the civic building establishes a symbiotic relationship with its ever-changing immediate and wider contexts. Attentive to the environment, it recognises the co-production and creative influence of natural as well as cultural forces. Discursive, it encourages social and political engagement, and the interaction of public and private lives. Inventive, it reimagines histories and narratives, creating new myths for a new city.

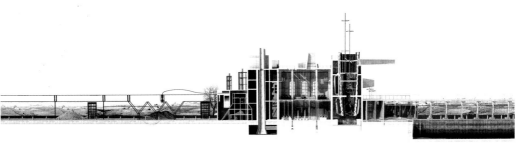

12.2

12.3

12.4

12.5

12.6

Fig. 12.1 Rodolfo Acevedo Rodriguez Y5, 'The House of Eros'. The home was once the microcosm of the ideal society, with love and charity replacing the capitalism of the outside world. Today, ancient mythology comes to life in Stewartby, relating the narratives of humans and deities, which together with contemporary technologies introduce a new activity and meaning to the already there. **Fig. 12.2 Adam Shapland** Y4, 'The Environment Agency Headquarters for Flooding'. The proposed building and surrounding landscape activates, and is activated by, the movement of flood water, which is re-directed south from the Great river Ouse at Bedford, in a seasonal relief effort. **Fig. 12.3 Akhil Bakhda** Y4, 'Manifest Destiny: The Case and Consequences of Colonising Mars'. In its preliminary stages, this project seeks to explore the story of American

Frontier history in seeking to understand the trajectory of how we will colonise Mars from 2030. **Fig. 12.4 Samiyah Bawamia** Y4, 'The Porcelain Foundation of Stewartby'. The Porcelain Foundation is perceived as an icon of luxury, replacing a polluted territory. It is a critique to Venturi's statement of 'Less is bore' and investigates the idea of the building being a crafted object, relating to shrines and follies. **Fig. 12.5 Ben Ferns** Y4, 'Solforico Consulate'. Through a composition of perverse juxtapositions and subverted hierarchies, the Italian Consulate is assembled from a montage of sulfur and brick. It questions Neapolitan identity, perception and transparency in hybrid spaces, revealing a sulfuric industry.

12.7

12.8

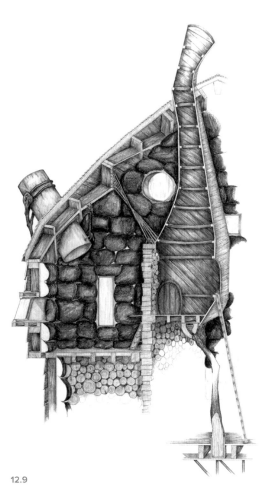

12.9

12.10

Fig. 12.6 **Helena Howard** Y4, 'The City Of Gastronomic Lichenology, Stewartby'. The city of Stewartby acts as the world centre for research into gastronomic lichen as a potential new source of nutrition, in order to alleviate the inevitable food crisis brought about by climate change. **Fig. 12.7 Larisa Cosmina Bulibasa** Y4, 'The Urban Forestry College'. The project engages with exploring symbiotic relationships between architecture and nature looking at a physical and a poetical level between the two of them. **Fig. 12.8 Tereza Kacerova** Y4 'Clay Nanocomposite Fabrication Ground For Emerging Airship Industry'. Following on the industrial heritage of the site, the project proposes an alternative for an existing resource – Oxford Clay. A clay nanocomposite membrane fabricated on site is further utilised in construction of a training centre for

airship pilots. **Fig. 12.9 Joseph Reilly** Y4, 'Anachronistic Forestry in the Near Future'. The project exists within the reforestation of Bedfordshire's post-industrial brickfields. The uncanny architecture combines crafted pieces of timber with reclaimed objects from the redundant brickworks factory. Within a vast burgeoning woodland an anachronistic sawmill and workshop building form the first and last elements of a new slower city. **Fig. 12.10 Alex Cotterill** Y4, '(Stewartby) Land Mill.' The landfill can be understood as both a place of shared social significance, a collective repository for discarded material and an essential resource for exhausted material goods; it is somewhere between these three that the project sits.

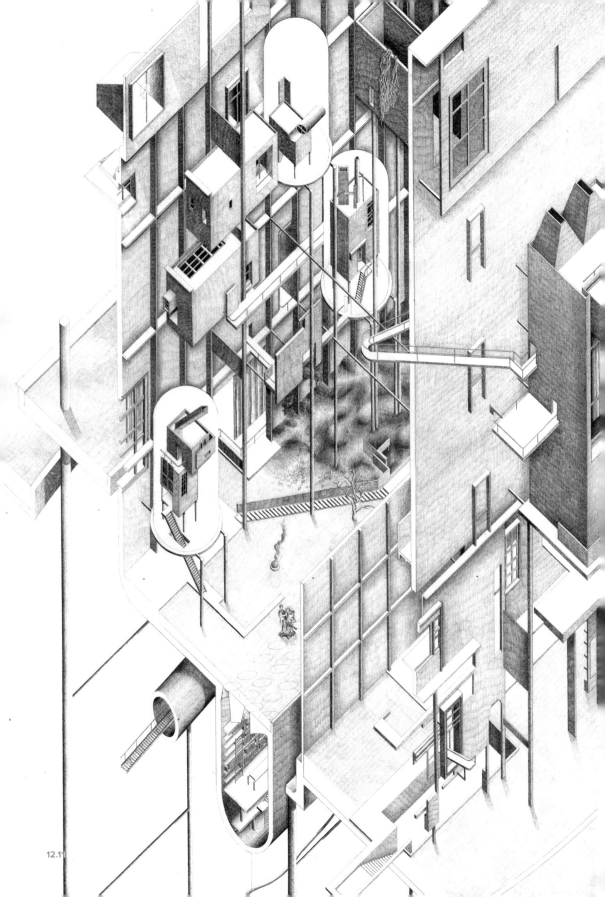

12.12

12.13

Fig. 12.11 Alastair King Y5, 'A Home, an Office and a University'. This project explores the identity of Sir Albert Richardson (1880-1964), a Modern Georgian Paradox, through multiple scales, times and modes of representation.
Fig. 12.12 Xuhong Zheng Y5, 'Wilderness Institute'. Situated on the edge of a disused clay quarry at Stewartby, the Wilderness Institute houses a community of researchers, ecologists, planners and artists who inhabit the sublime wilderness of both the landscape and the architecture, establishing a new research and planning centre. The building forms an inhabitable wall around the pit, controlling entry and views into the site whilst acting as a catalyst for wilderness to develop – through actions such as seed dispersal, wind funneling, rainwater collection and release. The journey through the

building is constructed as a journey through a landscape.
Fig. 12.13 Emma Clinton Y5, 'Cathedral of St Thomas, Cathedral of Doubt'. Using Doubting Thomas as a narrative device, the project is designed through a series of fragments, exploring theological themes of the body and soul. In a constant state of disrepair, it becomes a celebration of our mortality, suspending disbelief through a tactile experience, explored through a series of incomplete pencil studies and 1:1 models.

12.14

Fig. 12.14 **Daniel Wilkinson** Y5, 'The Courthouse of the 23rd Baroque'. This project speculates on Eugenio D'Ors' idea that the Baroque isn't a finite period in art history, but a recurrent disruptive artistic and political social cycle. Situated in the abandoned economic wastelands outside of Stewartby, the Court acts as the starting point for a new city which aesthetically turns away from the efficiencies and banalities of the structural celebrations which have dominated architecture for over a century. Acting as a landmark for its own logic, the Court structurally obscures itself through an ornamental irruption.

12.15

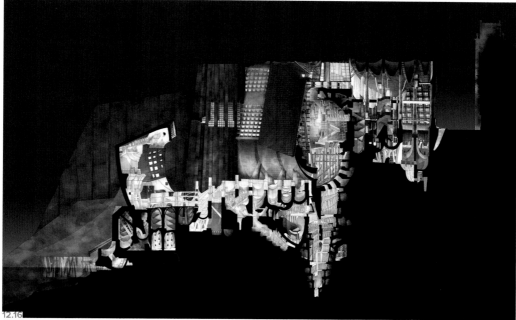

12.16

Fig. 12.15 Amy Sullivan Bodiam Y5 'The New Crystal Palace'. Located on Deptford's riverfront, the New Crystal Palace, a combination of the Master Shipwright's house and new Kaleido Park, is a monument to Deptford's industrial past and Sayes Court, London's lost garden. Live-work opportunities are offered in a community built on respect for nature, industry without drudgery, equality and well being for all, ideals that resonate with those of the 1960's counter culture. Small industries grow and sparkle like crystals as the Palace evolves. Festivals are held regularly to celebrate the rich tapestry of spaces and minds within the Palace. **Fig. 12.16 Leon Fenster** Y5, 'Exilic Landscapes'. The projects asks what an idiosyncratically Jewish architecture might look like and posits that it is one which embraces the notion of exile and the restlessness of uncertainty. A religious architecture not of the inaccessible sacred but of the disorder of human contradiction. A reading of history filled not with absolutes but with constant negotiation. As George Steiner puts it, 'this is an era in which increasingly large swathes of humanity are "becoming Jews," as defined by a consciousness of exile. Hence this approach to religious architecture is of great consequence for our age'.

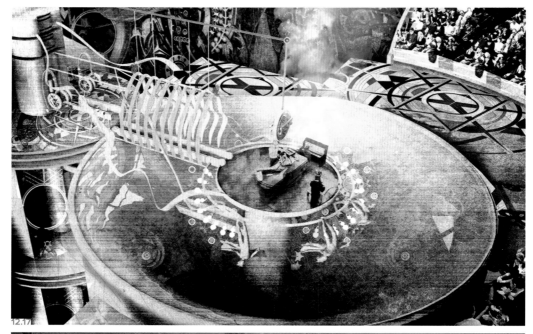

Fig. 12.17 – 12.18 **Samuel Rackham** Y5, 'The Royal Instituion'.
This project concerns the construction of a new home for
the Royal Institution on the Thames Southbank. The Royal
Institution was the flagship institution of Romantic Science,
where the arts and sciences were of equal importance and the
theatrical nature of science was celebrated. This project aims
to reintroduce these values and provide the foundation for a
relationship between these seemingly oppositional domains.
The institution will be given a new status as a representative
of both Science and Art and by displaying the excitement of
experimental science it can again become a part of the wider
public consciousness.

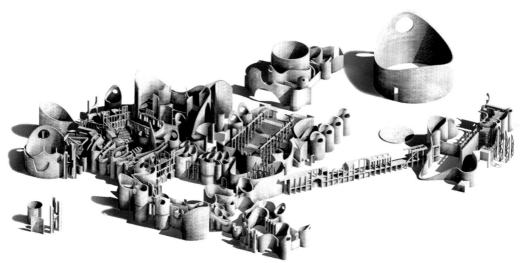

12.19

12.20

12.21

Fig. 12.19 **Jason Coe** Y5, 'The New Bedford Forum'. The New Bedford forum is the public and political centre of New Bedford, a democratic model city for the Bedford Cooperative Brickworks. The city implements a participatory form of governance for its local government, while the brickworks are jointly owned and managed by its citizens. Objects of democratic activity are articulated through the brickwork, which lay dormant awaiting their activation through social occupation. Fig. 12.20 – 12.21 **Louis Sullivan** Y5, 'The Living Dam'. A proposal towards a new typology of dam in response to the current anti-reservoir sentiment and the recent history of the world's large dams. A useful pyramid for the twenty-first century, an Arcology, away from the image of solitary hydrological infrastructures and towards a model which is not only integral but also integrated with society, environmentalism and ecology which may help alter the public perception of the essential infrastructures, re-instigate the principles of a hydraulic empire and encourage a cultural attitude towards beneficially living with dams.

Unit 14

Metamorphosis: Architectures of Ingenuity

Paul Bavister, James O'Leary

Year 4
Jiang Dong, Calum Alexander Macdonald, Heather McVicar, Louise Schmidt, Greg Storrar

Year 5
Kyveli Anastasiad, Seonghwan Cho, Petr Anthony Esposito, Yuan Ning, Alyssa Ohse , Jia Yuan Shen, Kok Kian Tew, Andrew Walker

We are grateful to our sponsors Kite & Laslett

Thank you to Dan Wright, our Design Realisation Tutor, structural consultant Andy Toohey, our environmental consultant Max Fordham and to our collaborators at Royal Holloway

Thanks also to our critics: Wesley Aelbrecht, Julia Backhaus, Gem Barton, Konstantinos Chalaris, Nat Chard, Illugi Eysteinsson, Ilona Gaynor, Alison Gibb, Ruairi Glynn, Fred Guttfield, Usman Haque, Christine Hawley, Sebastian Kite, Kristen Kreider, Tim Lucas, Patrick Lynch, Sam McElhinney, Mitch Mc Ewan, Ellen Page, Ollie Palmer, Bakul Patki, Eliot Payne, Price & Myers, Sophia Psarra, Kulveer Ranger, Richard Roberts, Rogers, Stirk Harbour + Partners, Florian Rothmayer, Ilona Sagar, Peter Scully, Catrina Stewart, Andy Toohey, Nick Wakefield, Melissa Woolford, Staff at Mike Kelley's Mobile Homestead and all Detroit activists. A special thank you is reserved for all Bartlett workshop staff

The post-industrial stage of capitalism has long-term implications for the cities we live in. Previously seen through the optimistic lens of modernist representation, the clean and fresh streets of architects' visualisations are, in some extreme cases, turning into living dystopias. Some of the more established cities of the industrial era that have lost their economic momentum are now blighted with swathes of urban necrosis, with previously lively neighbourhoods disappearing, reclaimed by nature, and growing wild. Today's cities are living organisms, a collection of autonomous components responding to localised conditions, each component thriving on the next, feeding on influxes of investment and societal needs. If left untended and starved of resource, areas of a city can die, leading to inevitable decay and the exodus of its host society.

————Yet with maintenance, sensitivity and care, these areas can be revitalised, bringing change and rebirth to fading urban conditions. This year, Unit 14 has been investigating strategies and tactics for replanting seeds of sustainable growth in the urban environment. We have been instigating modes of regeneration by way of critical interaction with a host environment. Using appropriate technologies, and working at 1:1 immersive scale, we seek to question existing design methodologies in the wider context of a macro-economic reality. How can intelligent architectural systems help to promote sustainable growth in these areas? What are the components that can define a sustainable response system? How can physical actions engender change outside of the studio environment?

————There is nowhere on the planet at present where the problems of the post-industrial city are laid bare more starkly than in the 'Motor City' of Detroit. The Unit visited Detroit to see first-hand examples of experimental work that aims toward a more sustainable urban future, meeting local artists and architects who are working to develop resilient forms of urban communities in challenging economic circumstances. We then travelled to New York, moving from a city in current state of dereliction to one in a condition of renaissance, stopping off along the way at architecture and design departments at Cranbrook, Cornell, Yale and Cooper Union. We conducted field research to see how ideas currently being tested in the urban laboratory of America's cities are changing their immediate environment.

————On our return to London, our Year 4 students developed new architectural propositions for sites located in Detroit. Our Year 5 students worked on highly tactical insertions, designing architectures of ingenuity that can engender new spatio-temporal conditions in the city, bringing about radical change. Architectural proposals from our research were tested through interventions, installations, prototypes, time-based media and drawings, leading to further speculative representations at an urban scale.

The Bartlett School of Architecture 2014

14.2

14.3

14.4

14.5

Fig. 14.1 Andrew Walker Y5. 'Edge Condition'. Situated in darkness, a bespoke system of interactive drawing machines equipped with dynamic, electroluminescent armatures translate occupant behaviour into a sequence of light events, transforming the space around them from a scotopic labyrinth to an inhabitable diagram of their own perception. Chance superimpositions of afterimages suggest edges and surfaces that exist as Illusory sub-architectures occupying the interstice between imagination, memory and objective reality.
Fig. 14.2 – 14.4 Jia Yuan Shen Y5, 'Co-operative Architecture'. A series of reconfigurable and extendable components designed to enable occupants to develop shared micro-gardening spaces through local co-operation. When erected, the structure is entirely self-contained, with irrigation systems powered by solar cells within the structure. **Fig. 14.5 Alyssa Ohse** Y5, 'A Caring Room'. The project investigates the role of responsive architecture within the healthcare system. A series of intelligent objects are created that work in ensemble to bring the sense of external conditions – light, sound, smell, the sky, to the interior space of a bed-bound patient. In the case illustrated here, a ceiling mounted array of actuated feathers reflects the motion of clouds scudding overhead.

14.6

14.7

14.8

Fig. 14.6 **Seonghwan Cho** Y5, 'PolySpace'. A head-mounted device that overlays projected images from one urban space (Detroit) over the reality of another (Times Square, New York). Fig. 14.7 – 14.8 **Seonghwan Cho** Y5, The project developed from these initial studies to a proposal for an architectural façade that is configured to translate and replay the actions of the BBC Symphony Orchestra in Maida Vale, London to the streetscape outside. Fig. 14.9 – 14.11 **Kyveli Anastasiad** Y5, 'Occupying Momentum'. A process of spatial analysis and creation that explores 'physical thinking' as a process of representation and making architectural spaces through data derived from interactions between a performer and a site. The resulting information – drawings, scans or sculptures – is used as a cognitive map of observed spatial

data and subsequently redefined as a set of instructions of how to design, inhabit or perform a given space. This is a form of examination and enquiry that is derived from the 'thinking body', where no external representation exists.

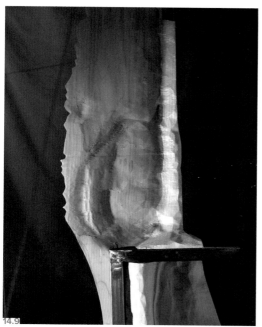

14.9

14.10

14.11

14.12

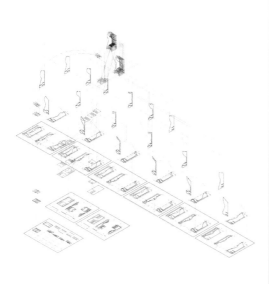

14.13

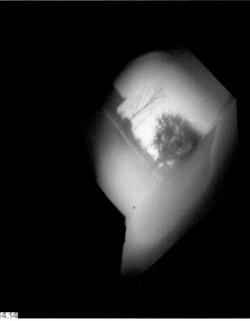

14.14

Fig. 14.12 **Louise Schmidt** Y4, 'Paper Trails'. Drawn to the cavernous and sprawling interior of the disused Packard car production plant in Detroit, the project investigates techniques for delicately defining and guiding human occupancy within the interior. Paper is used as a marker and modelling tool that suggests new architectural configurations with site-led material investigations. Fig. 14.13 **Calum Alexander Macdonald** Y4, 'Practice Gallery'. Exploded Axonometric tracing the incremental development and subtle modification of various tectonic components throughout the course of this project's construction phase. Fig. 14.14 **Heather McVicar** Y4, 'Photography Gallery with Dispersed Satellite Studios'. A series of architectural interventions that seeks to engage people in the act of reimaging Detroit. Located on the roof of Michigan

Central Station – the most photographed ruin in Detroit, the architecture of the gallery is constructed physically and symbolically as a journey which redirects the contemporary 'ruin gaze' back into the living city. This image above is constructed using a camera obscura that was made in London and deployed in various sites around Detroit to document their spatial and atmospheric conditions.

14.15

14.16

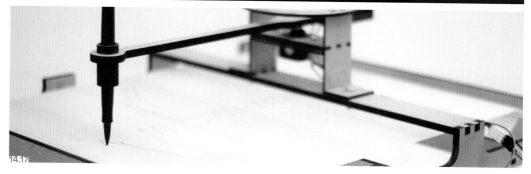

14.17

Fig. 14.15 **Jiang Dong** Y4, 'Floating in the Ruins'. An acoustic sentinel that 'listens' for sounds of occupation and approach within an abandoned factory in Detroit. This has been developed into a 1:1 prototype as illustrated here.

Fig. 14.16 – 14.17 **Greg Storrar** Y4, 'Share Detroit'. Siting the project firmly in the growing landscape of digital information, Greg develops a series of interface objects that encourage and collate information based on site and localised conditions. Actively seeking interaction from local users, a roaming QR code projector and Twitter response harvesting website are developed to generate discussion around the architectural direction of particular areas of the city.

Fig. 14.18 **Petr Anthony Esposito** Y5, 'Scattered Domesticity'.
The project investigates an architecture developed to better
the lives of people caught in a situation of either temporary
or chronic homelessness. The project proposed a network
of micro-architectures – a 'scattered domesticity' both for
houseless and housed across the city creating spaces of
inclusivity. The architecture activates their chosen sites,
challenging existing or forgotten uses with the aim of
provoking discussion about the role of social architecture
in the urban fabric. Fig. 14.19 **Yuan Ning** Y5, 'Camden Time
Folly'. The project seeks to unify a location's past with an
ever-changing present. It proposes a building that houses
a series of immersive spaces that gave viewers and occupants
new readings of the site via light-responsive panels and effects.

The content of the folly is created using both hand-crafted
casting processes, and contemporary digital manufacturing
techniques. Fig. 14.20 **Kok Kian Tew** Y5, 'Theatre of
Displacement'. An installation explores the notion of
displacement through the use of surveillance technology.
Live events and images are captured and manipulated, inviting
an occupant to inhabit two spaces at a time through a series of
spatialised projections and experiences. The installation takes
the form of a deployable structure that is able to provide a new
kind of psychological shelter and shared memory repository
that can present images of a lost space that has meaning to
an occupant.

14:20

The Bartlett School of Architecture 2014

Unit 15

Immediate Exposure

Maren Klasing, Stefan Rutzinger, Kristina Schinegger

Year 4
Wang Fung Chan, Yin Hui
Chung, Sam Dodsworth,
Shengyu Meng, Augustine
Ong Wing, Shinnosuke
Takayanagi, Jonas Weiss

Year 5
Jiyoon Bae, John Ju Hyung
Chun, Andrea Giordano,
Tsun Ming Ho, Stephen
Kenneth Johnson, Jihum
Kim, Kristoffer Mitchell,
Amanda Moore

Thanks to our consultants:
Francis Archer (Arup
Engineering) and Dominik
Strzelec

Thanks to our critics: Julia
Backhaus, Richard Beckett,
Roberto Bottazzi, Izaskun
Chinchilla, Marjan Coletti,
Marcos Cruz, Manuel
Jimenez Garcia, Carlos
Jimenez, James O'Leary,
Stefan Ritter, Hannes
Schaffelner, Seda Zirek

According to Reyner Banham, humans developed two basic ways of dealing with environmental conditions: the first was to simply ignore them and hide under a roof or stone, which led to conventional architecture as we know it today. The other was active interference with local meteorology, pictured in the form of the campfire. While the strategy of sheltering leads to permanence and stability, the campfire provides variability and freedom, yet is exposed and vulnerable. What Banham was predicting – new social and spatial organisation due to the invention of air conditioning – soon came into a crisis when it faced the limits of resources.

———This year we envisioned a third architectural condition beyond the categories of building and meteorology. The task for students was to understand architecture as a resilient and energised matter that can cope with changing environmental conditions, adapt or even bounce back.

———Our field trip took us to the vibrant metropolises of Seoul and Busan, where individual projects were sited. These booming urban agglomerations have long followed the slogan 'grow now, clean up later', yet are now embracing alternative solutions and possibilities of resilience. Students were asked to develop proposals that would be highly exposed to external and internal influences, flows, and conditions, thereby creating symbiotic systems and entangled formations that show integrated functionalities and multi-causal behaviours.

———The design method of Unit 15 is based on a systematic feedback between analogue material testing and digital experimentation which privileges an open-ended design method of probability and approximation. Thereby material (or matter) is understood as a complex system that can balance opposing influencing factors as well as adapt to external and internal conditions.

———The interest in self-organisation and material formation provides an 'aesthetic reserve' for architecture: by freeing the outcome from fixed intentions and interpretations, it can maintain an operational force and develop unexpected performances as well as a potential for adaption and unintended use. The main questions of the Unit are methodological: how to develop a precise and targeted design method that fosters and manipulates unpredictability? How to evaluate and categorise resulting spatial performances that by definition evade determination and fixation?

———Exposure is also a question of dose – from the homeopathic, the toxic to the mere-exposure effect. We are exposed unprotected to architecture and its effects. As a background to our everyday life it constantly surrounds us and often stays unnoticed, yet colours our emotions, thoughts and routines. Unit 15 investigates the immediacy of architecture and the corporeal and psychological effects of our exposure to it. We speculate about the atmospheric interaction between body and space, as well as the entanglement of our perception with material and geometry.

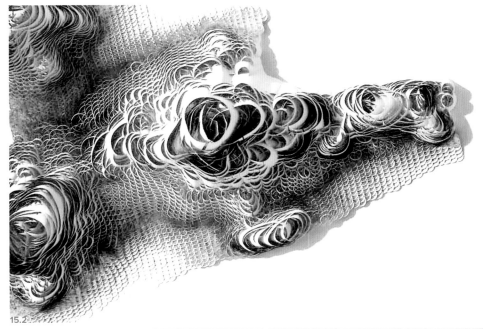

15.2

15.3

15.4

Fig. 15.1 **Shinnosuke Takayanagi** Y4, 'Sensing Intangibility', rendering. One of a series of digital stills and physical models inspired by the molecular process of salt crystallisation. Molecular behavior during crystallisation has been simulated in a digital environment to compute fibrous geometry at an architectural scale inorder to capture its intangible spatial qualities. **Fig. 15.2 Jiyoon Bae** Y5, 'Museum of Memory', rendering. The conceptual masterplan for the reconstructed landscape by dissolving historic objects in the museum quarter, Seoul. The historic site was originally a place of pine trees which provided materials to build the royal palace. Using this notion, the revival of old in the site is one technique to make the landscape an embodied place of relationship for the new Museum of Memory.

Fig. 15.3 **Andrea Giordano** Y5, 'Recomputing the Han River', 3D print and CNCed MDF. Intersecting shells of a recursively modelled digital artefact. **Fig. 15.4 Jiyoon Bae** Y5, 'Museum of Memory', rendering. The main gallery of the museum of memory in Seoul. The multiple route of visitors' space is also considered by creating a different height, depth and length for the exhibition space. This experimental place of memory enables embodied experience of remembering and forgetting as well when visitors walk through the path of Möbius strip, so finally the embodied experience connect the past and present by looking back on where they are coming from.

15.5

15.6

15.7

Fig. 15.5 **Kristoffer Mitchell** Y5, 'Architectural Faciality', rendering. Liquid simulation studies displaying signs of both asymmetry and symmetry. Multiple liquids inform each other's movement and create smaller pockets of intrigue in undefined areas. Fig. 15.6 **Shinnosuke Takayanagi** Y4, 'Sensing Intangibility', 3D print. An interior study showing a fibrous structure forming a variety of architectural elements. Fig. 15.7 **Shinnosuke Takayanagi** Y4, 'Sensing Intangibility', salt crystal on threads, photograph.

Fig. 15.8 **Andrea Giordano** Y5, 'EPS Exposed to Acetone covered in Black Tinted Latex', macro photograph. The culmination of experiments testing the formal potential of a material exposed to a liquid. Fig. 15.9 **Andrea Giordano** Y5, 'Recomputing the Han River', CNCed MDF. tool paths exposing varying heights of the topological riverside landscape. The first gestural geometry reconfiguring the riverbed of the Han River into a landscape augmented by formal principles observed in analogue in the experiments. Fig. 15.10 **Sam Dodsworth** Y4, 'Anisotropic Carpology', mixed media. Close-up photograph showing typical Seed Bank Silo Section.

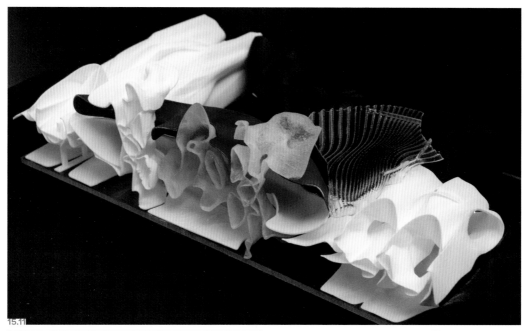

15.11

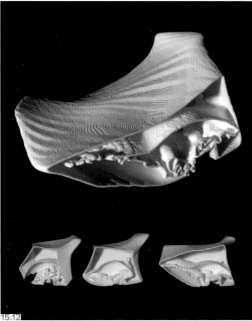

15.12

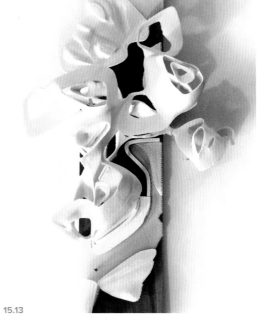

15.13

Fig. 15.11 **Kristoffer Mitchell** Y5, 'Architectural Faciality', 3D print, sectional model. Fig. 15.12 **Stephen Kenneth Johnson** Y5, 3D print. Study models utilising the same parametric process to produce a series of results that seek to create varying semi-internal void conditions, i.e. external performance space. Fig. 15.13 **Augustine Ong Wing** Y4, 'Bulyeog-Bae Maritime Heritage Museum', 3D print massing model. The geometry and form of the building evolved from a series of homeostat particle simulations conducted to explore the ideas of resilience and self-organisation in stochastic geometries. The building's relationship to the site is inspired the interplay of random and controlled spatial flows in liquids. These shifting boundaries become the basis of floating 'vessels' that merge with the surroundings into one complex whole.

Fig. 15.14 **Wang Fung Chan** Y4, 'Eroded Layers: A Korean Bathhouse', 3D print, sectional model. The atmospheric exquisiteness and delicacy of this excavated poolscape with its gradient of porosity is generated with fractal principles and controlled randomness on a layering system. **Fig 15.15 Amanda Moore** Y5, 'Sea Energy Centre: Deokjeokdo', South Korea, masterplan strategy to improve island resilience. The project replaces existing diesel generators with cleaner wave energy-capturing devices, as well as improving food security with seaweed farming and fishing and providing visitor facilities to the south. **Fig. 15.16 Stephen Kenneth Johnson** Y5, 'Traditional & Open Air Music Venue', 3D print and CNCed MDF. Aerial view of site model exhibiting internal arena space and the buildings 'light touch' relationship with the ground.

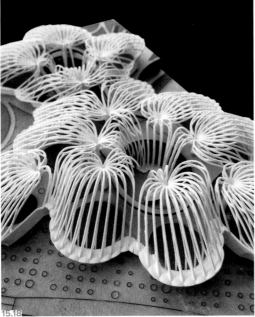

Fig. 15.17 **Jihum Kim** Y5, 'Sunken Courtyard Shopping, Leisure and Publication Centre', 3D print, sectional model of shopping centre in Seoul, South Korea. The expanding building elements blend into the surrounding context in a form of landscape, pavement and handrail. **Fig. 15.18 Ju Hyung Chun** Y5, 'Food-chitecture in Nodeul Island'. An architectural response to the twin challenges of global urbanisation and climate change by integrating both hydroponics and traditional farming practices. The building serves as a farm and a gathering place for the Seoul community. **Fig. 15.19 Jihum Kim** Y5, 'Rendering of Light Corridor.' The porous roof structure allows great deal of natural light in the tunnel which links the central atrium of publication centre and the sunken courtyard.

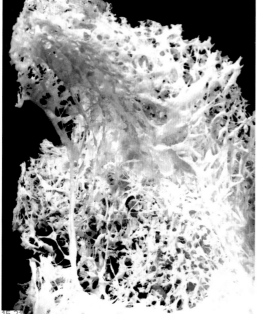

Fig. 15.20 **Tsun Ming Ho** Y5, 'Exposing Void', CNCed plywood, relief model photograph. An investigation of void formation under a field condition of multiple attractors. The resulting pattern shows the height of the underlying topography as well as the strength of the field. Fig. 15.21 **Jonas Weiss** Y4, 'Climate Cloud', acetone on styrofoam, photograph of artefact. Fig. 15.22 **Yin Hui Chung** Y4, 'Logic of Flow: Yongdusan Fungarium', 3D print. Conceptual model of urban massing strategy. Fluid spatial study generated from a fluid dynamics algorithm which adapts to different behaviours of fluid flows according to the local conditions of Yongdusan Park. The emergent viscous splash dynamics blossoms into multiple museum levels between parkscape and cityscape.

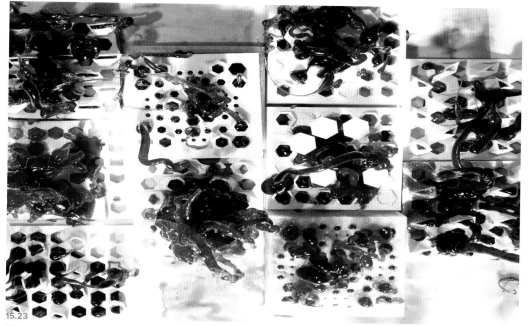

15.23

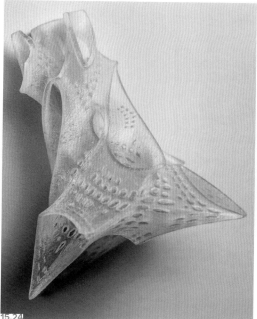

15.24

15.25

Fig. 15.23 **Augustine Ong Wing** Y4, 'Stochastic Exposure: Modulated Flow'. Analogue experiment investigating emergent stochastic formations through modulated flows of molten sugar. Naturally occurring resilient formations in various states of matter were investigated from an interest in self-organising systems. Complex formations were rationalised by pouring molten sugar at extreme temperatures through a series of parametrically generated 3D grid meshes. The resultant spectrum of complex stochastic formations are generated according to the logic of the grid parameters on the cooling liquid, which exhibit phenomena of nonlinearity, instability and adaptability. **Fig. 15.24 John Ju Hyung Chun** Y5, 'Labyrinth of Transparent Passages', 3D print, study model. **Fig. 15.25 Shengyu Meng** Y4, 'Busan Mushroom Museum', MDF.

Conceptual section model, Inspired by the process of solidification of melting wax, a spiralling system's potential has been explored to create vertical formation and organisation.

Adapt

Johan Berglund, Josep Miàs

Year 4
Leif Nader Buchmann, Jack
Morton Gransmore, Rebecca
Muirhead, Rachel Pickford,
Michael Pugh, Alex Sutton

Year 5
Benjamin Murray Allan,
Nathan Joseph Breeze,
James Alexander Bruce,
Robert Peter Burrows,
Natalia Eddy, Francis Roper,
Louise Sorensen, Richard
Winter

Thanks to Andrew Best,
Dean Pike and Happold
Consulting, and all of our
critics, supporters and
friends

Being a shrinking city and a quintessential modern site in flux, Detroit is a testing ground for experimentation and rethinking.[1]

Detroit is largely composed, today, of seemingly endless square miles of low-density failure.[2]

Unit 16 aims to exist in a close symbiosis between academic research and architectural practice, with constant testing and 'reflecting through action' to challenge the limits of architecture. We see architecture as an act of realisation, with both the power to transform and the responsibility to make sure we leave something positive behind.

Re-boot

On 18 July 2013, the city of Detroit filed for bankruptcy after a long history of economic struggle. The city, known for its booming car production during the twentieth century, has been falling into an extreme state of disrepair, and now must reinvent itself in order to survive. In order to generate personal positions in relation to this problem, the Unit explored the questions: How do you save a city? How do you decide what your legacy is when new developments move in? Is nostalgic preservation valuable in the evolution of cities?

The City of the Future

Parallel to our study of Detroit, we began to investigate ideas for future cities. As the world's population has increased in mobility, people migrate into cities in large quantities. Architects and urbanists will need to develop solutions for rapidly growing mega-cities, as well as sudden changes in growth or decline in other areas. We looked at current studies developed by planners, architects, sociologists, urbanists and economists, as well as fictional representations of the future city.

Cycles

We continued to develop ideas about the duration of our architecture, and encouraged students to look at extremes in order to find inventive architectural solutions. Our projects span from short-term interventions to aid mobilisation and relocation, to medium-term proposals dealing with the reconstruction of new Detroit, and long-term proposals that draw up future scenarios for the greater metropolitan area of Detroit. We visited the USA, traveling from Chicago, the city that gave birth to the skyscraper, to Detroit, the city that has become a symbol for its decline. We looked for utopian architectural proposals that question permanence, duration, and temporality; architectures that respond to and suggest contemporary and future modes of urban living; spaces that can evolve and change rather than being demolished or left to ruin as they become outdated.

1. Luis A. Croquer, www.mutualart.com
2. Jane Jacobs, *The Death and Life of Great American Cities* (NY: Vintage, 1993)

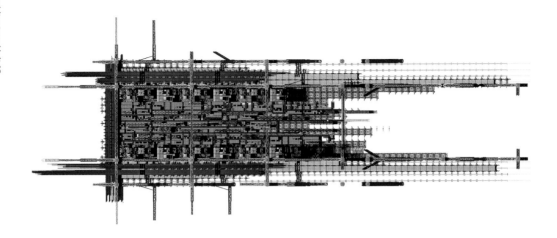

16.2

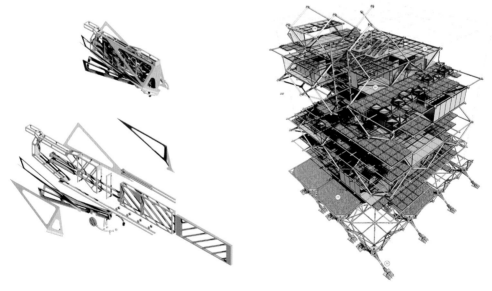

16.3   16.4

Fig. 16.1 – 16.5 **Francis Roper** Y5, 'Neo-Detroit'. A bold
proposal that erases the current city structure to make way for
a new flexible and re-configuable city structure. Through a
collection of clever prefabricated elements, the city is easily
built and unbuilt, and offers full flexibility to expand and
contract with the changing needs of the city and its residents.

16.5

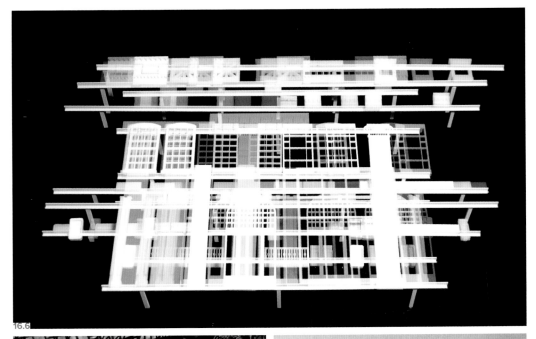

16.6

16.7

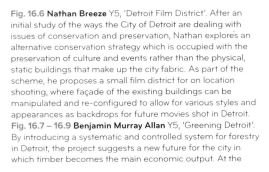

16.8

Fig. 16.6 Nathan Breeze Y5, 'Detroit Film District'. After an initial study of the ways the City of Detroit are dealing with issues of conservation and preservation, Nathan explore's an alternative conservation strategy which is occupied with the preservation of culture and events rather than the physical, static buildings that make up the city fabric. As part of the scheme, he proposes a small film district for on location shooting, where façade of the existing buildings can be manipulated and re-configured to allow for various styles and appearances as backdrops for future movies shot in Detroit.
Fig. 16.7 – 16.9 Benjamin Murray Allan Y5, 'Greening Detroit'. By introducing a systematic and controlled system for forestry in Detroit, the project suggests a new future for the city in which timber becomes the main economic output. At the

same time, the city shrinks to make way for large planted areas, turning Detroit into a city of forests. A focal point for this new development is the Timber Institute, a building nestled within the first forest plantation, from which the new financial initiative can be promoted and controlled.

16.9

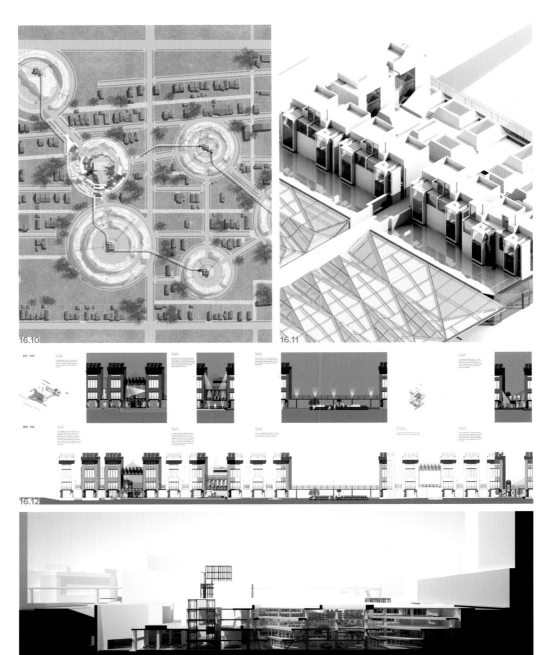

16.10

16.11

16.12

16.13

Fig. 16.10 Rebecca Muirhead Y4, 'Community Salt Mine'.
A study in how the residents of Detroit's suburban
neighbourhoods can utilise the loop holes in US legislation to
set up and operate their own small-scale mining cooperative.
Salt is an abundant resource in the Detroit area and a viable
business model for community growth and prosperity.
Fig. 16.11 Michael Pugh Y4, 'Eastern Market Artist Community'.
The project suggests an extension of the popular Eastern
Market, in order to accommodate facilities for a growing art
scene. It includes artist studios, a small gallery space, and
a public market area for selling and displaying artworks.
Fig. 16.12 Rachel Pickford Y4, 'A Living and Learning
Community'. An industrial, but inspired piece of architecture
that cleverly mixes residential units with spaces

for learning, both in the traditional sense but also for use in
home schooling groups, which is becoming more and more
common in the U.S. **Fig. 16.13 Alex Sutton** Y4, 'Detroit Hub'.
The project proposes the re-use of an existing underground
car park in downtown Detroit. Building on the growing trend
of shared workspace facilities and business incubators,
Alex carves out and reconfigures the car park into a great
subterranean office complex. **Fig. 16.14 Louise Sorensen** Y5,
'A Space for Sound and Performance'. A proposal for a new
masterplan for Corktown, where the re-introduction of the
historical creeks paves way for a regeneration of the area into
an engaging landscape design. By cutting into the building
and allowing it to be open to the elements, it seamlessly blends
into the watery landscape that surrounds it.

1448 Wabash Street, June 2035.
Third floor plan 1:250

16.14

16.15

16.16

16.17

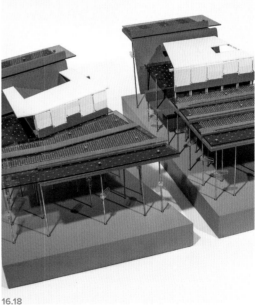

16.18

Fig. 16.15 **Richard Winter** Y5, 'Rouge River Car Recycling Plant'. Building on Detroit's automotive history and its need to regenerate its economy as well as its urban spaces, the project introduces a new car recycling plant along the river, where the public can interact and engage with the recycling processes. Fig. 16.16 **Robert Peter Burrows** Y5, 'Belle Isle Farm'. The project proposes the reinvigoration of what used to be Detroit's main park and recreation area. As the urban agriculture trend is growing in the city, the project sees the opportunity to expand this into a larger scale farmland complex, while education communities on farming techniques. Fig. 16.17 **Leif Nader Buchmann** Y4, 'New Centre Train Station'. A project for a new Amtrak station that connects to the US governments plans for extending the current rail network into a high speed rail system. The project builds on historical train station typologies while upgrading it to the twenty-first century in a playful manner. Fig. 16.18 **Jack Morton Gransmore** Y4, 'Stormwater Facility and Water Park'. A strategy for handling the storm water run off in Detroit, while at the same time creating new public spaces along the riverfront. A visitor centre lies within a concrete trench landscape, shifting up and down depending on the amount of water flowing through the artificial river.

16.19

16.20

Fig. 16.19 **Natalia Eddy** Y5, 'Steam Power Facility'. A proposal for a retrofit and upgrade of an exisiting steam power plant, which in the new iteration would be able to power a large part of central Detroit. Derelict skyscrapers become heat stores, large underground areas are utilised for heated public spaces, and the excavated rock from below ground is used to create new sculptural and imaginative public spaces above ground.
Fig. 16.20 **James Alexander Bruce** Y5 'Woodward Avenue Masterplan'. Following the City of Detroit's new initiative to create a new tram link along Woodward Avenue, the project proposes a masterplan along the avenue with new public spaces, mobile kiosks, pavilions, and temporary markets used to activate the area surrounding the Avenue, and to open up possibilities for future expansion of the neighbouring areas.

Unit 17

The Open Work

Yeoryia Manolopoulou, Níall McLaughlin, Michiko Sumi

Year 4
Emily Doll, Justine Dorion, André Kullmar, Jonathan Paley, Paloma Rua-Figueroa, Chris Worsfold

Year 5
Alastair Browning, Joel Cady, Alicia González-Lafita Pérez, Uieong To, William Tweddell, Kirsty Sarah Williams, Mika Helen Zacharias

Thank you to our consultant William Whitby and our Design Realisation Tutors Joseph Mackey, David Hemingway and Anne Schroell

Thanks also to our critics: Matthew Butcher, Hannah Corlett, Mary Duggan, Murray Fraser, Will Hunter, Jan Kattein, Constance Lau, Guan Lee, Sophia Psarra, Peg Rawes, Bob Sheil, Henning Stummell, Mike Tonkin, Victoria Watson

Thanks to Mihail Amariei, Alberto Redolfi, Emiliano Rizzotti, Carlo Ostorero, Alberto Pottenghi, Phil Tabor, and Jan-Christoph Zoels for their fieldtrip support

Unit 17 designs contextual buildings that interplay with the social, political and material cultures of specific places. Each project is research-based, aiming to construct an architectural thesis that is explicitly manifested in the design proposition. We are interested in each student's imagination and original voice, and seek diversity in the work produced by the Unit as a whole: projects complement and sometimes intentionally contradict each other to form a multilayered dialogue about the nature of architectural thought and practice today. Design iteration through drawing and making is a constant activity that we encourage. Stimulating fieldtrips, critical debates through open reviews and tutorials, and an osmosis of ideas and techniques in the studio are vital aspects of the Unit's culture.

————In *The Open Work* Umberto Eco discusses the role of openness in modern art by asking what it means for authors to understand their work as incomplete, left open to the public and to chance. We see buildings exactly in this way: as 'open works' experienced and changed over time. Buildings are exposed to accidents, the environment, myriads different interpretations and modes of occupation. They are vulnerable to decline and collapse, human intervention, extension and demolition. Prescribed programmes often change or become obsolete.

————Our degree of openness towards the evolution of buildings over time determines our design approach and eventually the kind of architecture and cities we produce.

————This year we questioned architecture's excessive programmatic specificity, welcoming propositions for buildings that are less 'programmed'. We explored buildings that have had different purposes over the course of time, gaining quality through enduring, despite changes of use and circumstance. In November we travelled to northern Italy, a place of contradictions that denies any singular or fixed meaning. We visited the Olivetti complex in Ivrea, and buildings by Nervi, Ponti, Terragni, Rossi, Mangiarotti and Grafton Architects among others.

————No matter how themes change from year to year, our emphasis is always on the design of buildings as spaces to experience, and as meaningful public artefacts in culture and in history. Excessive metaphors, narratives and other overloaded signifiers are questioned, since our view is that the building should not be explained but experienced. The relationships between ideas, materials, places, environment, political life and the contemporary everyday will continue to preoccupy us.

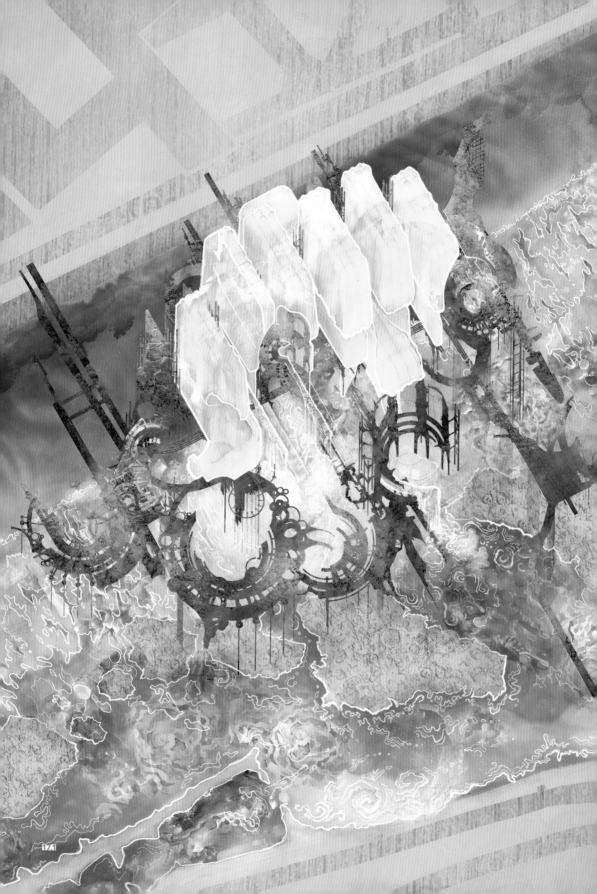

Fig. 17.1 Kirsty Sarah Williams Y5, 'Ivrea Natural History Museum'. The building is a celebration of production, a self-making factory powered by the meltwater of the Alps. It is an inversion of the city it occupies, Ivrea – a once notable industrial centre now stagnating. It is also a noteworthy place geologically, sitting at the heart of the most significant morainic amphitheatre in Europe. The project interrogates the relationship between a modern scientific institution using sophisticated digital techniques to reintroduce extinct species, and the inherent nostalgia of such an undertaking. This is done by producing traditional sculpted pieces using digital clay and 3D printing using wax, which is then electroplated. The museum is organised through the concept of time and focuses on the natural world surrounding Ivrea.

Fig. 17.2 – 17.4 Mika Helen Zacharias Y5, 'Banca di Valdo Fusi', Turin. The proposed bank is sited in a block of Turin's Roman Quarter and responds to the urban context by opening views to nearby piazzas which punctuate the city grid, as a space which is open to and effected by public use. The building is experienced through movement across courtyards and along meandering public walkways; meeting spaces are arranged to encourage social gatherings, exchange and chance encounters. Servers containing digital currencies are integrated into the building, giving money a physical presence. The building is constructed of both solid and temporary elements; glass and steel are inserted within a robust stone framework. It becomes a form which is malleable and can be subjected to the programmatic changes that will take place on the site over time.

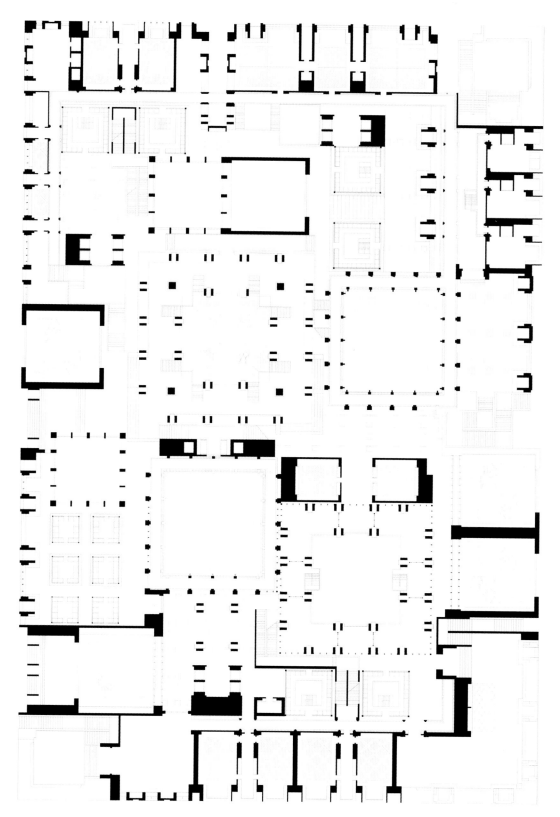

17.4

17.5

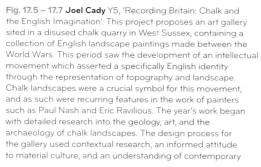

17.6

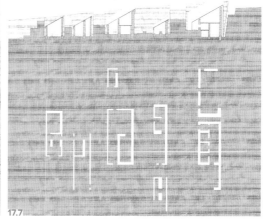

17.7

Fig. 17.5 – 17.7 **Joel Cady** Y5, 'Recording Britain: Chalk and the English Imagination'. This project proposes an art gallery sited in a disused chalk quarry in West Sussex, containing a collection of English landscape paintings made between the World Wars. This period saw the development of an intellectual movement which asserted a specifically English identity through the representation of topography and landscape. Chalk landscapes were a crucial symbol for this movement, and as such were recurring features in the work of painters such as Paul Nash and Eric Ravilious. The year's work began with detailed research into the geology, art, and the archaeology of chalk landscapes. The design process for the gallery used contextual research, an informed attitude to material culture, and an understanding of contemporary architecture in rural landscapes to develop a proposal which has a deep relationship with the materials, both imaginative and actual, from which places are made. The proposal carefully adapts the found spaces of the quarry and its relationship with the surrounding chalk escarpment to provide new 'ways in', both spatially and imaginatively, to the downland landscape. The gallery buildings, made predominantly from chalk, are inserted into new cuts in the quarry wall, and contain a series of evocative spaces designed to relate the paintings to the landscape around them. This is achieved through a combination of the visual and tactile qualities of chalk, carefully considered routes the landscape, and the charged light of the downs.

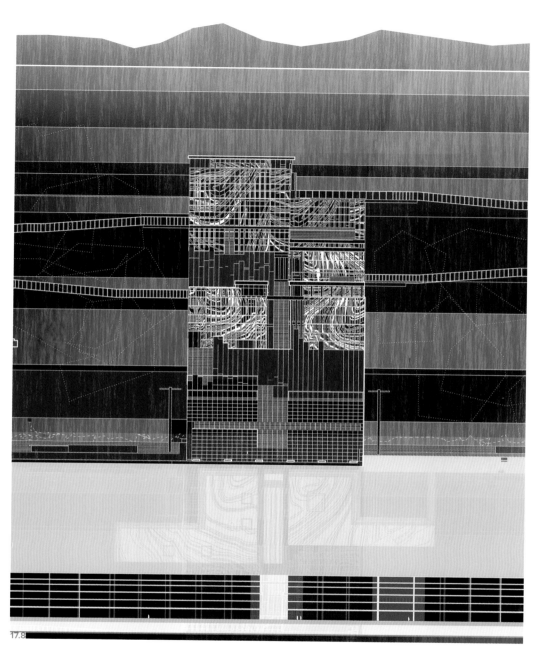

17.8

Fig. 17.8 **Alicia González-Lafita Pérez** Y5, 'Olivetti Research Centre', Ivrea. Camillo Olivetti founded the typewriter manufacturer company of the same name in Ivrea, where he and his son Adriano Olivetti developed the industrial city, primarily between 1933-1960. Adriano Olivetti built a city within a city, not only founding the factory to host the production of the typewriters but also providing housing for his employees and social facilities. Many of those projects did not successfully address their context or each other, rather becoming singular objects in the landscape. They were designed prioritising the plan over the section and ultimately over the experience of the building as a whole. The proposed Olivetti Reseach Centre and Cinema Archive addresses and critiques the aforementioned urban condition. The proposed building is positioned in response to a glazed factory located on Via Jervis, which was designed to bring in light and create a proximity to nature. The proposal acts as a gateway and explores the dichotomy between industrial and rural Ivrea. It is inserted in the hillside, into which it extends with a series of walkways – at ground level, a public square addresses the relationship between the existing Olivetti buildings. The northern façade filters views of the city whilst the south elevation directly opens onto the Evorese countryside. The modification of the landscape and the use of screening blurs these boundaries; the lattice follows the grided pattern of the Via Jervis façades and is overlaid with an Olivetti poster, reiterating Olivetti's use of architecture in advertising to depict 'utopian' life in Ivrea.

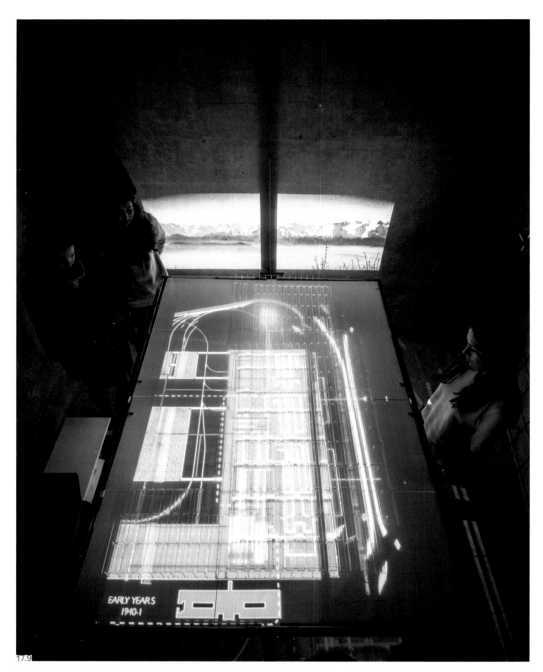

17.9

Fig. 17.9 – 17.10 **Alastair Browning** Y5, 'The Open-Plan'. Mirafiori, Turin. Located in a suburb of post-industrial Turin, once the 'Fordist world's most prototypical town', the project proposes a new university campus sited within the 20m x 20m grid of Fiat's behemoth Mirafiori Plant (1939). The flexible or 'generic' space of the Fordist factory, whilst born out of the necessity for the simplified movement of material alongside a predetermined form of human inhabitation, purveyed from the factory floor across many other built forms and typologies throughout the second half of the twentieth century.
This 'open-plan' influenced entire cities, demonstrating its suitability as the 'nth plan' of the tower blocks of the urban core, right through to the spaces of consumption that dominate the suburban periphery. The project is positioned as an exploration into the open-plan, balancing the 'generic' with the 'particular', interweaving new programmes and functions into the repetitive matrix of the existing concrete frame. The project positions the proposed high-speed railway link between Lyon, Turin and Budapest as a driving agent in repositioning post-industrial Turin within a wider European context. The design focuses on the sectional distribution of the masterplan: workshops, offices, lecture theatres and public squares are situated at ground level, whilst housing, communal facilities, nursery schools and shared gardens inhabit the building's roof. Occupying a site equivalent in size to the city's historic centre, the project envisages Mirafiori as a new city quarter articulated by the shifting presence of production, research, commerce and living.

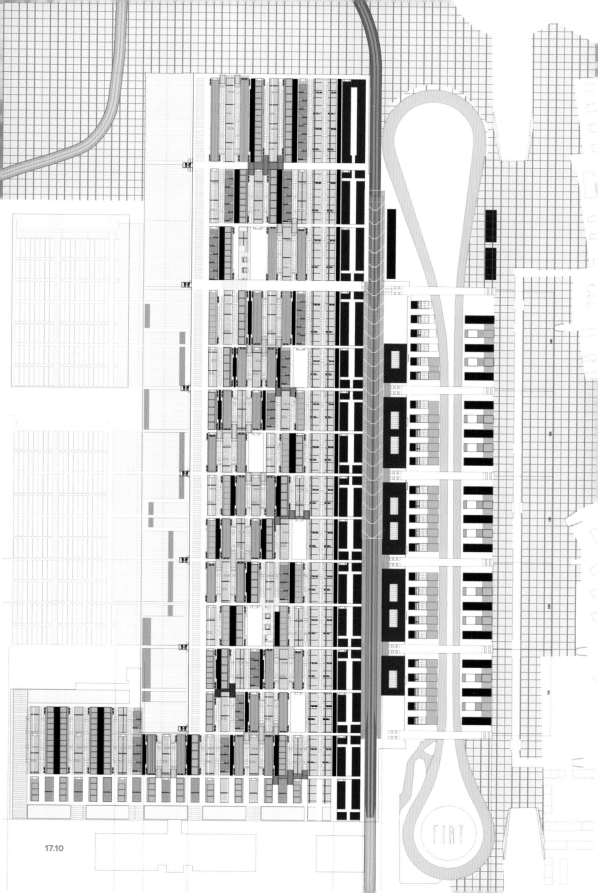

17.10

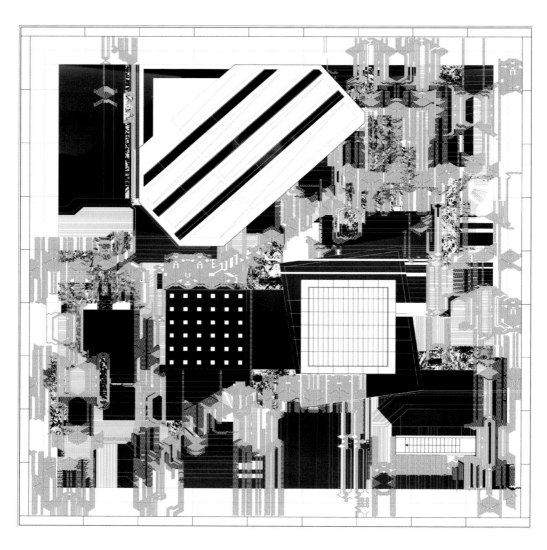

17.11

Fig. 17.11 William Twedell Y5, 'Casa dei Sindacati' is the final figure in the reinstatement of Giuseppe Terragni's Masterplan for Como, the idyllic pre-alpine city. The Casa del Fascio, the formative work of the seminal Fascist architect Giuseppe Terragni, serves as the antonymic counterpart to the proposal. The Trade Union superimposes an aesthetic language of the Ancient Greek Palaesta, to draw on its embodied ideologies. It was key to the development of young Athenians in learning through 'body practice' to become a part of the city and crucially naked, thus free and confident to express themselves. The building rises from the city textile, evidencing ruin and remnant seeking ground between formalism and looser, sculptural, tactile forms, in a bid to uncover a way of engaging with architecture in an acutely corporeal manner.

Fig. 17.12 Uieong To Y5, 'San Giovanni station', Como. The project is an extension to the border train station to accommodate the Como-Swiss commuters. A primary school and nursery are integrated into the proposal, exploring the live-work nature of the transnational family and the relationship between children and their mobile parents. Envisioned as a journey that resembles the trains, the primary school and nursery are stretched on a long plan with each occupying one side of the parallel structures running along the railway line. This concept is further reflected in the design of the continuous roof whose full length serves as the open ground for children's imagination and play. Fig. 17.13 left-right: Jonathan Paley, Emily Doll, André Kullmar Y4. Fig. 17.14 left-right: Paloma Rua-Figueroa, Chris Worsfold, Justine Dorion Y4.

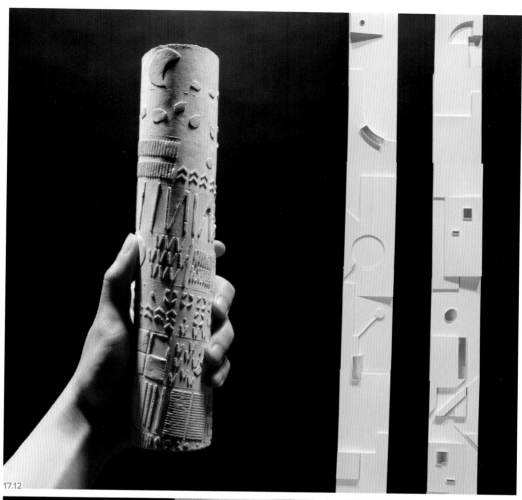

17.12

17.13

17.14

Unit 18

Carving a Giant

Nannette Jackowski, Ricardo de Ostos

Year 4
Christina Dahdaleh, Jingsi (Joyce) Li, Chi Hoon Seong, Shao Wang, Zhiying (Sean) Xu, Liang Zhou

Year 5
Sonal Balasuriya, Sing Sun (Ryan) Cheng, Anthony D'Auria, Anna Maria Janiak, Haaris Ramzan, Liang Shang, Anthanasios Varnavas

Thank you to our consultants: Ross Exo Adams, Ricardo Baptista, Jan Birksted, Anis Wan Kamaruddin, Sara Klomps, Guan Lee, Rob Partridge, Tania Sengupta, Simon Withers, Saman Ziaie

Thanks also to our guest critics: Jeroen van Armeijde, Julia Backhaus, Brendon Carlin, Ryan Dillon, Oliver Domeisen, Lawrence Friesen, Oliviu Lugojan-Ghenciu, Christine Hawley, Megha Chand Inglis, Manuel Jimenez, Sebastian Kite, Sara Klomps, Alice Labourel, Stephen Lau, Abel Maciel, Kaleigh Tirone Nunes, Claudia Pasquero, Vesna Petresin, Khyle Raja, Yael Reisner, Tania Sengupta, Marilena Skavara, Bob Sheil, Ellie Stathaki, Catrina Stewart, Robert Stuart-Smith, Aris Theodoropoulos, Lorenzo Vianello, Sam Welham, Young Wei Yang Chiu, Tim Yue, Brendan Woods

generationalphantoms.co.uk

The Bartlett School of Architecture 2014

This year Unit 18, or Generational Phantoms, continued to explore relationships between digital technologies and social structures. Furthering last year's understanding of cryptology as a way to generate architecture we specifically focused on the notion of the human body and its encryption into ornament.

————Firstly students investigated how in recent decades the body has been a fundamental benchmark for encoding information into buildings – as proportion, ornamentation, but also to communicate social structures. Utilising digital software and fabrication techniques students then developed their own concepts of the body, generating small-scale ornaments such as a vestigial rubber wisdom tooth, typewriter skins and a Morse Code hand ornament based on encryption strategies.

————In order to expand the notion of the individual body to the idea of a collective or collaborative body, we voyaged to Rajasthan, India to experience places of production and to study its social structures, known as guilds. We visited India's largest salt lake; a marble-extracting town covered by a thick layer of white marble dust; a city specialised in marble processing; a neighbourhood of storefront artisans; a clay brick factory whose kiln is made of the bricks that are being burnt; and an important trading region known for its ornately decorated residences.

————For the final project, students reconsidered their understanding of the body and the ornament in order to create a collaborative network in the form of a guild. To choose a context, students analysed specific scenarios of material extraction and manufacturing places in India where workers, corporations and more sophisticated fabrication methods overlap with endemic urban organisations and social inequalities.

————The 'Spiritual Guild' project by Sonal investigated a seasonal interaction between marble sculptors, Makrana city and its quarries. A series of narrow shafts allow for new places of production to rise directly out of the quarry, housing three generations of marble sculptors who make popular mini-temples using stone remains left on site. Athanasios created a compelling spatial narrative by designing an experiential journey along the Makrana quarry site rooted on India's rich mystical stories. Utilising earthworks, metal and concrete to shape each other and the idea of a vestigial ornament Anthony rearticulated the trade and technological possibilities of a nomadic guild, the Gadulia Lohar, by generating a building that is as much a shelter as a political space for identity.

————Along the journey, departing from the notion of the body, students uncovered a few architectural corpses and effected many digital autopsies, creating a dossier of projects where material and architecture go beyond the idea of the catalogue. Instead, material, technology and social networks opened new ways to the new collaborations between the visible and the invisible.

18.2

18.3

Fig. 18.1 Anthony D'Auria Y5, 'Vestigial Materialities / Vestigial Economies', cast site model. Vestigial steel from disused colonial railways near the Dolphur sandstone fields becomes the impetus for a seasonal waystation for the nomadic Gadulia Lohar blacksmiths. Steel is melted and cast into the landscape to create forges and covered market spaces that engage with the local economies of the agrarian and quarrying villages and the proposed tourist train that will traverse the region.
Fig. 18.2 Anthony D'Auria Y5, 'Vestigial Materialities / Vestigial Economies'. Section showing metal process at new site. The architecture follows the logic of the vestigial cycle as steel is transformed from obsolete railway to architectural armature to smithing tool and finally into saleable forged goods for distribution during the Gadulia Lohar's peripatetic season.

Fig. 18.3 **Athanasios Varnavas** Y5, 'Ariadne's Thread', aerial view of a cannibalised corpus. The project / book / labyrinth / body is nested on a Nave(l) in the City-Quarry of Makrana precisely located at 27°01'39" N 74°42'42" E. It envisions a series of operations on the existing Durga temple, where architecture transforms from 'static' Vitruvian proportions into a multilayered cannibalised, armored corpus of a Carved Giant. It seeks to challenge additive or weaving ('Penelope') processes in architecture through the subtractive thinking of carving ('Odysseus') and the uncanny of destruction, removing and releasing matter. The Blasphemous Guild explores these two processes (+-), blurring and merging so as to augment the surrounding landscape, operating between destruction and generation. **Fig. 18.4 Athanasios Varnavas** Y5, 'Ariadne's Thread', robotic carving, tombstone book. A fragment from the proposed spherical language based upon the 6-axis affinities of robotic carving ('the eye') simulated on a marble block. The spatial qualities sought by glyphs (that accumulate with time), form a space of memory and micro-niches, which temporarily accommodate the ashes from the 'sacrificed' quarry-workers. The ritual symbolically begins and ends based upon the circadian flooding of the quarry to further highlight the possibilities of an infinite book-labyrinth: a resurrected corpus.

18.5

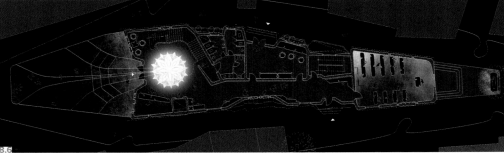

18.6

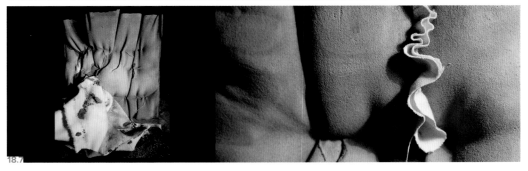

18.7

Fig. 18.5 **Chi Hoon Seong** Y4, 'Retreat Island'. The Island is a retreat from the harsh conditions created by the high salt content in Lake Sambhar in India; providing physical, spiritual and ecological regeneration through the creation of salt grottos and the play of light using ornamental roofs. Salt water absorbed from the site is used to crystallise the salt grottos, creating rehabilitation spaces for saltpan workers; and the marshes in pocket areas improve the ecological system of the lake. Fig. 18.6 **Liang Zhou** Y4, 'The Giant Sari Witness', Varanasi, India. The ground plan articulates the wedding ceremony centre and the context of the city, creating a street procession and generating narrow alleyways, in keeping with the city's morphological tradition. **Fig. 18.7 Liang Zhou** Y4, 'The Giant Sari Witness', Varanasi, India, fabric formwork test pieces.

The prototypes explore the retention of fabric in concrete crevices as part of an ornamental strategy.

Fig. 18.8 **Zhiying Xu** Y4, 'Varanasi Crematorium and Smoke Garden'. Model exploring multiple scales for a new crematorium in Varanasi, expanding the city streets into an elevated smoke garden enabling tourists to experience part of the ceremony without causing disruption to guild workers and families. **Fig. 18.9 Jingsi (Joyce) Li** Y4, 'Buddhist Pilgrimage in Sarnath'. Model exploring roof performance and light patterns. By utilising different types of paper and apertures based on symbolic Buddhist scriptures, the project explores the transition between performance and ornament. **Fig. 18.10 Christina Dahdaleh** Y4, 'Form Exploration'. Harvesting toxic waste present in one of the main marble quarries in the town of Makrana. The façade is developed to capture the Marble dust through the utilisation of updrafts onsite.

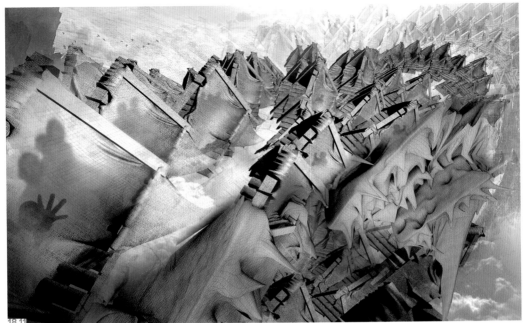

18.11

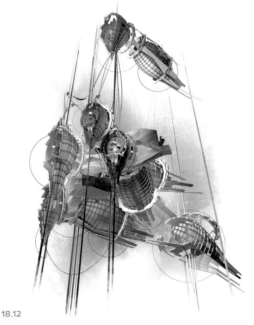

18.12

18.13

Fig. 18.11 **Haaris Ramzan** Y5, 'Guild of the Storyteller'. The Guild of the Storyteller proposes a fairytale retreat situated within the Valley of Kashmir. The retreat aims to provide the orphans of Kashmir with a moment of escape from the turbulence of a violent political conflict. The architectural language of the retreat mimics that of the menagerie of animals and beasts found within traditional Kashmiri fairytales. The journey through the retreat attempts to simulate the forgotten art of storytelling through an enchanted architectural language. Fig. 18.12 **Liang Shang** Y5, 'Guild of Identity – Call Centre Agent Village'. Digital render section of the call centre agents' work and living space: Five individual working units including one senior agent and four juniors. The cable connections indicate the 'office' network, forming a vertical

structure that acts as the 'façade' of the guild. Fig. 18.13 **Liang Shang** Y5, 'Guild of Identity – Call Centre Agent Village'. Sectional drawing exploring proposed guild social structure and its relationship with the local context. Open markets extend the sightline towards the IT campus, and the prayer room utilises the Gudawara concept of tolerance for all religions, providing a welcoming collective space as a new village centre.

18.14

18.15

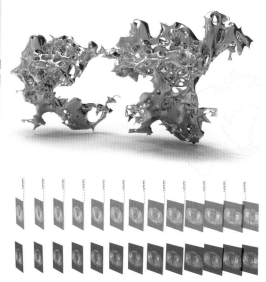

18.16

Fig. 18.14 **Anna Maria Janiak** Y5, 'The Architecture of Mathematical Rituals'. The project aims to explore ideas of order and chaos in architectural creation in New Delhi. Order is represented by the beauty of forms generated using ancient geometric formulas. Chaos refers to the social and environmental issues connected with e-waste recycling. The final architectural output is an ever-growing temple constructed out of reused metals slowly emerging from the waters of Yamuna River. Fig. 18.15 **Sing Sun (Ryan) Cheng** Y5, 'Perceiving an Erroneous Landscape'. Camouflage garden situated in-between the disputed mine boundaries in Goa, India. The architecture is generated by glitches in Google Earth, in which the landscape is misinterpreted as a malformed forest, concealing the local community's unlawful mining activities from satellite surveillance. Fig. 18.16 **Sing Sun (Ryan) Cheng** Y5, 'Perceiving an Erroneous Landscape'. Digital errors are physically manifested to reinvent the process of translating the human body in ornamentation for the digital age.

Fig. 18.17 **Sonal Balasuriya** Y5, 'The Spiritual Guild', Makrana, Rajasthan. The project proposes the migration of contemporary stone carving guilds of Jaipur, to Makrana, where white marble has been quarried for centuries creating a landscape of gigantic proportions. These craftsmen will inhabit self-built shafts that rise from the depths of the quarry, attempting to link the liberated with the non-liberated along the cosmic axis. The stone carving workshops will be located along this axis, creating sacred ornaments, mini temples capable of provoking thoughts of liberation or 'moksha'.

Fig. 18.18 **Sonal Balasuriya** Y5, 'The Spiritual Guild', Makrana, Rajasthan. 1:10 prototype of the workshop façade, milled in white Makrana marble. The façade detail shows the perforated nature of marble at a much larger scale with the agglomeration of mini temples that alter and reconfigure the porosity of the façade. Fig. 18.19 – 18.20 **Sonal Balasuriya** Y5, 'The Spiritual Guild, Makrana', Rajasthan.

Unit 19

The Living Spaces of the Algorithmics

Mollie Claypool, Manuel Jiménez Garcia, Philippe Morel

Year 4
Shi Qi An, Maria-Cristina Banceanu, Yuan Xing (Lisa) Liu, Yiting Lu, Annabel Monk, Stacy Peh Li Lin, Ran Shu, Tomas Tvarijonas

Year 5
Stuart Colaco, Matthew Lacey, Jeffrey Lim, Liu Meng, Sang Yong Seok, Shuo Zhang

Thank you to our Design Realisation Tutor Manja van der Worp, and thanks to Vicente Soler for technical support

Thanks also to our critics: Nuria Alvarez Lombardero, Sebastian Andia, Torsted Broeder, Matthew Butcher, Brendon Carlin, Marcos Cruz, Marjan Colletti, Apostolis Despotidis, Ryan Dillon, Vidal Fernandez, Evan Greenberg, Christine Hawley, Carlos Jimenez, Katya Larina, Jorge Mendez, Drew Merkle, Gilles Retsin, Yael Reisner, Pablo Ros, Stefan Rutzinger, Carles Sala, Thibault Schwartz, Kristina Schinegger, Vicente Soler, Claudia Pasquero, Jeroen van Ameijde, Manja van de Worp, Naiara Vegara, Michael Weinstock, Manja van der Worp, Emmannouil Zaroukas

Many thanks for the generosity of our critics over the course of the year, the workshop and DPL staff for their support as well as students of GAD RC5 and the Y5 students' thesis tutors

In 2014 the largest problem we face as designers is how to house the world's exponentially increasing population. In 2050 it is estimated that the world population will surpass 10 billion and the world will become the most dense, and most temporal, it has ever been. Where will we house all of those people? How will we house them? What kinds of needs will they have? This year, we have continued a research agenda into the problem of housing, situating ourselves in Sicily, a site which has been a important geographic fulcrum for population shifts throughout history due to its position in the Mediterranean: it is the gateway to Europe from Africa and parts of the Middle East. Its ever-changing population due to migration has resulted in a new kind of domesticity and housing becoming necessary, one which must be continuously in flux, adaptive and temporal, as well as sensitive in terms of economic and social relationships.

———As a means of opening this as a design research problem, we began the year studying patterns of delinquency, nomadism, escapism, alienation, isolation and exile, and how this relates to these shifts and variances in population architecturally and spatially. With an exponential increase in the ways in which architects can understand the world due to the computational revolution, architects now have the capacity to design for this variability as well as difference. Each student designed a 1:1, 1:5 or 1:10 apparatus which had to transform mechanically, with several uses or functions designed into the piece. This was then simulated using algorithmic processes, and a structural, geometric or material logic was abstracted. This logic was used as the main driver in design research into novel material strategies, adaptable and kinetic structures and geometries and novel fabrication technologies, with the design of a housing 'unit' being the output of this work. As a result, almost all of the projects designed for a single inhabitable housing unit to be capable of being differentiated within an overall logic, enabling the same logic to be utilised for different functions. A single unit can achieve different kinds of inhabitable spaces when aggregated with density logics to form housing 'clusters' and then, on a larger scale, an urban strategy for housing. Each project brief is individual to the student's own interests within housing, ranging from short-term or longer-term solutions for the housing crisis we are now in. For Year 5 this is a continuation of research begun in the unit last year and is tied to the work done for the Thesis. For Year 4 it was tied to the Design Realisation project as well as building a clear research agenda to take into Year 5 next year.

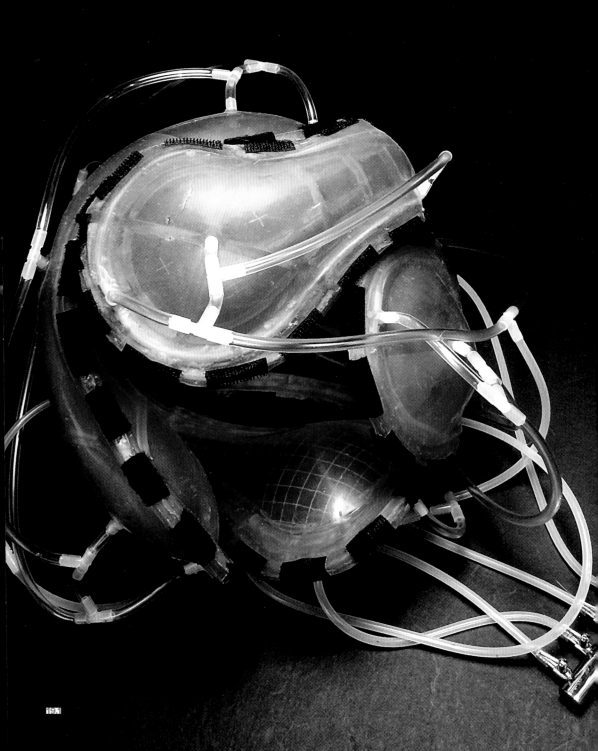

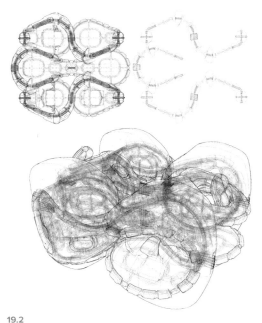

19.2

19.3

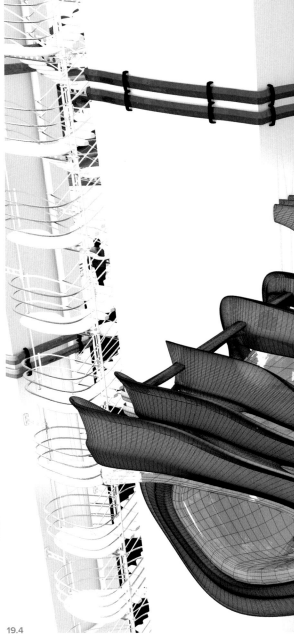

19.4

Fig. 19.1 **Liu Meng** Y5, inflatable prototype model study for a housing unit made of cast latex and silicon, part of a series of test models made during Unit 19's prototyping workshop in Term 2. **Fig. 19.2 Liu Meng** Y5, drawings of inflatable housing unit, clustered (top left), unrolled (top right) and the structural frame (bottom). **Fig. 19.3 Tomas Tvarijonas** Y4, 3D prints made of a latex cast exploring ways to fabricate lattices which could then be inflated to be made structural, or embedded with mechanical technologies **Fig. 19.4 Tomas Tvarijonas** Y4, overall view of materially-intelligent prototypical system deployed on site on the underside of unused highway infrastructure, showing public space (foreground) and housing clusters (background).

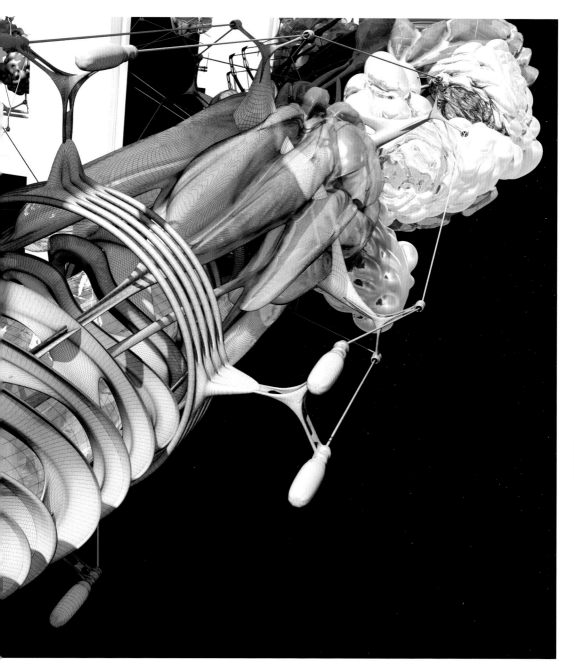

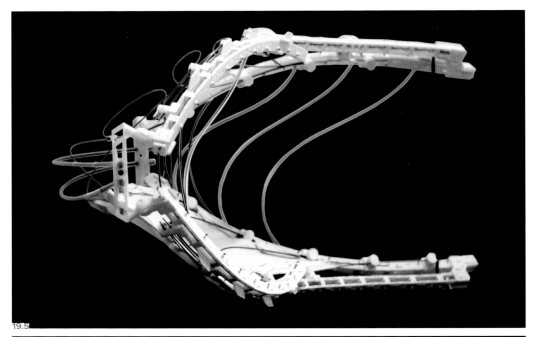

19.5

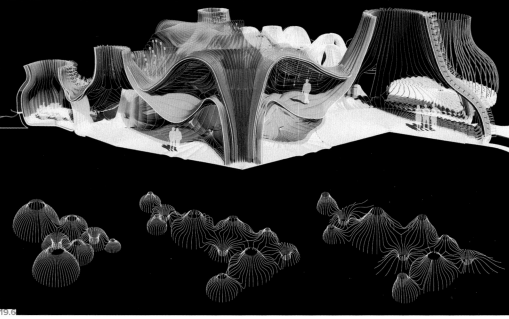

19.6

Fig. 19.5 **Stuart Colaco** Y5, model of frame of prototypical housing unit in deployed state showing spline system. Fig. 19.6 **Matthew Lacey** Y5, sectional perspective showing corrogation of skin, interaction between forms and interior spaces. Fig. 19.7 **Annabel Monk** Y4, prototype of structural strategy for catenary system using inflating to deploy. Fig. 19.8 **Yiting Lu** Y4, early studies of flat pack system for deployment of the structure for a single unit. Fig. 19.9 **Sang Yong Seok** Y5, plans of modules for housing.

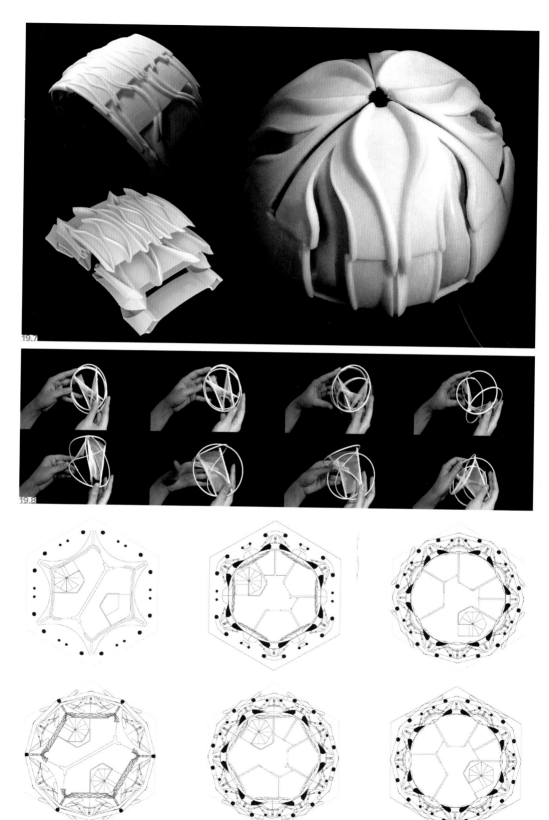

19.7

19.8

19.9

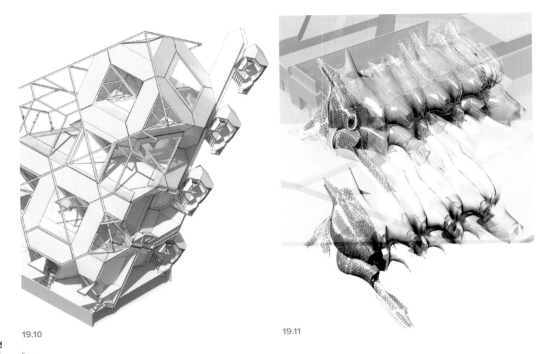

19.10

19.11

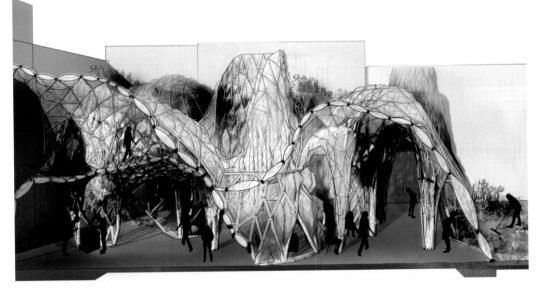

19.12

Fig. 19.10 **Maria-Cristina Banceanu** Y4, view of one of four
scenarios for the deployment of housing module within overall
structural frame. Fig. 19.11 **Jeffrey Lim** Y5, overall view of
capsule housing system deployment in deactive (above)
and active (below) states. Fig. 19.12 **Yuan Xing (Lisa) Liu** Y4,
sectional perspective through inflated expandable column
system on site. Fig. 19.13 **Ran Shu** Y4, exploded axometric of
housing unit showing structure and panel system. Fig. 19.14
Shi Qi An Y4, studies for deployment strategies of a housing
unit onstructuted of a series of foldable lines with varying fold
patterns. Fig. 19.15 **Stacy Peh Li Lin** Y4, view of housing units
deployed on site in Mazara del Vallo.

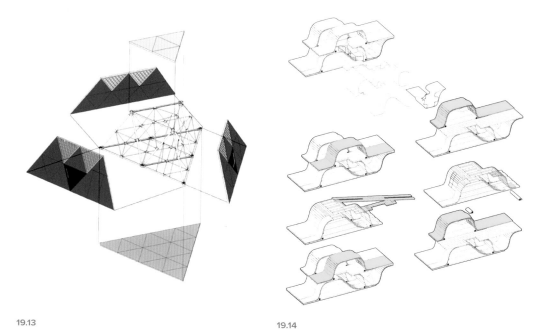

19.13

19.14

19.15

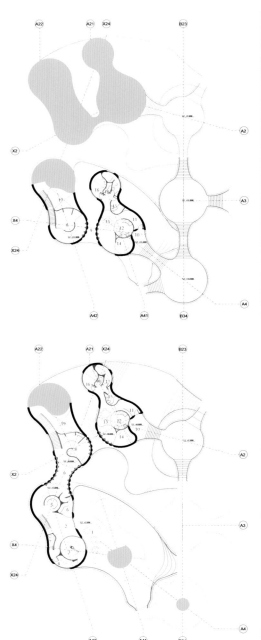

19.16

19.17

Fig. 19.16 – 19.17 **Shuo Zhang** Y5, plans and model of
transitionary spaces between live and work units in
prototypical scenario.

Unit 20 **Newtopia**

Richard Beckett, Marjan Colletti, Marcos Cruz

Year 4
Maria Esteban-Casañas,
Chris Falla, Jianze (Arthur)
Hao, Wiktor Kidziak,
Jonathan Wilson

Year 5
Anahita Chouhan, Daphnie
Costi, Judith Shiow Yin
Gillespie, Thomas Hopkins,
Wai Yue (Ruby) Law, Olivia
Pearson, Sam Rigby, Javier
Ruiz, Emily Yan

Thanks to Justin Nicholls
and Maria Eugenia Villafañe

The Bartlett School of Architecture 2014

Unit 20 is interested in crossing the boundaries of traditional architectural practice and envisioning innovative conditions in design. By considering a wide range of topics from science and art, students are encouraged to develop a two-year research study that is both individual and collaborative. Projects in the Unit aim to be poetic, people-centric and always multi-layered. They are developed with a focus on contemporary means of design and production while establishing an architecture that is built up upon social, cultural and historic strata.

Dwelling (boundaries, curtilage, proximity...)

This year the Unit explored the underlying geometries of dwelling within our cities. Dwelling is essential to human existence, and today more than ever it is at the centre of our architectural and environmental preoccupations. In a time where the world population is rapidly growing and with the majority of people living in cities, the need to house the basic needs of such a large quantity of people is unprecedented. Dwelling is not to be confused with housing. It is a broader concept that is at the heart of phenomenological thinking. It questions how we occupy, reside and inhabit the spaces of our contemporary city. It is a condition of primal importance that touches upon notions of identity, proximity, functionality, comfort and protection.

Novel Geometries (configurations, relationships, typo-morphologies, lattices...)

Underlying all of these notions are the socio-politics of space, the fragility of our environment and a new geometric language of architecture that will determine the way in which we will inhabit our future buildings and cities. This year's brief advances previous studies from last year, which investigated 'Porosity: A Material Shift Towards an Architecture of Permeability'. The generation and expression of novel geometries, developed with the aid of contemporary digital and computational techniques, allows for open, porous, permeable and fibrous spaces to be configured – towards a higher degree of spatial complexity, material intelligence and cultural phenomena.

Trade (pearls, oil, spices...)

This year, Unit 20 studied one of the most fascinating and fast-developing areas of the world today: the Gulf. We explored various cities in the region which offered a great variety of historic layers, geo-political complexity, cultural specificity, environmental beauty and fragility. We toured Dubai and Abu Dhabi, through deserts and oases, along the fortifications of the old spice and pearl trade via the Strait of Hormuz to Muscat in Oman – the most strategically important checkpoint of oil trade in the world. Two students continued with their previous lines of research in the context of Hong Kong.

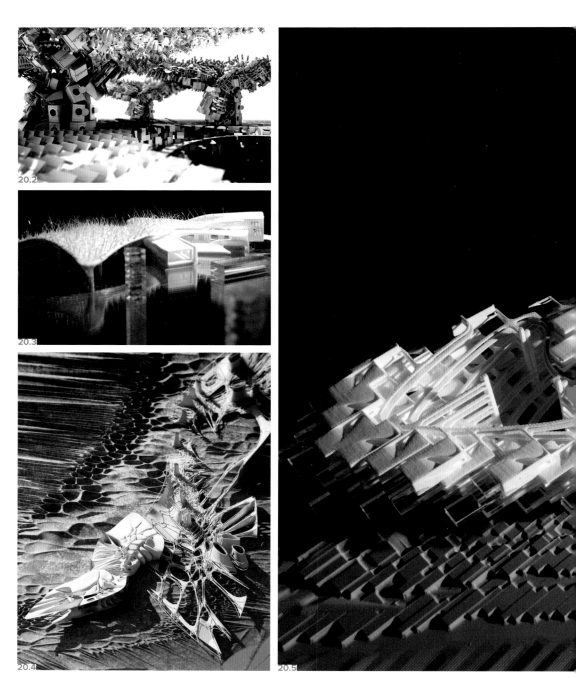

Fig. 20.1 **Thomas Hopkins** Y5, 'The Dubai Amphitheatre', UAE. The proposal is a multi-disciplinary sports complex and camel track located at the centre of the old creek district of Dubai. The varying patternisation within the canopies, inspired from the composition of ancient mashrabiyas, is optimised according to solar gain within specific time periods. They achieve environmental thermal comfort through the use of non-deterministic and performance-based design. The typo-morphologies subsequently produced help to create a new composition of space leading to a more homogenous integration of the building within its landscape. **Fig. 20.2 Wiktor Kidziak** Y4, 'Recycled Baroque', Dubai UAE. Scanned voxellised landscapes are transformed into urban shading devices constructed out of assemblies of objects that are constantly rearranged to make up market spaces of Dubai. **Fig. 20.3 Jianze (Arthur) Hao** Y4, 'Dubai Cooking School', UAE. The new Cooking School uses natural intelligence and cultural signs from Middle Eastern plants to simulate the form of the building, which is, at the same time, environmentally sensitive to its surrounding. The consumption of natural resources is reduced by the collection of dew and through balancing interior air condition to create a comfortable environment for cooking education, shopping, rest and catering. **Fig. 20.4 Jonathan Wilson** Y4, Dubai Marine Ecological Centre, UAE. Situated between the urban fringe of Al Ras district and the Creek, an aquarium and coral farm hinge the transforming urban and natural ecologies of Dubai. Cellular organisations and morphological gradients respond to the wide scope and

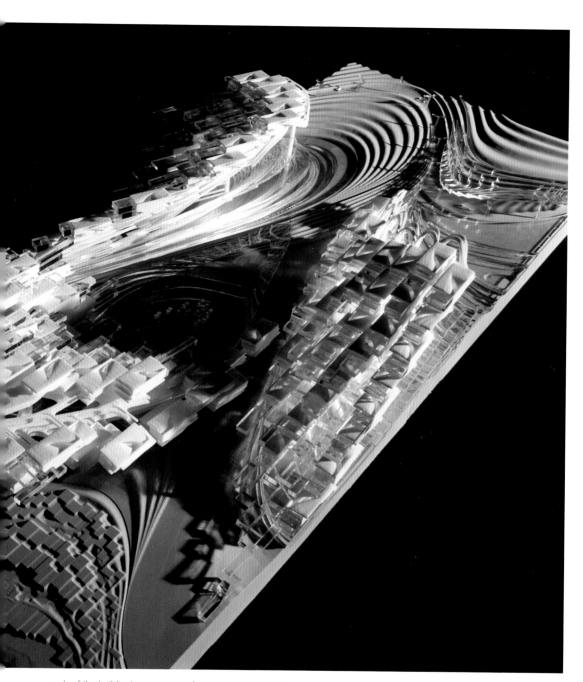

scale of the building's programme; from its integration with the urban infrastructure to the growth of endangered coral species and marine life. **Fig. 20.5 Emily Yan** Y5, 'Domestic Agglomeration: Urban Oasis', Muscat, Oman. The beauty of Muscat lies largely in its voluptuous topography of mountains and valleys that create the backdrop of this agglomerative housing project. Grounded on Arabic cultural living patterns and people-centric design, a typological 'kernel' creates the core of each housing unit with a variable peripheral bounding veil. Through computational scripting a gradual transition of typologies respond to given parameters such as family size, visual distances, sunlight/shading, porosity and prevailing winds; resulting in a culturally and environmentally sensitive hybridised cluster of domestic spaces.

20.6

20.7

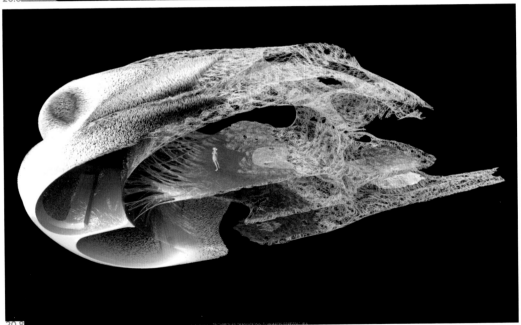

20.8

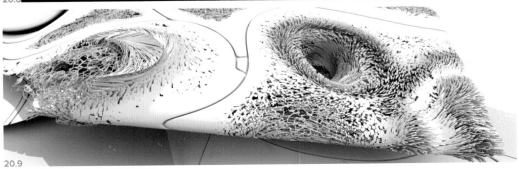

20.9

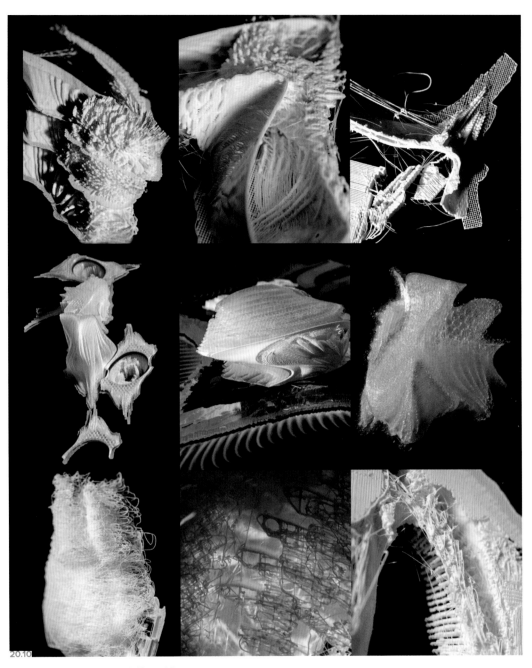

20.10

Fig. 20.6 – 20.9 **Javier Ruiz** Y5, 'Spatial Sprezzatura,
Architecture of Gradients and Transitions', Hong Kong.
Material, light, structure, space, geometry and conditions
of visibility shift gradually from an opaque, smooth and
continuous surface to a highly porous and volatile structural
fabric creating a highly variable and ambiguous in-transition
space. **Fig. 20.10 Olivia Pearson** Y5, 'Fibrous Lusters –
Iridescent Trade Centre,' Abu Dhabi, UAE. The project focuses
on fibrous studies that are generated through analogue and
digital algorithm feedback loops. It develops an intricate and
innovative design language that integrates hybrid material
responses between fundamental resources of Abu Dhabi pearl
and oil. Located in the National Mangrove Park, the bulding is
materiliased through the iridescence of its 3D envelope.

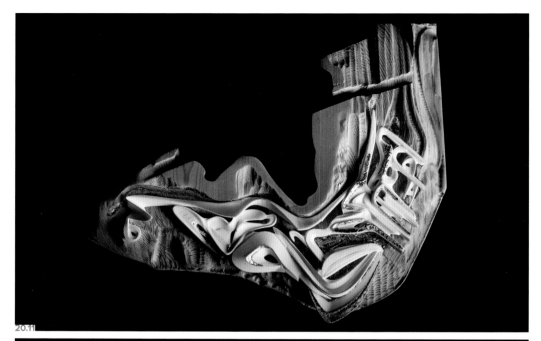

20.11

20.12

Fig. 20.11 Judith Shiow Yin Gillespie Y5, 'In_Scribing Architecture: The National Library of Oman'. 'Read, for your Lord is most beneficent, who taught by the pen, taught man what he did not know' (Qur'an, 96:3-5). Calligraphy is one of the most important elements of Islamic culture. The architecture and language of the new National Library of Oman challenges how space can be redefined by the dialogue of 1) an extruded calligraphy and 2) the subsequent integration of its gestural meaningfulness into the surrounding topography. Using a set of traditional phrases specific to Islam, the Library shields its content by engraving it into the landscape and coating its externalised volumes with gold (reviving the traditional techniques of gild carvings). **Fig. 20.12 – Fig. 20.13 Sam Rigby** Y5, 'A Reinterpretation of Sullivan's City: Ornament, Reform and the Extension of Dubai', UAE. Through the study of Louis Sullivan's ornament, the project traverses a variety of scales, as an infrastructural development and new system of dwelling exploring layering, density and porosity. In an attempt to piece together and weave within the fabric of Dubai's disparate urban environment, the building proposal addresses typical notions of public and private space in an International Cultural House of America. Commenting on the current cultural identity and parallels with previous cities and epochs, it challenges the potential of introverted urbanism, as a typological condition, proposed for a city defined by its segregated societies and cultures.

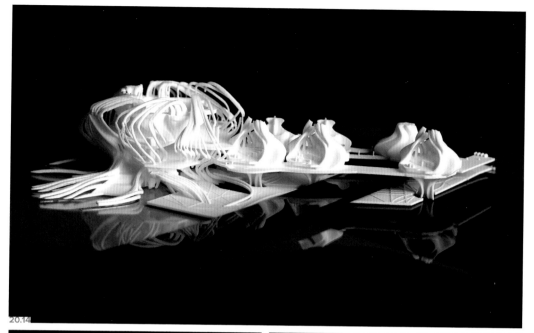

Fig. 20.14 – 20.15 **Anahita Chouhan** Y5, 'The Oriental Court
of Dubai', UAE. Dealing with a rapidly growing ex-patriate
population and contemporary issues arising as a result
of British imperialism and the Orientalist attitudes of the
eighteenth century, the Oriental Court of Dubai helps to
define a new era of architecture for the city. The programme
addresses issues surrounding methods of Sharia law imposed
on 90% of non-Emirati citizens of Dubai. The Courthouse uses
a British model of precedent law in order to judge crimes, from
civil to criminal in a non-Islamic system. The form and design
principles for the court stem from Middle Eastern influences
in order to help redefine cultural aesthetics in the region.

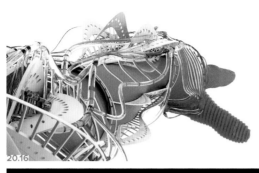

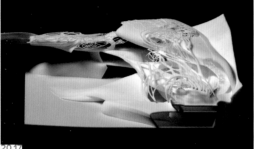

Fig. 20.16 – 20.17 Daphnie Costi Y5, 'Skin Clinic', Hong Kong. The project of a Skin Clinic on the Island of Ma Wan exaggerates the existing widespread trend of cosmetic surgery in Hong Kong and China. It formulates an extreme scenario in the future, suggesting a 'beauty factory' where people undergo extreme body modification controlled by programmed technology. The clinic encompasses a voluntary initiative carried out by individuals who are willing to alter their bodies in the sake of beauty and eternal youth. Patients consider the body to be a flexible material on which they can act: a transformable, improvable and augmentable entity. **Fig. 20.18 Chris Falla** Y4, 'Trans.Market – Hybrid Trade Infrastructure', Dubai, UAE. Derived through a superposition of history and computational swarm optimisation, traces of trade and culture are reinterpreted into a fibrous new passage across the creek, facilitating trade in various hybrid and contemporary forms. **Fig. 20.19 Maria Esteban-Casañas** Y4, 'Water-Based Morphologies', Dubai, UAE. Reacting against a future of oil depletion, the proposal invests in a new trade of bio-fuel. The Salicornia Plant Nursery provides the seeds for plantation in the salt flats of the Gulf. The building and landscape design emerges from the logic of water irrigation systems and studies of plant growth. The building's roof explores the multiplicity of possibilities of patterns through repetition, variation and deformation of a morphing hexagonal grid. The computational variability within this repetitive system allows for unexpected geometries to occur. **Fig. 20.20 Wai Yue (Ruby) Law** Y5, 'Centre for Dharmic Faiths', Muscat, Oman. Located along

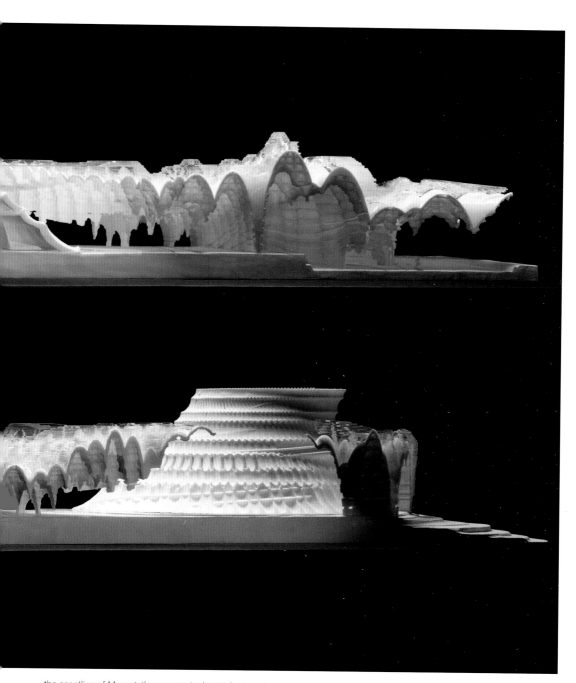

the coastline of Muscat, the new centre hosts the temples of five Indian religions, encouraging respect, communication and discussion among the groups within a shared community. The building is proposed to be built out of a loam-concrete composite that triggers the revival of earth-bound architecture in the Gulf. It determines the building's geometrical, tectonic and ornamental complexity. The project also aims at reinventing the traditional program with a neo-materialistic approach, marking the ambition to escape from virtual digital architectural visions.

Unit 21

Alternative Inputs

Abigail Ashton, Andrew Porter

Year 4
Jamie Lilley, William Molho, Jens Kongstad Olesen, Francesca Pringle, Charlotte Reynolds, James Simcock

Year 5
Emma Louise Carter, Naomi Gibson, Wai Hong Hew, Yu Chien (Wendy) Lin, Risa Nagasaki, Simona Schroeder, Sayan Skandarajah, Tess Martin, Antonina Tkachenko

Thank you to our Practice Tutor Tom Holberton and Engineer Brian Eckersley

Thanks to our consultants and critics: Peter Cook, Rachel Cruise, Stephen Gage, Christine Hawley, Tom Holberton, Luke Pearson, Godofredo Pereira, Nick Tyson

Physical change in the contemporary city is inevitably slow. Building stock has a slow turnover and such change is measured in decades or even centuries. However, there are other systems and forces at work in the city that are fast changing and far-reaching in their impact. Communication technology, information systems and networks have a much more profound impact on us now than traditional architectural space. This year Unit 21 continued to investigate how these fundamental influences can motivate and initiate new architectural space.

————Long-established building techniques still predominate and the processes of advanced industrialisation are still very limited within much of the building industry. The Unit recognises that advanced techniques of digitised fabrication will change this and we relish the opportunities that are implicit within these realms. Whilst this lag in technology and the economies of scale which preserve the current situation remain, the Unit continued to speculate on how such futures could emerge.

————Urban space is defined evermore by invisible systems of force, action and event. Contemporary technology such as datasets and networks of communication and information are one such system. But there are also the invisible forces of a political, cultural and economic nature which can be identified. In addition there are environmental systems of both natural phenomena such as weather, and artificial systems which have outputs as varied as sound, smell and pollution. The Unit continued to develop new tools to represent and interpret such systems. In particular, we investigated methods of representation that reflect the slippage and distortions that occur between these translations from drawing to building; and these methods and processes were treated as a creative opportunities that both developed and represented new models of architectural space.

————The Unit initially embarked on a three-week drawing investigation. This exercise was both about identifying an invisible system of organisation or communication within the city, and inventing a method of drawing to represent this. Both then became generators for the year's work. We then visited the city of Copenhagen to look at reclaimed lands and egalitarian societies. Year 4 worked on a project for the redesign of the 'Scene and Heard' theatre in Somers Town, Camden, which they later used for their design realisation. Both year groups worked on projects in Copenhagen, for differing timescales.

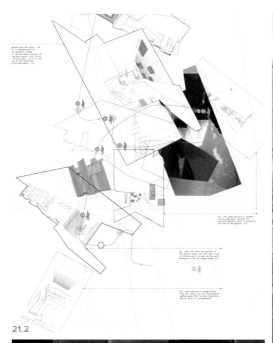

21.2

21.4

21.3

21.5

Fig. 21.1 & 21.6 **Tess Martin** Y5, 'Cruise Copenhagen'. Cruise Copenhagen aims to improve the currently unsustainable and parasitic relationship between the cruise industry and the city through the provision of a new port-side experience and two inner-city destinations for cruise passengers, residents and tourists alike. **Fig. 21.2 Yu Chien (Wendy) Lin** Y5, 'Copenhagen Exchange School'. The scheme aims to revitalise Christiania by attracting youths back into the area with the Exchange School's barter skill classes, self-built student accommodation and interactive learning spaces. The architectural language is based upon three behaviours that are central to the realisation of this scheme from conception to building construction and usage. **Fig. 21.3 Wai Hong Hew** Y5, 'Museum of Cartography / Reconstructing Copenhagen'. **Fig. 21.4 William Molho** Y4,

Somers Walls, London, A series of stills were extracted from 'Somers Walls', a filmed continuous elevation of Somers Town Boundaries. **Fig. 21.5 Risa Nagasaki** Y5, 'Time-Based Landscape: Bridging, Floating, Staging Copenhagen'. The project extends the city of Copenhagen, bridging the harbour. The landscape transforms with seasons, tides, and operas.

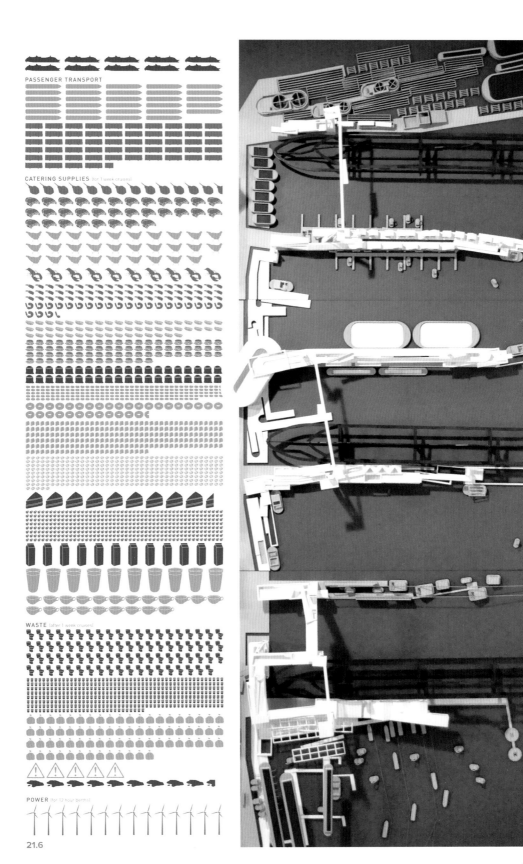

PASSENGER TRANSPORT

CATERING SUPPLIES (for 1 week cruises)

WASTE (after 1 week cruises)

POWER (for 12 hour berths)

21.6

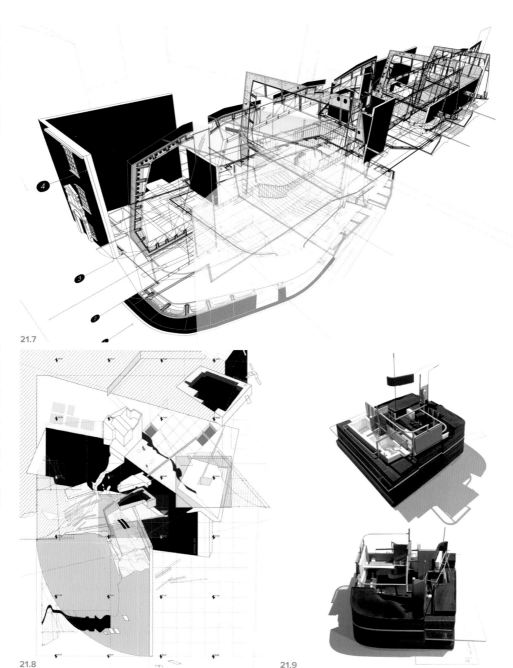

21.7

21.8

21.9

Fig. 21.7 **Jens Kongstad Olesen** Y4, 'A Record of Change'. A Radiographic perspective. Redevelopment plan for a local community theatre in Somers Town. Incorporating the previous life cycles and history of the existing building in the new design proposal. **Fig. 21.8 – 21.9 Charlotte Reynolds** Y4, 'The Pocket Park Prototype', Copenhagen. Setting out a precedent for government funded 'pocket parks' to provide public space in designated vacant urban plots under 5000sqm, responding to the artificial construct of the city. Manipulation of the existing artificial land produces a series of incremental and 'unfinished' parks across Copenhagen of which certain elements will be inherited by future site development. A language of excavation and relocation of earth allows the site mass to remain constant throughout.

Fig. 21.10 **Antonia Tkachenko** Y5, 'Copenhagen Arts Terrain'. Exploration of an architectural language derived from mobile experiences of the urban fabric. This approach is employed in revitalising a disused railway terrain in Copenhagen's Vesterbro into a vibrant terrain dedicated to local arts initiatives. Architectural space is derived from a series of moving viewpoints and frames, such as the railway carriage. The proposal forms a dual relationship with the users, engaging with both the global and neighbourhood speeds and timescales.

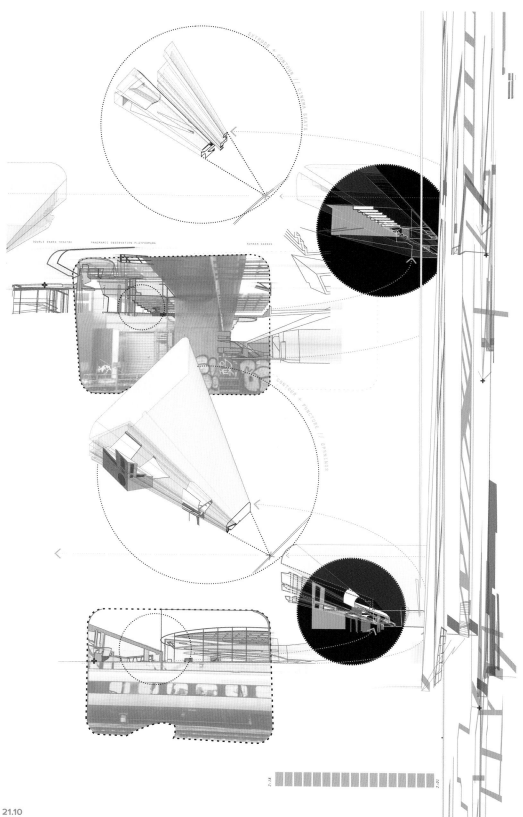

DOUBLE ENDED THEATRE   PANORAMIC OBSERVATION PLATFFORMS   SUNKEN GARDEN

EXTRUDE + CONTOUR // CINEMA SETS

CONTOUR + PUNCTURE // OPENINGS

21.10

Fig. 21.11 – 21.14 Sayan Skandarajah Y5, 'Curating an Egalitarian Territory', Copenhagen. Responding to the geopolitical and archaeological slippage between territory and equality in Copenhagen, the project seeks to define an exclusivity in architectural identity through the proposal of an emergent nine-square enclave in the heart of the city. Using egalitarian principles of order, distribution and composition, six architectural interventions and their associated infrastructures are defined, containing at their scale the principles and vocabulary of the enclave as a whole. The project thus reflects the tensions of the inevitable territorial exclusivity of a society that is founded upon principles of equality.

Fig. 21.15 – 21.16 **Naomi Gibson** Y5, 'The Performing Ground of Fragmented Identity.' This proposition uses the microcosmic act of performance and the socio-spatial qualities of stage typologies to re-imagine local activities and transform the socio-political tensions of Nørrebro, a culturally diverse district of Copenhagen. Centered around and based upon two sites of local collective memory – the void site of Jagtvej 69 and a deconsecrated corner of Assistens Cemetery – locals are invited to meet and explore 'other' both peacefully and agonistically, and to celebrate local heterogeneity. **Fig. 21.17** **Simona Schroeder** Y5, 'Building for the Invisible: Rethinking the Concept of Danish Asylum Centres'. Transforming the Folkets Park in Copenhagen, it becomes a user-driven urban park for asylum seekers and citizens of Copenhagen alike. The landscape also performs as a community centre uniting the neighbourhood. Various activities encourage a social and cultural exchange between the participants regenerating the area and integrating asylum seekers. **Fig. 21.18** **Jamie Lilley** Y4, 'Semiotics'. An investigation into the creation of an alternative street scape. The symbology of a street is depicted through plotting the longitude of the signs origin against of the street datum. **Fig. 21.19** **Emma Louise Carter** Y5, 'Better Building: The Incremental House'. The proposal discusses the beneficial development of floating incrementally built family houses. A house begins as a small, structural service core that is developed over time through the addition of timber plug-in spaces chosen, manufactured and constructed at a time that suits each individual household financially and socially.

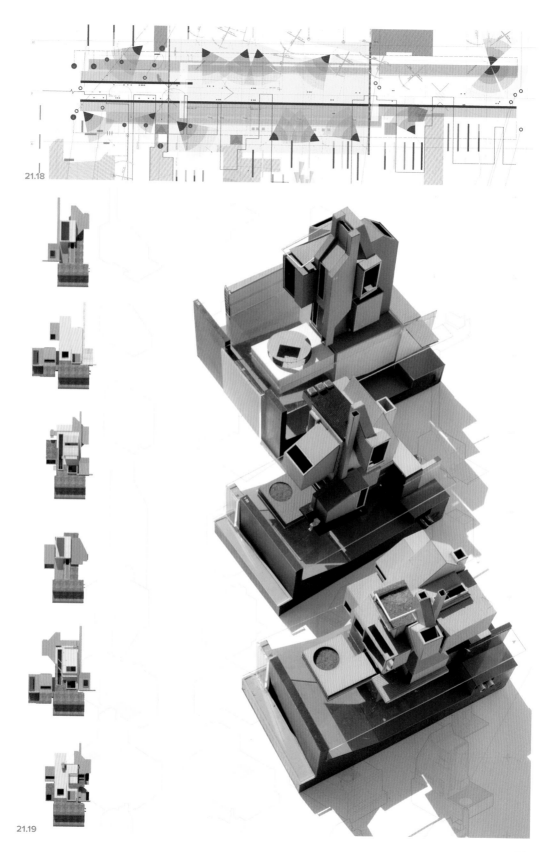

21.18

21.19

Unit 22

Designing the Future: Architecture as Hypothesis vs. Hypothesis as Synthesis

Izaskun Chinchilla, Carlos Jimenez

Year 4
Xiao Ying Lin, Sirisan Nivatvongs, Jiao Peng, Joshua Thomas, Han (John) Wu

Year 5
Akmal Afani Azhar, Victoria Bateman, Ko Wai Cheung, Sarah Firth, Yuen Sar (Lillian) Lam, Zhiyu Huang, Hisham Abdullah Muazzam, Jose Ignacio Ortiz-Muñoz, Joanne Preston

Thanks to our supporters Vidal Associates and the Faculty of Architecture, Chiang Mai University, Thailand

Thank you to Pedro Gil, our Design Realisation practice tutor and Roberto Marin, our structural consultant

Thanks also to our critics: Julia Bauhaus, Nerea Calvillo, Freya Cobbin, Gonzalo Coello de Portugal, Christine Hawley, Gonzalo Herrero Delicado, Jan Kattein, Lulu Le Li, Sophia Psarra, Peter Scully, Anthony Staples

Our field trip to Thailand, where we developed the Future Natural workshop, was supported by Faculty of Architecture, Chiang Mai University (Thailand), Ajarn Sant, Julian Huang and 16 Thai students with their knowledge and generosity

The Bartlett School of Architecture 2014

Many architects define their design work as a synthesis of the present. Projects encompass the availability of local technologies, climate conditions, cultural preferences, contemporary aesthetic tendencies, and much more. History invites us to study buildings as a way to understand a period. The advanced version of this understanding gives synthesis the role of helping humans adapt to context. Christian Norbert-Schultz declared 'modern architecture came into existence to help man feel at home in a new world'. [1]

————Several factors trouble this peaceful academic perspective. Firstly, the speed of change has suffered the 'acceleration of history'. [2] Even while implementing a building, original ideas might become outdated. Secondly, our building technologies mix within the same body items that may reach obsolescence within different rhythms. Thirdly, the performance of a building can change dramatically throughout its life. [3] The notion of sustainability challenges any previous ignorance of the building's evolution. Education demands students make decisions without knowing what is to come.

Unit 22 works on a radically different premise, designing not from synthesis but from a consciously built hypothesis of what may lie ahead:

————The architect tests whether he/she might be wrong. Her/his principal task is checking, comparing scenarios, providing alternative solutions or even finding ways to demolish parts.

————There is not a simplistic vision of the problem-solving capacity of architecture. Wendell Berry proposes designs should act as a pattern; [4] solving several problems simultaneously, while minimising the creation of new ones.

————Direct cause-effect relationships are broken.

————Architects are more aware when they are imagining or building their own definitions of reality.

The methodology for designing from hypothesis gives new opportunities for innovation. It encourages starting from the 'state of the art', avoids 'design amnesia' and values gradual innovation. [5] It helps integration of functions. It avoids potential innovation being rejected for not matching the puzzle. It allows true and subversive experimentation to take place.

1. C. Norbert-Schultz, *Principles of Modern Architecture*, (London: Andreas Papadakis, 2000), p.6
2. Lester R. Brown uses this term in *Eco-Economy: Building and Economy of the Earth*, (NY: W. W. Norton & Co., 2001)
3. E. Hollis, *The Secret Lives of Buildings: From the Parthenon to the Vegas Strip in Thirteen Stories* (NY: Metropolitan, 2010)
4. See 'Solving for Pattern' by Wendell Berry in *The Gift of Good Land: Further Essays Cultural & Agricultural* (NY: North Point Press, 1981)
5. A. Snodgrass & R. Coyne, *Interpretation in Architecture: Design as a way of thinking* (Abingdon: Routledge, 2006)

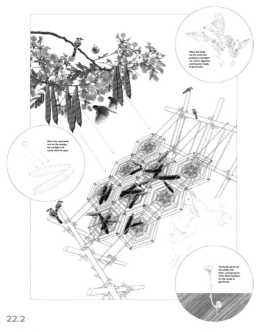

22.2

22.3

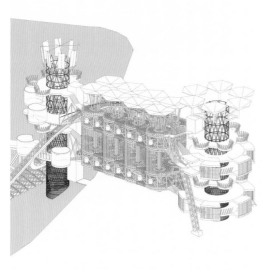

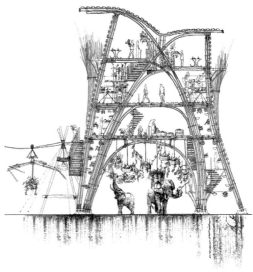

22.4

22.5

Fig. 22.1 **Ko Wai Cheung** Y5, 'House of the Future – Hong Kong 2047'. Elevated walkways connect skyscrapers in Hong Kong, the ground level often becomes hazy and forgotten. Connected to an elevated walkway, the proposal explores the possibilities for innovations in a family. Flexible living spaces use exchanged components for constructing a home with the specific needs for each family. The house is an integration of technology, materials, ideas and innovations. **Fig. 22.2 – 22.3 Sarah Firth** Y5, **Zhiyu Huang** Y5, **Joshua Thomas**, Y4 and students from FACMU, 'Future Nature – Canopy Group'. In December 2013, 13 Students from Unit 22 joined the Faculty of Architecture at Chiang Mai University on a 7-day intensive design and fabrication workshop to revisit the design of curtains, parasols, louvres, canopies and carpets. These architectural interfaces act not only as protection mechanism for inhabitants inside the building, but also as wider protection strategies for nature against human actions. **Fig. 22.4 Jiao Peng** Y4, 'Student Accommodation'. This project is targeted at students in Hongcun City, China. The building provides accommodation for local students, collects rainwater to satisfy the daily demands, and encourages tourists to cherish the water resources. **Fig. 22.5 Xiao Ying Lin** Y4, 'The Elephant Embassy', section of the Interactive Feeding Station. The proposal aims to retain the elephants' natural living habitats in Bangkok. The Bamboo structure is a temporary residence and a medical centre for the elephants. The higher level contains a cafe, food workshop, and nutrition lab. The lower level contains an interactive space to feed the elephants passing through.

22.6

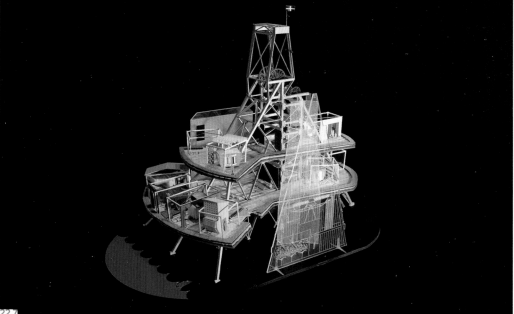

22.7

Fig. 22.6 Sirisan Nivatvongs Y4, 'Bangkok Noi Flood Shelter'. A 1:20 Scale Model to investigate hanging floor structures and innovate traditional façades. The proposal makes use of elevated public infrastructures to host a series of ephemeral floating structures to provide living and temporary shelters for a flooded Bangkok Noi District in 2050. The architecture seeks to innovate local sensibilities, vernacular techniques to interact to its bio-climatic conditions. **Fig. 22.7 Joshua Thomas** Y4, 'Citizenry Association Hotel', Penzance. Four coastal towns in Cornwall have been chosen to host Citizenry Associations in 'Special Tourism Areas', which contain the most affluent economies in the county. Inflated land values, however, make access to activity, property and work difficult for local people. The founding structure in Penzance aims to move local life, decision-making institutions and government offices and skilled jobs back into the town, therefore empowering residents to partake in the discussion, distribution and use of the land and resources in their region.

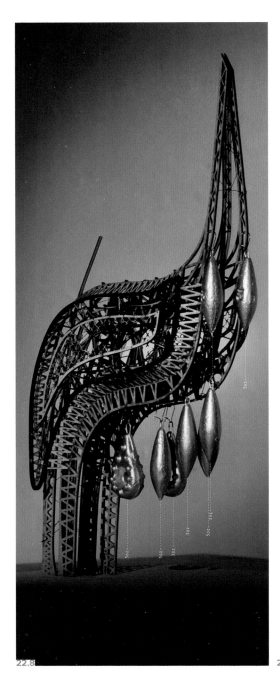

22.8

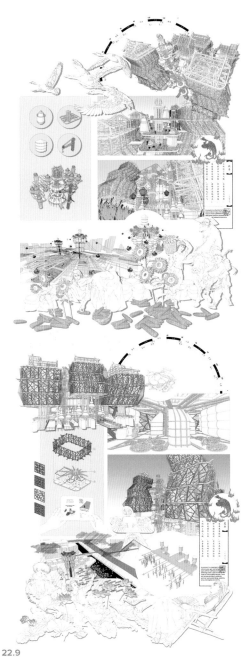

22.9

Fig. 22.8 Jose Ignacio Ortiz-Muñoz Y5, Photo showing the tested structure as a layered inhabitable volume, allowing for cross-ventilation. Set in 2080, this project is based on a hypothetical vision of the city of Murcia in south east Spain. It aims to find an optimised archetype to improve the environment and meet the demands of an increasingly saturated city, respecting its best traditions and culture. The project looks at geometries and ventilation of spaces and structures as a way to achieve to stop the dependence on air conditioning, abused at present by its increasing population. Four main towers rise from in between the existing buildings to compose an 'Upper City' landscape: The Water Tower, the Orchard Tower, the Kitchen Tower and the Sleeping Tower.

Fig. 22.9 Zhiyu Huang Y5, 'The New Urban Village, Shenzhen'. A reconstruction of the unique settlements occupied by migrant workers, promoting sustainable living and the value of agriculture. The knowledge of urban villagers is harvested to tackle the crisis and challenges faced by the city. The architecture is a response to the seasons and 24 solar terms, which is an ancient calendar that guides people's daily routine according to the climate and the ecliptic coordinate system.

22.10

22.11

Fig. 22.10 **Hisham Abdullah Muazzam** Y5, 'Dhaka Adaptive Factory Typologies for Manufacturing Welfare'. A detailed axonometric drawing showing the infrastructural, technical and spatial programme layout of the proposed new garment factory typology in Bangladesh. The drawing envisages building above and around existing skyscrapers in the heart of the dense urban Dhaka landscape. Vertical expansion and flexible architecture is key to ensuring sustainable growth in the booming garments industry in 2050. The innovations present a more symbiotic relationship between consumers and producers within the industry by promoting positive dialogue through direct interactions and trading. Fig. 22.11 **Akmal Afani Azhar** Y5, 'The New House of the Future in Malaysia', Assemblage of 'Train House', 'Bicycle House', 'Suitcase House',

'Flying House' and 'Floating House'. The designs are derived from one hypothesis: in the year 2050, human mobility will increase following the existing pattern of movement in the country from rural to urban areas. This future scenario challenges societies conservative perception of a 'house' being rooted in one place. New House of the Future in Malaysia deals with different cultural issues such as, bathing traditions, food culture, traditional performance and alternative healthcare influenced by multiple contextual and multicultural population of the country.

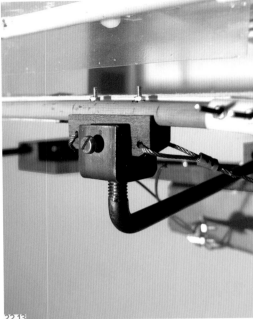

Fig. 22.12 – 22.15 **Ko Wai Cheung** Y5, 'Innovation Catalogue Component Kits'. In the proposed masterplan of the Lok Ma Chau Loop in Hong Kong, the government uses a non-plan approach to encourage re-industrialisation in the rural parts of the New Territories with Shenzhen, the border. Villagers in allocated plots of land can choose kits from the catalogue of innovation to construct their own homes and industries within the limitation of the government's main structure. This provides flexibility in function and freedom for further development, as kits can be reassembled and are highly adaptable. The kit of components combines advanced technology with indigenous techniques and materials to suggest an innovative approach to the future. **Fig. 22.16 Sarah Firth, Joanne Preston** Y5, 'Group Project', 1:10 physical model. In response to London's housing crisis, a new typology of vertical dwelling is proposed for disused brownfield sites such as old quarries, farmsteads, and golf courses within the London Metropolitan Greenbelt. Modular units are stacked to form a vertical terraces, with modest individual house plans and generous shared spaces which allow for home working, shared recreation and dining.

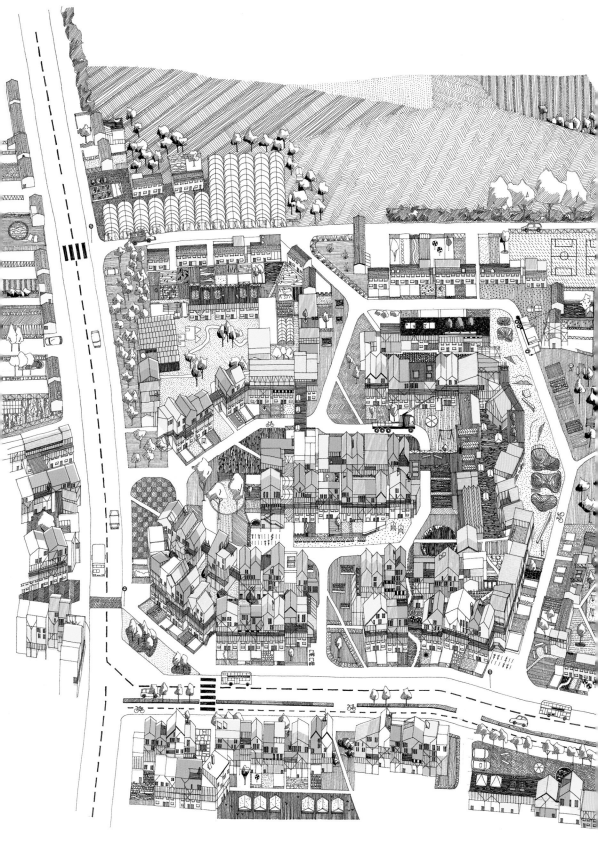

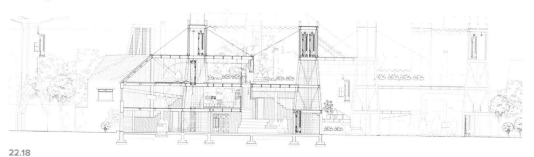

22.18

22.19

Fig. 22.17 Sarah Firth Y5, 'Negotiation and the Future of the New Town'. Showing Neighbourhood Block's 30 years of growth (from top left, clockwise). Investigating the potential of government New Town, suburban Hemel Hempstead, to respond to the current housing crisis through densification by means of localism. **Fig. 22.18 Joanne Preston** Y5, 'Garden Cities of "To-morrow": A Manifesto for the UK's Garden Cities of 2050'. 1:50 Section Hybrid Typology, Welwyn Garden City, UK. Based on a more transient idea of 'home', a future is envisaged where everyone can have a place to call home in the city the, greenbelt and the suburb. **Fig. 22.19 Joanne Preston** Y5, 'Desk Buggy', 1:25 plan. A new infrastructure is linked with existing rail networks and made habitable by kinetic walls and furniture modules. These innovations bring together childcare

and working from home, that have been separated through the failures of Ebenezer Howard's 1898 model. Influenced by Howard's Cul-de-Sac formations, the tessellation of the proposed typology forms a patchwork landscape of contained gardens and terraces. The dwellings are designed to accommodate a community rather than a 'nuclear family'. Divisions between one dwelling and the next are made unclear inorder to encourage neighbourly interaction.

Unit 23

Neither Here nor There: Supernatural Architecture

Kate Davies, Bob Sheil, Emmanuel Vercruysse

Year 4
Negin Amiridahaj, Luke Bowler, Joshua Broomer, Nicholas Debruyne, Gary Edwards, Grigor Rosenov Grigorov, Matthew Hudspith, Glenn Wooldridge, Liang Zhang

Year 5
Atilla Ali Tasan, Gladys Yanyi Ching, Aleksandra Natalia Cicha, Oliver Farmer, Rory Keenan, Hyder Mohsin, Richard Northcroft, Thomas Pearce, Eliza De Silva

Thanks to our consultants and critics: William Bondin, Matthew Butcher, Mario Carpo, Mollie Claypool, Stephen Gage, Ilona Gaynor, Bastian Glaessner, Jon Goldbun, Penelope Haralambidou, Colin Herperger, Andy Hudson-Smith, Francesca Hughes, Guan Lee, Tom Lomax, Oli Oliviu Lugojan-Ghenciu, Andy MacFee, Ed Moseley, Shaun Murray, Tim Norman, Chris Pierce, Caroline Rabourdin, Gilles Retsin, Rupert Scott, Peter Scully, Christina Seely, Matt Shaw, Will Trossell, Peter Vaughan, Graeme Williamson, Simon Withers

Unit 23 is a forum for in-depth design investigation. We pride ourselves on our hands-on approach to design through making and direct experimentation. Closely aligned with the workshop, it spans the gulf between the speculative and the tangible and places a strong emphasis on the exploration of ideas through elaborations of craft, rigorous physical testing and experimental production in order to test and explore directly the material consequences of our inventions. The Unit evolves as a design laboratory exploring the frontiers of dispersed spatiality and dissolved materiality as the increasingly blurred relationship between representation and the represented continues. We occupy the liminal territories of saturated space as drawn and built works have been devised to challenge the stability and meaning of the physical and the immaterial, the analogue and the digital, the real and the unreal.

————Fuelling this experiment is the Unit's intimate association with the Bartlett Workshops (now known as B-Made) and their progressive investment in new technologies that expand the role of designers into makers of architecture. Exploring the actions of design at the point of production, Term 1 was defined by projects in casting, 3D scanning, mechanics, and electronics. Each was led by a day's instruction, practice, and critique, and followed by two weeks of design experimentation, documentation, tutorials and research.

————Midway through these projects the Unit embarked on a European road trip that began with the artist Stelarc visiting our studio for a discussion, followed by a convoy to Theo Jansen's Strandbeest workshop in Ypenburg. From there we headed to Paris via the work of Jean Tinguely, Gerrit van Bakel, and others. In Paris, we tracked down the clandestine group Untergunther, the team that famously restored the Pantheon's clock. Along our way we visited and scanned abandoned railways, surrealist parks, subterranean habitats, a 1930s concrete silo, and Disneyland. All that we visited became a testing ground for the year's projects, where individuals explored ideas of the supernatural, the unreal, hyperreal, half-imagined, invented, fictional, and fantastic. The Unit also travelled to Zurich in February to attend Fabricate 2014 – the Bartlett-founded international conference on making digital architecture. Running alongside these ventures Year 4 students collaborated to build a large-scale prototype as an invited contribution to the international Solar Decathlon in Versailles.

23.2

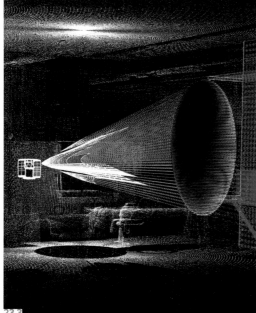

23.3

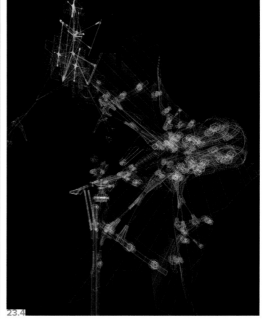

23.4

Fig. 23.1 **Richard Northcroft** Y5, 'Materialising Ghosts', photogrammetry camera rig for the Institute of Invisible Geometry, Walbrook Square, City of London [2016]. The project reveals the invisible and ever-shifting archaeology of the Walbook Valley, made famous by the discovery of the Temple of Mithras on the Bucklesbury House site in 1954. Manifested as a tactile 3D scan, the proposition inhabits a new gallery as a collection of infra-thin skinned spaces that reveal the historical architectural layers of the site, blurring the distinction between the authentic and reconstructed artefact.

Fig. 23.2 – 23.4 **Thomas Pearce** Y5, 'Orchestrating The Edge'. This investigation reverse-engineers the phenomenon of edge noise. Mixed measurements appear in the 3D scanner's point cloud when the laser beam hits the edge of an object and creates 'ghost points' between foreground and background. These mixed measurements, normally seen as anomalous artefacts to be filtered out of the point cloud, are instead appropriated. The project devises masks or screens that, through the high resolution of their encoded perforation, become 'all edge'. The resulting edge cloud inserts counterfactual geometries a series of sites along. Fig. 23.5 **Thomas Pearce** Y5, 'Fleet Street in the City of London'. The scale model, built around one scanning origin on the street, becomes an instrument for the fabrication of the fictional edge cloud, scaled up and planted within the scanned city archive. The screens dissolve into high-tech surrealist mirages that deconstruct the veracity of the scanner and inject fragments of the imaginary into its representation of the city.

23.5

23.6

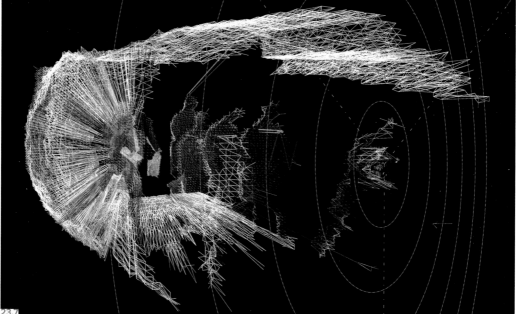

23.7

Fig. 23.6 – 23.7 **Oliver Farmer** Y5, 'The Next Best Liar'. The 3D scan has become currency for truth and evidence but will it grow into a medium for fakery and deception? Is the scanner the next best liar? 3D scans have become evidence; scans are collected data; data can be corrupted, manipulated and altered; the evidence cannot be seized and maintained in its original or in situ state. At bank station a crime is committed. The scanned evidence is corrupted through a designed particle choreography. The suspect is masked, the object is hidden, only fragments remain.

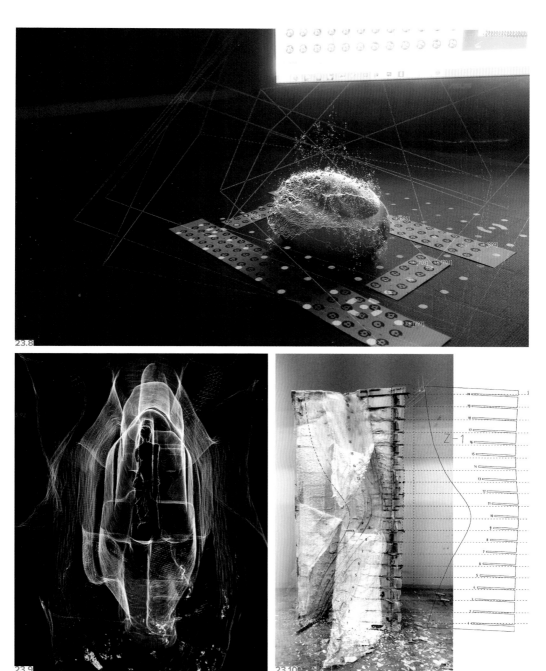

Fig. 23.8 – 23.9 **Eliza de Silva** Y5, 'Venus de Milo and the Flood'. The anticipation of the next great flood in Paris is the backdrop to the re-curation of artworks that are housed in the institutions along the banks of the Seine. The work speculates on the consequences of the city's unstable water table, orchestrating the intersection of a very physical disruption with the almost mythical status of key cultural commodities. Through the interrogation of fragile thresholds, the project conjures a condition that integrates, instead of isolates, art from extreme environmental conditions. **Fig. 23.10 Atilla Ali Tasan** Y5, 'Material Prototype for a Continuous Cast'. The proposal describes the transformation of a disused railway – the Petit Ceinture in Paris – into an ever evolving public space. A machine running on the existing track establishes the framework for stigmergic space-making. Each unit in the convoy serves as a fabrication hub and provides infrastructure for an insurgent construction scheme in post-industrial Paris, stitching an area on the deprived periphery into a wealthier neighbourhood across the tracks. The occupiers create novel ways to utilise the public space and propose complex spatial engagements in the cityscape.

23.11

23.12

23.13

Fig. 23.11 – 23.12 **Hyder Mohsin** Y5, 'Percussing the Sky: New Horizons' Conducting experimental tests for the design of the Ultrasonic Mist Control Array in a proposed weather experimentation facility, the project imagines a future where newfound insecurity in Europe provokes France to initiate an experimental science-city dedicated to weather control. Situated in agricultural land outside Orléans, the project explores the technologies and theories of rain capture and weather control and through physical tests and experiments engineers the subtle visual qualities of weather. It proposes weather modification on a vast scale and speculates on its geopolitical consequences. Weather stations are designed for rain steering and capture; engaging mist and humidity as agents, constructing a phenomenological landscape.

Fig. 23.13 **Rory Keenan** Y5, 'Covert Cartography'. Ubiquitous mapping technologies are increasingly used to survey and surveil our movements and actions. This project seeks to interfere in the mapping data set, turning to the world of military decoys for inspiration. A carbon fibre cocoon is slowly woven over the gardens of the Royal Geographical Society in Kensington by quadcopters, creating an evolving drawing for the eye of Google Earth over time. The image shows a prototype of a drone-woven carbon fibre cocoon.

Fig. 23.14 Aleksandra Cicha Y5, 'Biorealities'. Using cinematic near future scenarios, Aleksandra asks us to imagine how the merging of mobile networks and biotechnology might change the way we inhabit the city. A series of short films speculates on a future where data about our psychological and medical health (including whether we are lying) is collected by our mobile devices and starts to form a live online database that charts citizens' identity, bodily condition, emotional health and mood swings. The image shows the Moral Amplifier being fitted to a patient. Designed to know if you are being truthful, it is a device which sits in judgement over our daily decisions.
Fig. 23.15 Gladys Yanyi Ching Y5, 'Searching for Sonic Interference'. The project directly investigates the redistributing radio transmissions of Hertzian Space. The experiments test

the creation of two different conditions; a tangible presence and a void. For the first, electromagnetic signals are translated into sound signals, constructing a sensed landscape of transmission and forging a tangibile space from something invisible but instrumental to our daily lives. The second is a void within this transmission landscape, constructed from interference patterns. It asks whether the absence of signal might be a desirable and manipulable spatial quality in itself. The installation pictured acts as a scale model of the topography of transmissions.

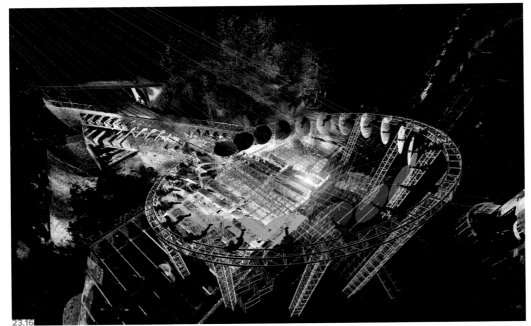

23.16

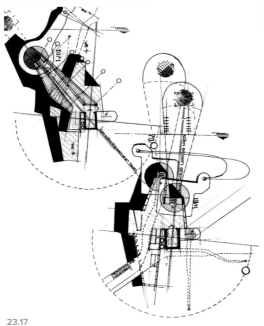

23.17

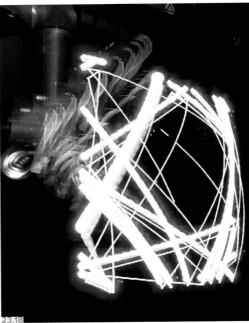

23.18

Fig. 23.16 **Glenn Wooldridge** Y4, 'Solar Redirection'. As cities become ever denser, the project conjurs a future Paris where responsive systems redirect light around buildings into public spaces and parks. Robotic arms fitted with reflective panels create heliostatic systems attached to tall buildings in order to bend light around them. **Fig. 23.17 Neguin Amiridahaj** Y4, 'Urban Space and Indeterminacy'. Positioned in a sensitive public space – where unusual objects might arouse suspicion – this viewing device allows room for a personal interpretation of the scene pictured within it. It heightens the perception of a public urban space, both through its very presence and through the selective, distorted and obscured views it offers. **Fig. 23.18 Group Research** Y4, 'Shadow Lines: an installation for the Solar Decathlon, Versailles'. A fabrication project, using

large scale robotic depositioning to build a 1:1 installation, to be shipped and installed in Versailles in June 2014. The geometry was visualised as a light path prior to printing using a UR10 robot.

23.19

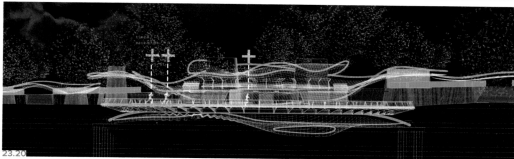

23.20

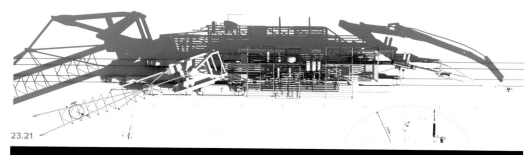

23.21

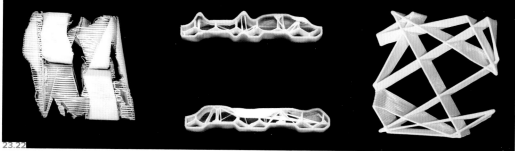

23.22

Fig. 23.19 Matthew Hudspith Y4, 'Chateau Buttes Chaumont'. The urban winery seeks to bring the production of France's most celebrated export back to the city and into the hands of the population. Anyone with the capacity to grow grapes is given the opportunity to produce a bottle of wine, blurring the boundary between consumer and producer. **Fig. 23.20 Nick DeBruyne** Y4, 'Buttes Chaumont Running Pavilion'. A high performance running track perches over the city of Paris; vibrations from the running track are transmitted into a massive climbing net where visitors experience the sensation of floating above the city. **Fig. 23.21 Liang Zhang** Y4, 'A Landscape Sculpting Machine'. The project transforms the landscape of the Petit Ceinture railway through an inhabitable printing machine. The drawing illustrates a plan view of the

proposition whereby material is deposited at the front and back, and the landscape of the track can be constantly adapted and re-inhabited. **Fig. 23.22 Group Research** Y4, 'Shadow Lines'. A series of iterative models test material performance, tooling paths, fabrication geometry, and structural performance. Generations are passed seamlessly from desktop MakerBots to full scale prototypes using the KUKA KR60 robot. The work seeks to expand the functionality and utilisation of regular technologies and redistribute their default position from factory to studio.

Unit 24

Remember the Future

Penelope Haralambidou, Simon Kennedy, Michael Tite

The Bartlett School of Architecture 2014

Year 4
Behnaz Berengi, Ka Tsun Kelvin Ip, Emir Tigrel, Angeliki Vasileiou, Kai Yu, Cai Wei (Amy) Zhao

Year 5
Kairo Baden-Powell, Daniel Cotton, Liam Davis, Jonathan Holmes, Steven Howson, Keiichi Iwamoto, Edward Mascarenhas, Rintaro Yoshida

Thanks to our partners: Factory Fifteen, Hal Currey of Arup Associates, Kevin Pollard, Andrew Gow of Raindog Films, Ali Carter of Max Fordham and Ben Sheterline of Price & Myers

Thanks to our critics: Dimitris Argyros, Julia Backhaus, Greg Blee, Kyle Buchanan, Luke Chandresinghe, Nat Chard, Hal Currey, Jo Dejardin, Richard Difford, Daniel Dale, Tom Ebdon, Douglas Fenton, Andrew Gancikov, Christophe Gerard, Tilo Gunther, Christine Hawley, Timo Haedrich, Colin Heperger, Jonathan Hill, Chee-Kit Lai, Sean Macintosh, Tim Norman, James O'Leary, Pravin Muthiah, Luke Pearson, Sophia Psarra, Kim Quazi, Merjin Royards, Matt Shaw, Gabby Shawcross, Bob Sheil, Mark Smout

Unit 24 employs film, video, animation, drawing and virtual/physical modelling techniques to generate architectural propositions. Acknowledging the continuing absence of a dominant socio-political design regime, and inspired by cinema, television, photography, literature and computer games, the Unit seeks to challenge the empty formalist pursuit currently prevalent in the production of built form in search of a critical and politically engaged role for the architect.
————Inspired by historical cinematic visions of the future (Fritz Lang's *Metropolis*), contemporary urban fantasies (Wim Wenders' *Wings of Desire*), and past versions of the present (Walter Ruttman's *Berlin: Die Sinfonie der Großstadt*), this year the Unit's studies were focused on Berlin.
————Beginning by studying Berlin from afar, the first phase of the year, 'Berlin Dream', saw students use a number of short, time-based projects to develop an informed visual and cultural attitude to Berlin. A site was identified, an intervention proposed, and new techniques of spatio-temporal design and representation were explored.
————The field trip to Berlin, 'Berlin Travelogue', took the form of an intense study of both the site chosen in the first phase of the year, and of Berlin as a whole. The students collaborated with ScanLAB to create highly detailed 3D scans of extraordinary spaces, and produced experimental film work to further refine their design ambitions and their approach to an individual spatial practice.
————For the main project of the year, which we called 'Berlin Symphony', Year 4 students designed a detailed, 'filmic' building which sought to draw on cultural, physical, economic and historical peculiarities, resolving an architecture that sought to challenge and subvert the fabric of Berlin. This design then became the protagonist in a final, time-based exploration. Year 5 students refined their explorations into speculative cinematic architectural projects, generating architectural films and filmic architectures, spatio-temporal graphics and cinematic architectural drawings, all supported and enriched by the written thesis document. The completion of Year 5 enables students to develop particular personal design methodologies with the moving image as a key parameter.

Creative Practice

Unit 24 benefits from a broad network of associated professionals working across the creative sectors. This year students benefited from frequent masterclasses from architectural filmmakers Factory Fifteen, from sound workshops with film composer Kevin Pollard, from scriptwriting and narrative direction from Andrew Gow of Raindog Films, from scanning workshops by Matt Shaw of ScanLAB, and from inspirational lectures from digital design agency Studio Output, dynamic young practices Patrick Lewis Architects and Haptic Architects, and architectural visionary and practitioner Felix Robbins.

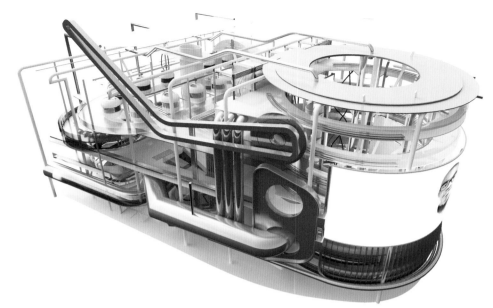

24.2

24.3

24.4

Fig. 24.1 **Liam Davis** Y5, 'Agitprop (agitation propaganda)'. The film represents the dissemination of social and political conflict in public space through architectural and cinematic montage. It traces the design and production of a dialectic structure, constructed from culturally significant icons to incite emotional associations through a process of superimposition and superadjacency. Fig. 24.2 **Steven Howson** Y5, 'Accelerated Serendipity'. The project proposes a speculative work space for the creative digital technology industry in East London's Tech City. The film is an ironic take on corporate promotional shorts satirically proposing an architectural iconography inspired by electronic devices. Fig. 24.3 **Aggeliki Vasileiou** Y4, 'Staging Weather'. Oscillating between reality and dream, the theatre sited on the bank of the river Spree in Berlin entraps the indeterminacy of the weather by simulating different environmental conditions within the interior of three auditoria. Fig. 24.4 **Emir Tigrel** Y4, 'New Bank and School of Economics'. The building is sited within a redundant ice factory, featuring a dynamic roof 'vault' system that stores digital and physical currency, harnessing socio-economic nuances to trigger an architectural response that encourages entrepreneurialism and change. Fig. 24.5 **Jonathan Holmes** Y5, 'Tempelhofer Lu(f/s)twerk'. A wind and hydro-powered recreational wetland transforms Tempelhof Airport into a landscape of the sublime. The physical processes on site spawn programmatic opportunities and cause natural phenomena. The film uses the motion-picturesque architectural framework to cast the site in parallel cinematic universe.

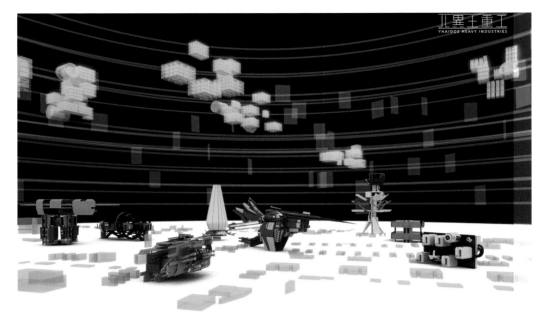

24.6

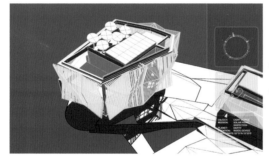

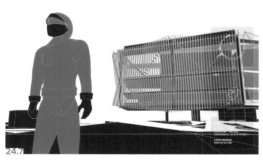

24.7

24.8

Fig. 24.6 Rintaro Yoshida Y5, 'The Parasphere Architect'. The film proposes an archaeological museum/garden of cyberspace grafted on physical uncanny urban structures that resemble 'Tomason' which suddenly appear in the city. The design explores the early iconography of cyberspace before digital media became all-pervasive, in a series of brightly coloured toy-like digital follies, each representing a seminal cyberspace novel. **Fig. 24.7 Cai Wei (Amy) Zhao** Y4, 'Cross-Media Centre: A Light Device'. Sited in the Media Spree Development Corridor in Berlin, the building features a dynamic glass façade that filters natural light as well as being self-illuminating at night. Using the music video genre and featuring Kraftwerk's classic piece, *Home Computer*, the film recasts the building in a humorous alien invasion narrative.

Fig. 24.8 Kelvin Ip Y4, 'Blossoming Bridge'. The project proposes an ornamental movable bridge housing a hybrid programme of a post office/shopping arcade. Soft ornaments grow and expand in response to both environmental and functional cycles mimicking the blossoming of flowers creating a decorative choreography. **Fig. 24.9 Keiichi Iwamoto** Y5, 'Berlin Estrangement'. Exploring Berlin's underground, a space that has strong associations with both fear (bunkers and wartime bombing) and freedom (tunnelling under the Berlin Wall to escape), the project imagines an allegorical 'deep underground' and constructs a utopian future that challenges, inverts and expands the current urban reality of the city.

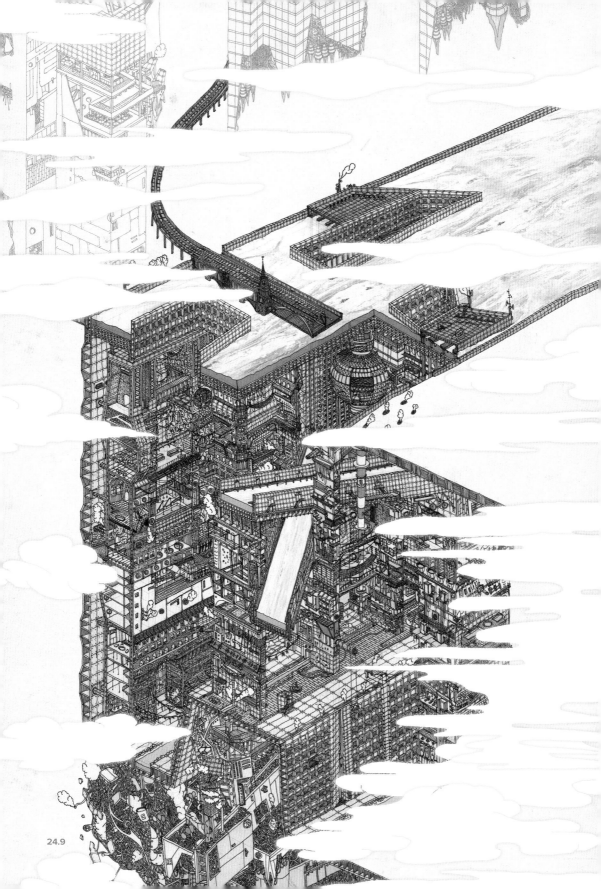

24.10

Fig. 24.10 Edward Mascarenhas Y5, 'Barbecana'. Inspired by Constant's *New Babylon* and re-appropriating the spaces of The Barbican Estate, the project proposes a game that reflects on architecture's relationship to play. This new pervasive game creates a space that mediates between real and simulated urban experience. Through immersive gameplay Barbecana destabilises and blurs the spatial temporal nature of the site.

Fig. 24.11 Dan Cotton Y5, 'Wates House'. A building narrates its own life story in a short film that explores the multifarious nature of our lived-in spaces and comments on the role of memory in our experience of space. Projection-mapped animations uncover hidden narratives – drawn from material collected through interviews with its inhabitants – and replayed on the walls of the soon to be demolished Wates House.

Fig. 24.12 Kairo Baden-Powell Y5, 'Fictional Constructs'. Set in Kraftwerk, Berlin, the film constructs a fictional image of the site where hyper-real design interventions conceal various levels of deception of scale, time and place. The design proposes a new open film studio/public space that constantly evolves, grows and performs, acts and expands, merging the boundaries between the everyday and the iconic, the real city and its representation in film.

24.12

MArch Design Realisation

Dirk Krolikowski, James O'Leary

We would like to thank our lecturers: Damian Eley (Arup Structures) Andrew Sedgwick (Arup Services), Joanna Pencakowski (Rogers Stirk Harbour + Partners), Sara Klomps (Zaha Hadid Architects), Xavier De Kestelier (Foster + Partners), Hareth Pochee (Max Fordham), Klaus Bode (BDSP/AA), Thomas Vietzke (Zaha Hadid Architects), Daniel Bosia (AKT), Jan Guell (Rogers Stirk Harbour + Partners), Susan Ware (The Bartlett), Simon Allford (Allford Hall Monaghan Morris) Dirk Krolikowski (The Bartlett / Rogers Stirk Harbour + Partners), James O'Leary (The Bartlett)

Thanks to our practice tutors: Simon Dickens (Youmeheshe), Sara Klomps (Zaha Hadid Architects), John Lyall (Lyall, Bills & Young Architects), Manja Van Der Worp (Nous), James Hampton (Studio Egret West), Justin Nichols (Make), Daniel Wright (Rogers Stirk Harbour + Partners), Tom Holberton (Rick Mather Architects), Soma, Pedro Gil (Studio Gil Architects), Dean Pike (Dean Pike Architecture), Peter Vaughan (Asif Khan), Michael Tite (The Bartlett / Walters & Cohen Architects), Anne Schroell, Joseph Mackey, David Hemingway (Niall McLaughlin Architects)

Thanks to all the Structural Consultants that have worked with individual Units to realise their projects, and to Max Fordham, Environmental Consultants

The Design Realisation course provides the opportunity for all Year 4 MArch Architecture students to consider how buildings are designed, constructed and delivered. Students are asked to reflect upon their relationship to technology, the environment and the profession. This is explored through an iterative critical examination of the major building design project, taught within the context of individual design Units in Year 4. Students are supported by an extensive lecture series, seminars and cross-unit crits. The course forms bridges between the world of academia and practice, engaging with many internationally renowned design and consultancy practices. A dedicated practice-based architect, structural engineer and environmental engineer support each design Unit, working individually with students to develop their work throughout the duration of the programme.

———We award the Design Technology Prize for the project with the most potential for developing innovative processes and systems in architectural design. The prizewinner is provided with financial and in-kind support from The Bartlett to extend the scope of the research initially developed through the Design Realisation programme. In 2013 the winner was Andrew Walker, who presented his work at the ACADIA conference in Canada in November 2013 and exhibited in the Innovation in Technology Prizewinners' Exhibition at The Bartlett in January 2014. Andrew's work explores the relationship between spatial definition and spatial perception, through the development of highly articulated armatures that dynamically change the edge conditions of the space they occupy over time. Highly crafted and responsive, Andrew's work spans the realms of kinetic intelligent architectures, drawing machines, coded space, digital manufacturing, space perception, memory and afterimage.

———The Design Technology Prize this year goes to Marcus Stockton, for his 'SÄNTIS:MET/GEOstn' project, an off-grid, user deployable mountainside base in the Swiss Alps. The project aims to create a cluster of research spaces that are designed to tackle extreme levels of exposure to wind and snowfall. It addresses the temporary nature of camps and remote inhabitation, specifically looking at the environmental implications of how sites are erected and abandoned. As the project is completely off-grid, ingenious methods are deployed to tackle waste and sanitation systems for the base. A further constraint is the fact that all building materials for the project need to be hauled up the mountain by the occupants, necessitating a complete re-assessment of archetypal building elements from foundations upwards, resulting in an inventive and unique response to non-standard site conditions.

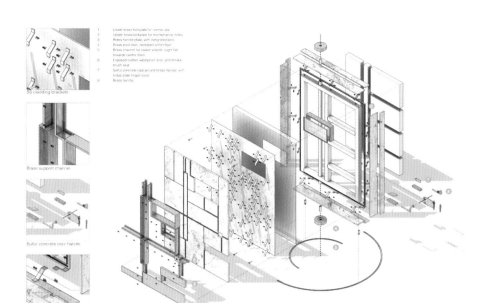

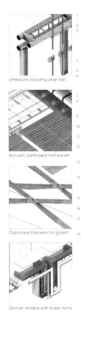

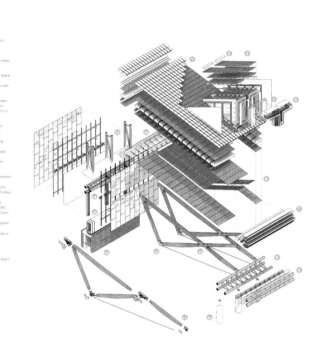

Ben Ferns Unit 12, Y4, 'Solforico Consulate',
Exploded Roof and Door Details.

MArch Year 5 Thesis

Peg Rawes, Mark Smout, Oliver Wilton

The Thesis enables Year 5 students to define the intellectual position which underpins their work, engaging with architectural disciplines and from the visual arts, humanities, physical or social sciences, including: physics, healthcare and housing policy, environmental philosophy, anthropology or political theory, structural engineering or computation. Individual theses therefore synthesis a student's chosen research approach into a 10,000-word study. Work from the module has won the RIBA President's Medals Dissertation Prize (e.g. Tamsin Hanke in 2013; Matthew Leung in 2012), and from this year's academic cohort we anticipate a number of theses to be developed into external publications.

Thesis Tutors
Hector Altamirano, Paul Bavister, Jan Birksted, Iain Borden, Jason Bruges, David Buck, Ben Campkin, Nat Chard, Mollie Claypool, Edward Denison, Christian Derix, Oliver Domeisen, Ross Exo Adams, Luis Fernandez, Murray Fraser, Daisy Froud, Stephen Gage, Ruairi Glynn, Jon Goodbun, Gary Grant Penelope Haralambidou, Bill Hodgson, Andy Hudson-Smith, Adrian Lahoud, Guan Lee, Stephen Lorimer, Luke Lowings, Tim Lucas, Anna Mavrogianni, Hareth Pochee, Hilary Powell, Sophia Psarra, Rokia Raslan, Peg Rawes, Jane Rendell, Tania Sengupta, Bob Sheil, Jason Slocombe, Mark Smout, Nina Vollenbroker, Tim Waterman, Finn Williams, Robin Wilson, Oliver Wilton, Simon Withers, Brendan Woods

The Bartlett School of Architecture 2014

Leon Fenster

*Exilic Landscapes: Synagogues and Jewish
Architectural Identity in 1870s Britain*
Thesis Tutor: Murray Fraser

When Jews in Florence submitted plans for a new Great Synagogue in 1872, the designs were rejected not on the usual religious or political grounds, but for stylistic reasons. The Accademie del Arti Delle Disegno, the body tasked with regulating Florentine artistic endeavours explained that the proposed neo-classical design was not of a 'Jewish enough' style and should rather evoke 'the dates and places that are of most interest for this religion'. The Florentine Jews were, however, at a loss as to what constitutes 'Jewish style'. This thesis revisits that particular historical problem, asking what relevance such debates might have today.

———The most acute call for monumental Jewish architecture in Europe came following Napoleon's real and metaphorical toppling of the ghetto walls. But what types of buildings were needed? A prayer service can, according to Jewish law, take place wherever a quorum of ten Jews is gathered.

———The subsequent unimportance of grand architecture has led most synagogues to be designed in styles borrowed from surrounding buildings. Where synagogues do stand out, they have sometimes been designed according to memories of synagogues in previous places in which that particular community once dwelled. Bevis Marks, the oldest remaining synagogue established after Jews were readmitted to England, contains both traits. Built by a Quaker architect for primarily Dutch Jews, the building externally resembles a Georgian church while the interior is modelled after Amsterdam's Great Synagogue.

———It follows, therefore, that synagogues have hitherto remained on the fringes of architectural discourse. In Banister Fletcher's seminal categorisation of world architecture, synagogues were only referred to in passing, as examples of prevailing architectural styles. Fletcher only concedes a Jewish architectural canon when discussing ancient architecture. Compared to other religious groups in Britain in the 1870s, Judaism seemed to have virtually no established framework through which to seek a cohesive style, resulting in synagogues in styles ranging from neo-Classical to Egyptian Revival to Moresque. This thesis considers how the architecture of synagogues in Britain in the 1870s contributed to the dramatisation of the Jewish worldview that took place within them. It focuses on five important 'cathedral' synagogues during this decade. The seeming absence of a Jewish architectural canon is shown to belie consistently hybridised synagogues which reflect the culture's embrace of an exilic reading of history.

Image: Orientalist Fantasy. The apse of the Bradford Synagogue, 1880

Ruby Law

The Architecture of Loam-Concrete Composite:
a material study on thermal and structural
performance in the Middle East
Thesis Tutor: Tim Lucas

More than half of the world's architecture is built with earth and this accommodates around one-third of the global population. Earth is widely available and it can be an affordable and low environmental impact option for building construction. Also many buildings in hot, dry parts of the world utilise earth extensively due to its thermal mass and the benefits of relative thermal stability that this can bring.

———Despite the benefits to the use of earth in building construction, it is not widely used in modern forms of construction as it is not a standardised building material and modern building codes for earth architecture have generally not been developed. Instead, generic Western technologies have tended to predominate, often with the utilisation of outdated building codes, and principally using concrete construction which tends to be more costly and uses far more carbon than traditional earth methods.

———The thesis documents an investigation of loam, the technical term for earth used as a building material, through history and goes on to propose, research, test and develop a new hybrid construction system whereby the use of concrete augments the performance of loam, providing structural integrity and protection from excessive weathering. The role of digital design and fabrication methods in this new system is investigated, and these methods are also used extensively in the development and prototyping of the system that is documented within the thesis.

———Case studies include an examination of the use of loam material in Muscat (Oman), where the design project is located, providing insights on modern revitalisations of the material. Modern technologies are briefly introduced in relation to loam material and reinterpreted to create a new design prototype. Material performance properties of loam and concrete are investigated in terms of composition, thermal and structural properties. A series of sample tests are undertaken in order to directly investigate the material properties of loam.

———At the heart of the thesis is a sequence of progressive physical prototyping activities utilising CADCAM technology and incorporating lessons learned from the initial material studies. These commence with investigations on how a mechanical connection might be achieved between loam and concrete utilising different geometries and accounting for differential shrinkage, etc. Various fibrous admixes to loam are investigated at this stage to improve tensile strength and help control cracking. The hybrid loam-concrete architecture is then developed further by prototyping areas of the proposed building design at a scale of 1:10, indicating the potential of the system and revealing some remarkable tactile results that link the architecture to the earth that it stands on.

Image: Loam-Concrete Composite Prototype – Scale 1:10. Fibre and polystyrene additive loam rammed on reinforced concrete with CNC fabricated mould

The Bartlett School of Architecture 2014

Jennifer Dyne
Debunking the Bunker: Strangelove, Strangelet, Swisslet
Thesis Tutor: Peg Rawes

During the Cold War era, very few Americans actually built fallout shelters, whilst Switzerland, even without the threat of mutually assured destruction (MAD), can boast capacity for 114% of its population in their national shelter network. The Swiss, a nation prepared to fight despite neutrality, bunker-ready without nuclear warheads, and who remain isolated whilst indisputably landlocked, present a unique environment where bunkers are not speculative proposals but policy required buildings.

———Exploring the language of duplicity, dualisms and defence, Switzerland establishes itself as a platform for bunker revivalism. In spite of a stable western Europe, territorial invasion sits at their border – where once Nazi Germany threatened to claim the Alps and beyond, a theoretical killer particle known as the Strangelet now lies – anticipating ejection into the Swiss landscape from the Large Hadron Collider.

———Switzerland, a positively neutral country, is unfailingly armed for military threat, so what of the scientific? The Strangelet represents the unknown anxiety, where its unstable particle structure threatens to transform all life on Earth into degenerate matter – doomsday as we know it – providing further ammunition for the Swiss's seemingly continuous cold era of Alpine defence.

———By learning from Cold War shelters, current Swiss defence objectives, and futuristic spaceship 'bunkers', the bunker is redefined as a platform for discussion through *Dr. Strangelove* – a darkly satirical take on political anxiety. Dr. Strangelove, the title character in Stanley Kubrick's 1964 film, advocates a higher female to male ratio in America's underground fallout community. By allowing sex and society to inform the highly gendered realm of the post-bunker world, the realities of how to repopulate the planet and recreate Swissness in the shelter are inevitably questioned: acts of bunk(er)ing.

———From Strangelove idealisms, to debunking the architectural language of defence, the invisibility of anxiety, imitation, preparedness and population are unearthed. Heaviness is defunct and a new bunker typology appears (quite literally) out of thin air, born from the 21st century's doomsday device, with a super-sized, super-Swiss expression of preparedness. The pre- and post- states of this new model create a paradoxical landscape of escapism, where the tourist alpine lodge can be transformed from sparse and luxurious holiday, to dense Strangelet survival mode. This exploration of shelter, Strangelove, Switzerland and society forms the bunker manifesto for Swiss Defenscape – an alpine fortress of skiing, sex and sometimes Strangelets.

Image: Strangelet Defenchalets. Luxurious holiday lodges transform into dense survival mode, creating a Swisslet population in the Alps complete with mini Matterhorn and numerous Swiss imitations, concealments and dualities – the Swiss Army Knife of bunkers.

BSc Year 1 field trip to Mies Pavilion, Barcelona, Spain

MA Architectural History at the Southbank Centre, London
(photo Bernadette Devilat)

B-Pro: MArch Graduate Architectural Design

Programme Leader: Alisa Andrasek

Report Coordinator:
Stephen Gage

Research Clusters
RC1:
Alisa Andrasek,
Daghan Cam
RC2:
Isaïe Bloch, Moa Carlsson
RC3:
Ruairi Glynn, Christopher
Leung, Ollie Palmer
RC4:
Manuel Jimenez Garcia,
Gilles Retsin
RC5:
Philippe Morel,
Thibault Schwartz
RC6:
Stefan Basig, Soomeen
Hahm, Daniel Widrig

The Masters programme in Graduate Architectural Design (GAD) is a 12-month full-time post-professional course, leading to a Masters of Architecture (MArch) degree. It is part of B-Pro, the umbrella structure for post-professional Masters programmes at The Bartlett School of Architecture, directed by Professor Frédéric Migayrou. The Six GAD Research Clusters deliver diverse yet focused strands of speculative research, emphasising the key role computation plays within complex design ecologies.

————Design has a long tradition of mastery in complex synthesis, and presently it is harvesting acute resources of science and technology for complex constructed environments within accelerated condition of convergence of matter and information. While data visualisation exposes the hidden beauty and complexity of observed systems, data materialisation can produce such beauty and complexity within new synthetic fields. The boundaries of disciplines are increasingly porous, giving architecture and design an expanded agency at the centre of open synthesis applicable to a myriad of complex domains.

————GAD research recognises the synthetic power of design at the core of complex ecologies, and its ability to bind a plethora of agencies. Through computational resources, architects have increased access to the physics of materials and structures at different orders of scale. These physics of matter are embedded in the design-search process, incorporating the constraints and inputs of manufacturing and constructability. Research Clusters explore the latest approaches to robotics, CNC fabrication, 3D printing, supercomputing, simulation, generative design, interactivity, advanced algorithms, extensive material experiments and links to material science. GAD engages critically with such developments, which are already radically changing the landscape of architecture, its social and economical role and its effectiveness as an active agency, particularly within urban ecologies.

————The programme is structured so that students are introduced to theoretical concepts through lectures and initial design projects supported by computational and robotics skills building workshops. During the second stage students work in small teams or individually, according to the methodology of each Cluster, allowing the student to focus on their individual interests in advanced design research and the development of a design project. There is a continuous evaluation of work via tutorials with regular design reviews organised between Clusters which include external critics.

————Alongside cutting-edge research, GAD hosts a series of public events, which this year included *Plexus, Material Matters* and *n_Salon*. Apart from in-house events open to the larger community, the exceptional pool of the GAD faculty includes some of the most prominent young practitioners and researchers in the field and beyond.

Image: Team Phylametrics, MArch GAD RC4, 'Space Wires'

B-Pro: MArch Urban Design

Programme Leader: Adrian Lahoud

UDI

UDI Stream Leader
Adrian Lahoud

History & Theory
Coordinator
Godofredo Pereira

Research Clusters
RC11:
Sam Jacoby, Adrian Lahoud
RC12:
Peter Besley, Hannah
Corlett, Jonathan Kendalll
RC14:
Platon Issaias, Camila
Sotomayor
RC15:
Ross Exo Adams, Beth
Hughes, Davide Sacconi

UDII

UDI Stream Leader
Claudia Pasquero

Coding and Media tutors
Immanuel Koh, Iker Mugarra

History and Theory tutors
Emmanouil Zaroukas,
Mollie Claypool

Research Clusters
RC16:
Claudia Pasquero,
Marco Poletto
RC17:
Ulrika Karlsson,
Maj Plemenitas
RC18:
Eduardo Rico, Enriqueta
Llabres, Zachary Flucker

The MArch Urban Design (UD) programme brings together a new generation of designers and thinkers from across the world in order to provide a rich and challenging space for long-term research on urbanisation and design. It is part of B-Pro, the umbrella structure for post-professional Masters programmes at The Bartlett School of Architecture, directed by Professor Frédéric Migayrou. Studio inquiry ranges across an expansive set of scales and bodies of knowledge culminating with a design project and thesis. Environmental and ecological questions are prioritised within a critical structure that embraces the dispersed, often paradoxical nature of contemporary urbanism. The curriculum introduces students to various fields such as archaeology, anthropology, ecological history, governance, law, media, philosophy, planning and political theory. Cross-studio dialogue is emphasised, as is a collective work ethic.

There are two streams within Urban Design, UDI and UDII.

MArch Urban Design (UD)I: The Project for the Mediterranean

Comprising 25 nation states, 13 language groups, and almost half a billion people, the Mediterranean defines the encounter between Africa, Europe and Asia. Its shores are caught by two fundamental and ongoing transformations: the Arab Spring and the financial crisis. At the same time, the Mediterranean Sea has become the most highly policed waterway on earth as the European Union attempts to insulate itself from flows of migrants from Africa and Asia. Add to this the unprecedented levels of diaspora and conflict in the Levant and there is no other space with more at stake in terms of coexistence between human beings and with their natural environment. Furthermore, in a number of different ways the Mediterranean manifests the problem of the 'weak state', whether through financial crisis, corporate dominance, institutional failure or military rule. Simultaneously then, a number of new non- and extra-governmental polities are emerging, raising important questions to do with citizenship, belonging and the idea of a public. These mutations, while placing new constraints on urban transformation, also open new spaces of financial investment evidenced by opportunistic flows of capital, especially from the Persian Gulf and resource revenues from the North of Africa.

Beginning in September 2012 and concluding in September 2015, 'The Project for the Mediterranean' consists of three one-year design studios with an accompanying public calendar of symposia, conferences, lectures and roundtables. The project aims to build a community of academic, professional and public interest around the agency of design and its role in transforming the future of this region.

MArch UDII: Urban Morphogenesis

MArch Urban Design (UD)II engages urban design as a computational practice to prefigure alternative models of the city represented as a complex dynamic system. The ambition of the stream is to stimulate a transdisciplinary discourse that reaches wider academic research networks as well as scientific organisations involved in the study of the city as a living system and in the development of future bio-digital technologies.

———The stream adopts analogue, biological and digital computational design to draw terrains of negotiation between strategic and tactical forms of intervention. Algorithmic coding enables the study of biological models and the testing of iterative, adaptive and resilient design solutions applicable to a broader eco-social domain, generating a multiplicity of responses and effects, ranging scales and regimes, from the molecular to the territorial, from the quasi-instantaneous to the geological.

———UDII is strictly studio-based and students are encouraged to work in teams and to engage with design as a form of research; current research clusters focus on the urban application of models of collective intelligence inspired by ants, corals and slime moulds, on the development of resilient and distributed bio-energy infrastructures, on the engineering of bio-digital soil remediation, urban landscapes and on the material articulation of adaptive water management territories.

———While escaping conventional urban categorisation, the Research Clusters engage specific regions that are gaining a new centrality, as both producers of the resources absorbed by existing global cities and as receivers of the surplus to society – the human and material waste which is a necessary byproduct of the contemporary capitalist system. Current locations include the copper mining corridor in Arizona, USA, the Tar Sands region in Alberta, Canada and the water basin of Manaus, Brazil.

MA Architectural History

Programme Director: Adrian Forty

Teaching staff:
Iain Borden, Ben Campkin,
Barbara Penner, Jane
Rendell, Peg Rawes, Amy
Thomas , Robin Wilson

The Bartlett School of Architecture 2014

Architecture consists not only of buildings and projects, but also of the life that takes place within them, and of the ideas and discussions that they give rise to. It is the business of the MA Architectural History to interrogate these discussions, to extend them, and possibly to reframe them in terms of broader debates about culture, history and politics.

We encourage our students to be experimental, to try out ideas from different fields, and to see whether bringing them to bear on architecture changes the way we think about buildings, cities and the life within them. Each one of the projects listed here is a small experiment, in which some particular architectural phenomenon has been put under the microscope and examined in the light of a particular theory or set of ideas, to see whether our view of it might change – or, alternatively, whether a theory might need to be reassessed.

The one-year Masters programme in Architectural History, which has been running for 30 years, is partly a taught programme that prepares people for research, and partly a research programme, in which people undertake a self-selected and self-directed research project – two examples are included here.

2012-13

Anna Andersen
Translation Transposition Translocation: The Development of a Phenomenology of Architecture by Christian Norberg-Schulz, 1973-1980

Sarah Cheema
Lubetkin's Staircases: Symbols of Visual, Poetic and Social Encounters

Simon England
'Not a Church as you know it': The Case of Cyril Mardall's Finnish Seamen's Mission

Sevcan Ercan
The Production of Space in Sites of Evictions

Catarina Castro Henriques
Church of the Sacred Heart: A Building of Resistance

Adriana Keramida Strahl
Reading the Skyline: A Semiotic Study of Framing London's Views

Carlo Menon
The Missing Decade? Architectural Magazines of the 1990s

Vyta Pivoriunate
Designing the Man of the Future:
Archigram's Domestic Architecture, 1960-70

Mrinal Rammohan
The Relative Freedom of Ambiguity: A Critical Examination of Satire in the Writings of Rem Koolhaas

Ishita Shah
Displacement of the Traditional: A Study of the Different Actors and their Voices in the Making of post-colonial Ahmedabad

Eda Soyal
Constructing Ambivalence: Modern Turkish Identity and Apartmentalisation in Nisantasi Istanbul

Davide Spina
America and the Sign Economy of Post-War Italy: The ENI Building in Rome

Neli Vasileva
On the Instability of Monuments. Monuments in Bulgaria from the period of the Communist Regime 1944-1989

Magd Zahran
Spaces of Urban Revolution: An Investigation of Revolutionary Rehearsals, Spaces in Cairo's El-Tahrir Square

18.4.79. "Translation"

stone building (e.g. classical) translated
into wood becomes a "box" (e.g. my own hous[e]
"translation" ←→ "transposition"
translocation.
preserve
import
export

translation is a tool for gathering
Arch. as language.   cf. mirror-play

Anna Ulrikke Andersen
*Translation Transposition Transposition:
The Development of a Phenomenology of
Architecture in Christian Norberg-Schulz, 1973-1980*

'Architecture is born from the dialectic of departure and return' Christian Norberg-Schulz, 1980

———In an archival box in the Norberg-Schulz archive in Oslo, a folder marked 'The 70s' contains a stack of assorted papers that are Thorvald Christian Norberg-Schulz's (1926-2000) personal, handwritten notes from the decade. The 1970s were fruitful years for the young professor. With the book *Intentions in Architecture* (1963) he had established himself within the international scene of architectural theory. He was invited to speak at the RIBA, The University of Cambridge, Yale University and MIT, along with being the editor of the Norwegian architectural journal *Byggekunst* and continuously publishing articles in international journals. In 1973 he moved to Rome to research his next book Genius Loci. After his first serious encounter with the phenomenology of Martin Heidegger in 1974, he developed what is considered to be his landmark treatise *Genius Loci: Towards a Phenomenology of Architecture* (1980). The notes from this period are remarkable, addressing several issues that are vital to his thinking: place, landscape, language, philosophy and architecture. Less known, and therefore intriguing, are the keywords 'translation', 'transposition', 'translocation', which appear in one of the notes from the period, dated 18.04.1979, headed 'Translation' (see image above).

———This report offers an analysis of the hitherto unknown document 'Translation' and investigates the role translation, transposition and translocation played in Norberg-Schulz's theoretical formation and link this to the reality of his life, by uncovering his references. How does the document fit into a larger tradition of architectural theory?

———The Norberg-Schulz Archive owes part of its inaccessibility to the demands it places upon the language skills of its visitors. Norberg-Schulz both read and wrote in English, German, Italian and Norwegian, and on occasions communicated in French. One of the most intriguing examples of his multilingualism is seen in a notebook from 1957. Within the range of a few pages, he switches between the four languages, depending on what he had read. It is obvious that Norberg-Schulz was comfortable reading literature in its original language and moved easily in the landscape between languages. Nevertheless, this makes the archive difficult to encounter and read in the way it deserves, leaving the archive relatively unexplored. Besides Otero-Pailos' archive-based study in *Architecture's Historical Turn*, no major archive-based study of Norberg-Schulz has been conducted. Most studies, Norwegian included, rely on published material. The archive invites further research.

Carlo Menon
*The Missing Decade? Architectural Magazines
of the 1990s*

From the perspective of today, it is common to consider that the 'golden age' of architectural magazines was in the 1960s and 70s, when thanks to more accessible reproduction technologies in printing, a host of 'little' magazines, fanzines and other kinds of ephemeral publications became the 'natural' vehicle for a polemical approach against all established values and customs. These experiments in new forms of architecture and criticism generate as much longing and nostalgia as does the other 'heroic' moment in the history of architectural periodicals, the avant-garde magazines of the 1920s, when Theo Van Doesburg was publishing *De Stijl* and Le Corbusier was shaping his audience through *L'Esprit Nouveau.*

———At first glance, the periodicals of the 1990s lack anything like the same kind of appeal and imageability. In the usual meta-narrative of the subject, this represents the 'missing decade' of architectural journals. One thinks of the typical 1990s architectural magazine as something ugly, glossy, commercially-driven, especially when compared to the variety of magazines published today. In a period, today, of renewed interest in the purpose and meaning of the printed page, the act of looking back at this 'missing decade', figuring out what were the main characteristics of the magazines around in those years, could reveal the good seeds and the bad weeds on which the new printed

magazines of the twenty-first century founded their existence.

———This report is therefore an attempt to seize some tendencies displayed in the mid-1990s through a close reading and a comparative, transversal approach to the printed material of five geographically and intellectually diverse architectural magazines which started publication in those years: *ANY, Terrazzo, Le Visiteur, UME* and *Zodiac.*

———Avoiding event-based accounts of the editorial backdrop to each magazine (side stories and so on), it focuses on what can be learnt from the printed pages of those magazines. A series of similarities and oppositions will be traced via various thematic tropes: enthusiasm towards the digital age, nostalgia for the loss of a more 'profound' past, preciousness of the object, the question of what is original, an enlarged space for discourse, and, perhaps surprisingly, the multiform legacy of *Oppositions* (New York, 1973-1984, 26 issues) within most of the magazines studied.

Davide Spina
*America and the Sign Economy of post-war Italy:
the ENI Building in Rome*

Approaching the city of Rome by car along via Cristoforo Colombo, after a pleasant sloping stretch cutting through a leafy park with sparse buildings, the landscape widens and one swiftly crosses a big artificial lake. Before being able to make sense of this sudden change of scenario the driver is already on the other side of the bridge, where the road is enveloped again by vegetation and buildings. During the short ride across the bridge a dark shadow slides into the driver's peripheral vision. You are probably not paying attention to it and just keep driving, absorbed by your own business, but, if out of curiosity you happen to turn your head to it, you would distractedly notice a big building. Then, if curiosity is further aroused and you decide to stop by the lakeside to look at it more carefully, you would have an entirely different experience. A distant, isolated, screen-like glass building dominates the landscape, shockingly attracting your gaze. As the shock progressively gives way to contemplation, anxiety mounts. What is this looming, featureless object doing here? This object, the ENI building of 1959-62, is there to tell a story about how a relatively underdeveloped country devised and negotiated a project of development. It is a story about the economic miracle in post-war Italy, but it also has much to say about the crisis the country is going through today.

————If all that is modern in Italy is 'foreign', predominantly American, and all that is American comes as an image, the formation of a (post-Fascist) modern Italian subjectivity is a business depending on deceptive identifications with, and interpretations of, images produced elsewhere, in the United States. As a consequence, the projects of development devised under these epistemological conditions are dependent on image-based knowledge with the foreign – again, American – objects and practices they employ. But because ultimately what is being borrowed is not a material thing, but an image, the significance of such objects and practices in the social fabric of their origin is ignored. This is evident in an architectural historian's remark on American solutions in post-war Italy, adopted 'not so much for their workability but for their potential significance in a context under intense transformation'. If we read this through semiotics, foreign motifs are adopted more for their sign value rather than for their use value, in other words, for the social currency they secure in their new context of application rather than for their capacity to carry out specific functions. To quote Guy Debord, as every object 'draw[s] its immediate prestige and its ultimate function' as an image, these projects take on a strong spectacular bent.

MPhil/PhD
Architectural Design

Programme Director: Professor Jonathan Hill
Programme Coordinator: Dr Penelope Haralambidou

Current Students:
Yota Adilenidou, Bihter Almac, Luisa Silva Alpalhão, Nicola Antaki, Anna Andersen, Alessandro Ayuso, Jaime Bartolome Yllera, Katy Beinart, Joanne Bristol, David Buck, Matthew Butcher, Niccolo Casas, Ines Dantas Ribeiro Bernardes, Bernadette Devilat, Pavlos Fereos, Pablo Gil, Ruairi Glynn, Polly Gould, Mohamad Hafeda, Colin Herperger, Bill Hodgson, Popi Iacovou, Christiana Ioannou, Nahed Jawad, Tae Young Kim, Dionysia Kypraiou, Hina Lad, Felipe Lanuza Rilling, Tea Lim, Jane Madsen, Samar Maqusi, Igor Marjanovic, Matteo Melioli, Oliver Palmer, Christos Papastergiou, Luke Pearson, Mariana Pestana, Henri Praeger, Felix Robbins, David Roberts, Natalia Romik, Merijn Royaards, Wiltrud Simbuerger, Eva Sopeoglou, Camila Sotomayor, Ro Spankie, Theo Spyropoulos, Theodoros Themistokleous, Quynh Vantu, Cindy Walters, Stefan White, Michael Wihart, Alex Zambelli, Seda Zirek, Fiona Zisch

Graduating Students:
Adam Adamis, Rachel Armstrong, Emma Cheatle, Guan Lee, Malca Mizrahi

Leading to a PhD in Architecture, the MPhil/PhD Architectural Design allows especially able and reflective designers to undertake research within The Bartlett School of Architecture's speculative and experimental ethos. The first to be established in the UK, the Bartlett MPhil/PhD Architectural Design is internationally recognised as one of the most influential doctoral programmes dedicated to architectural design.

⸻ The programme draws on the strengths of design teaching and doctoral research at The Bartlett, encouraging the development of architectural research through the interaction of designing and writing. An architectural design doctoral thesis has two inter-related elements of equal importance – a project and a text – that share a research theme and a productive relationship. The project may be drawn, filmed, built, or use whatever media is appropriate.

⸻ UCL's multidisciplinary environment offers a stimulating and varied research culture that connects research by architectural design to developments in other disciplines, such as anthropology, art, digital media, geography and medicine. The PhD Architectural Design programme is intended for graduates of architecture and other disciplines who wish to pursue research by architectural design. 55 students from over 20 countries are currently enrolled.

⸻ The Bartlett School of Architecture's two PhD programmes organise a number of annual events for doctoral students. *PhD Research Projects*, an exhibition and conference with presentations by current practice-based PhD students in UCL and the Royal Academy of Music, is held in Term 2. Invited critics in 2014 were Dr Sarah Callis (Royal Academy of Music), Dr Emma Cheatle (University of Westminster), Dr Roy Kozlovsky (Tel Aviv University), Professor Perry Kulper (University of Michigan), Professor John Macarthur (University of Queensland), and Dr Nina Vollenbröker (UCL). Throughout the year, *PhD Research Conversations* seminars are an opportunity for doctoral candidates to present work in progress.

Current Supervisors
Professor Peter Bishop, Dr Camillo Boano, Professor Iain Borden, Dr Victor Buchli, Dr Ben Campkin, Dr Marjan Colletti, Professor Sir Peter Cook, Dr Marcos Cruz, Professor Murray Fraser, Professor Stephen Gage, Professor Ranulph Glanville, Dr Sean Hanna, Dr Penelope Haralambidou, Professor Christine Hawley, Professor Jonathan Hill, Dr Adrian Lahoud, Dr Yeoryia Manolopoulou, Professor Sebastian Ourselin, Jayne Parker, Dr Barbara Penner, Dr Sophia Psarra, Dr Peg Rawes, Professor Jane Rendell, Professor Bob Sheil, Mark Smout, Professor Philip Steadman, Dr Hugo Spiers, Professor Neil Spiller, Professor Philip Tabor

Adam Theodoros Adamis
*Liquid Architecture, the Philosophy of Gilles Deleuze
and the Films of David Lynch*
Principal Supervisor: Professor Jonathan Hill
Subsidiary Supervisor: Professor Jane Rendell

The thesis explores the nature and impact of liquid concepts with a particular focus on the liquid architecture movement, dually interpreted through the thinking of Gilles Deleuze and the cinematic works of David Lynch. The text begins with a consideration of how architecture was until recently expected to be stable and solid. Following this, it introduces liquid concepts and what can be understood by this term, before discussing the stimuli that led to the expression of liquid thinking through liquid architecture. An introduction to the thinking of Gilles Deleuze and Félix Guattari follows, with a selective focus placed on ideas of relevance to liquid concepts. The central part of the text discusses liquid architecture, mentioning several key figures within the movement, including Lars Spuybroek, Kas Oosterhuis and Marcos Novak. This is followed by the presentation of several projects, both those of other architects and the projects forming part of this design thesis. The latter section is concerned with the definition of cinematic space and its function, and the work of David Lynch. It considers connections between Lynch and liquid concepts, and presents relevant themes and tools that feature prominently in his films. The final part of the thesis is dedicated to a discussion of the Liquid House design project, exploring the influences on the design process of the various strands considered in this thesis, and in particular of the work of Deleuze and of Lynch, ultimately affirming that the project is liquid in its design approach. The text concludes that while liquid architecture is mostly concerned with matters relating to design, liquid concepts are about ways of thinking, and further, the current expressions of liquid architecture are not the full extent of the developments in architecture, which may be expected to become even more liquid.

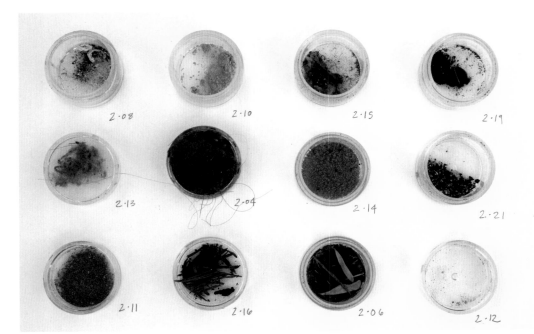

2·08   2·10   2·15   2·19
2·13   2·04   2·14   2·21
2·11   2·16   2·06   2·12

Emma Cheatle
*Part-architecture: The Maison de Verre through
the Large Glass*
Principal Supervisor: Dr Penelope Haralambidou
Subsidiary Supervisor: Professor Jane Rendell

My thesis is an examination of a building, the Maison de Verre (Pierre Chareau, 1928-32), through an artwork, the *Large Glass* (Marcel Duchamp, 1915-23). Aligning the two works materially, historically and conceptually, I challenge the accepted architectural descriptions of the *Maison de Verre*, and make original spatial and social accounts of its use and inhabitation in 1930s Paris.

——————The *Maison de Verre* is historiographically regarded as an iconic modern house. Designed for politically progressive gynaecologist Dr Jean Dalsace and his avant-garde wife, Annie Dalsace, the building comprises a 'free-plan' layout veiled by glass walls. A gynaecology clinic occupies most of the ground floor. In the 1930s numerous women must have visited it, seeking treatment or advice, including contraception and abortion. Due to the context of extreme pronatalism and illegality of contraception and abortion, their histories remained necessarily unrecorded. Further, twentieth century architectural historiography has not been concerned with socio-spatial analyses of buildings.

——————My thesis is inspired by the presence of the clinic and the historiographic absence it produces. In order to explore the role of sexuality in the *Maison de Verre*, I situate the *Large Glass* as a context for rereading it. A glass construction depicting unconsummated sexual relations it is, I argue, Duchamp's response to 1910-20s Parisian sexual mores.

——————I interrogate these ideas through a method for which I have coined the term 'part-architecture', developed from psychoanalytic theories on the 'L Schema' and 'part-object' (Freud, Lacan) and Rosalind Krauss' reinterpretation of them in an art history context. Part-architecture is an original interdisciplinary method of architectural history writing that combines rigorous academic research with design research to recover the lost social and sexual interactions occurring in the *Maison de Verre*. Firstly, I analyse modernist historiography, questioning the limits of accepted descriptions of the building. Then, I engage subjects marginal to modernist history – female sexuality, health and occupations – consulting multiple sources from different disciplines (social, philosophical, medical, photographic and fictional). When I reach evidential limits, I utilise innovative design research. Drawn and written investigations made over several periods on site at the *Maison de Verre*, and with the *Large Glass* and its archive, inspire speculative drawing, fiction, book arts and audio projects rereading the building.

——————Identifying three key materials present in the Large Glass, I structure the thesis through the chapters 'Glass', 'Dust' and 'Air'. In each, a history theory text and associated design projects rethink the *Large Glass* and recover the inhabitation of the *Maison de Verre*. Theory and design become interrelated, supporting each other as forms of thinking.

Guan Lee
*Cast and Camera: An Intimate Engagement with
Making at Grymsdyke Farm*
Principal Supervisor: Dr Yeoryia Manolopoulou
Subsidiary Supervisor: Professor Jonathan Hill

My research is practice-led and focuses on processes of casting through ongoing and hands-on experimentation at full scale. Set within the workshops of Grymsdyke Farm, it engages with materials in a direct and intimate manner. Photography is employed as a practical documentation tool but also as a physical and theoretical counterpart to casting, and with the photographs becoming design works in themselves. Casting and photography share tactile and spatial relationships with architecture, yet little discourse exists around them. Casting, like analogue photography, may soon become obsolete because of digital 3D scanning and 3D printing. Given this potentially bleak future of casting in architecture, this research and design project on casting offers resistance to its potential demise, specifically by consolidating its many innovative and culturally rich architectural contributions.

⸺This thesis studies the individual properties of both practices and how they correlate, bringing to light new observations about how they overlap with architecture. It examines works by different practitioners, such as the inventor of photography William Henry Fox Talbot, architects and builders Pier Luigi Nervi and Mark West, and the artist Medardo Rosso, to show how the synergy of shared

properties in casting and photography can deepen our understanding of architecture in terms of time and preservation, fluid and solid form, copy and reproducibility, positive and negative space. As digital processes prevail in contemporary architectural practice, inspiration taken from nature through mathematical and abstract constructs often lacks a necessary relationship to the physical realities of making. How can an intimate knowledge of material processes be relevant in architectural practice today? How can situated modes of craft be integrated meaningfully into ever-evolving forms of design production?

⸺At Grymsdyke Farm, the realms of inspiration, execution and place are not distinct but inseparable. All research projects presented in this thesis are integrated into the physical reality of the place. In addition Grymsdyke Farm hosts a number of site-specific works built with visiting architecture students and other practitioners. Grymsdyke Farm is a live-work environment that aims to establish a diverse collective. Through the constant exchange and sharing of ideas, experiences and expertise it becomes a place moulded over time, capturing individual and collaborative design in the making.

Malca Mizrahi
*Lyrical Space: The Construction of Space
in Contemporary Architecture, Art and Literature
in Argentina*
Principal Supervisor: Professor Philip Tabor
Subsidiary Supervisor: Professor Penny Florence

This thesis proposes that since 1990 a significant part of contemporary Argentine literature, art and architecture has been characterised by an identifiable quality: spatial lyricism. This new quality manifests in the spatial the aesthetic values that identify the lyric principle, normally related to sound and the verbal.

———The aim is to define 'lyrical space', and to show that space-making processes that validate introspective approaches in literature and visual arts can lead to the emergence of new form and content in architectural space, giving relevance to subjective experience and to the affective response induced in the user.

———Framed in neo-baroque aesthetics, the evidence positions experience, emotion, memory and identity as the critical material for the construction of space, inducing an 'exceptional' state of mind in the user/reader/spectator that recaptures the subjective dimension of seventeenth century Baroque. A selection of short stories by Jorge Luis Borges and Julio Cortázar, several novellas by César Aira, and a lyrical essay by Alejandra Pizarnik, are read in relation to the visual work of Guillermo Kuitca, Fabián Marcaccio, Lucio Fontana, Leandro Erlich, Dino Bruzzone, Tomás Saraceno and my own.

———The investigation explores the literary principles on lyricism, linking Hegel's aesthetics to post-structuralist thinking, and the category of the figural. To support the analysis further, interviews conducted by myself and by others are also used.

———Several aspects are unique about the project. The literary is located in the spatial, while the material is located between the spatial and the self. This collision of reading literary work centred on the construction of space, with the reading of spatial qualities in the visual and the verbal in terms of their aesthetic affective response – the emotional effect it arouses – has not been attempted before. The aesthetic affinities that emerge from the interdisciplinary analysis are also new.

Rachel Armstrong
Vibrant Architecture: How 'Vibrant Matter'
may Raise the Status of the Material World in
Architectural Design Practice and be Recognised
as a Codesigner of our Living Spaces
Principal Supervisor: Professor Neil Spiller
Subsidiary Supervisors: Professor Stephen Gage,
Professor Martin Hanczyc

This thesis aims to recognise the liveliness of matter to account for and technologise its contributions in architectural design practice. My multidisciplinary research establishes how it may be possible to work synergistically with the material realm by establishing fertile metabolic networks and build ecological relationships through the production of architecture. This proposition is experimentally tested using different species of lifelike chemistries at non-equilibrium states that serve as model systems for vibrant matter. Findings indicated that dynamic chemistries could spontaneously produce a new kind of operating system called an 'assemblage' that could be technologically operationalised. Assemblages provided an alternative theoretical and practical lens, and technological platform to machines, with different sets of associated concepts, operating principles and qualitatively distinctive outcomes. Design tactics were formulated as a result of these investigations, which were practically explored in the *Hylozoic Ground* installation by producing a series of responsive chemistries as a prototype assemblage technology. Further experimental and speculative development of the assemblage operating system was explored through project work in 'Vibrant Venice', which proposes to grow an artificial limestone reef underneath the foundations of the city, and 'Vibrant Cities', through the production of synthetic soils in under used and poorly imagined sites within urban environments. These technical and design studies suggested that the theory and practice of vibrant matter may give rise to new kinds of material solutions within the practice of the built environment that may be applied to architectural design as 'vibrant architecture', which is stochastic and life-promoting. Vibrant architecture may enable architects to codesign in partnership with human and nonhuman collectives, to produce buildings that enliven construction sites through the production of post-natural landscapes. Vibrant architecture consists of varied communities of loosely cooperating, heterogeneous bodies that are united through a common ontology of stardust. Yet, despite the diversity within assemblages, their collective behaviours may be coordinated through 'natural computing' approaches which harness the computational properties of the natural world and underpin the practice of vibrant architectural design. Ultimately vibrant architecture may operate as an ecological platform for human development that augments the liveliness of our planet, rather than diminishes it.

MPhil/PhD Architectural History & Theory

Course Director: Dr Barbara Penner
Course Coordinator: Dr Penelope Haralambidou

Current Students:
Wesley Aelbrecht, Tilo Amhoff, Kalliopi Amygdalou, Sabina Andron, Pinar Aykac, Tal Bar, Eva Branscome, Eray Cayli, Stylianos Giamarelos, Kate Jordan, Irene Kelly, Jeong Hye Kim, Torsten Lange, Claudio Leoni, Abigail Lockey, Kieran Mahon, Carlo Menon, Dragan Pavlovic, Matthew Poulter, Regner Ramos Ramirez, Sophie Read, Sarah Riviere, Ozayr Saloojee, Huda Tayob, Amy Thomas, Freya Wigzell, Danielle Willkens

Graduating Students:
María del Pilar Sánchez-Beltrán, Nicholas Jewell, Thomas-Bernard Kenniff, Brent Pilkey, Nina Vollenbröker

The Bartlett School of Architecture's MPhil/PhD Architectural History & Theory programme allows students to conduct an exhaustive piece of research into an area of their own selection and definition. Great importance is placed on the originality of information uncovered, the creativity of the interpretations made, and the rigour of the methodological procedures adopted.

Approximately 20-30 students from around the world are enrolled at any one time for MPhil/PhD research in this field. The range of research topics undertaken is broad, but most explore the history and theory of architecture and cities from c.1800 to the present day, with an emphasis on the critical reading of these subjects from cultural, political and experiential viewpoints.

The MPhil/PhD Architectural History & Theory programme draws on the expertise and experience of the Bartlett School of Architecture's team of architectural historians and theorists, who are recognised internationally for their contributions to the field. The programme itself is very dynamic with an active series of talks, seminars, and conferences. In keeping with UCL's multidisciplinary ethos, connections between architectural research and other fields are encouraged, and there are active collaborations with the Departments of Anthropology, Fine Art, and UCL Urban Lab. We have established regular research exchanges with the Royal Academy of Music and Cornell University, and have a longstanding partnership with the Canadian Centre for Architecture through the Collection Research Grant programme.

Current Supervisors

Dr Jan Birksted, Professor Iain Borden, Dr Ben Campkin, Professor Mario Carpo, Professor Adrian Forty, Professor Murray Fraser, Dr Penelope Haralambidou, Professor Jonathan Hill, Dr Adrian Lahoud, Dr Barbara Penner, Dr Peg Rawes, Professor Jane Rendell, Dr Sophia Psarra, Dr Tania Sengupta

Other Supervisors

Dr Victor Buchli and Dr Ruth Mandel, UCL Anthropology; Professor Julio Davila Silva, Bartlett Development Planning Unit; Dr Stephanie Schwartz, UCL History of Art

Nicholas Jewell
*Socialism and Shopping: The Role of the
Shopping Mall in the Formation of Public Space
in Modern China*
Principal Supervisor: Professor Murray Fraser
Subsidiary Supervisor: Professor Adrian Forty

China's recent rise as an economic superpower
has been inescapable. As the urban nuclei
spearheading its modernisation become
increasingly globalised, one of their keystones of
development is the shopping mall. The presence of
a building type which embodies Western capitalism
makes explicit the tensions between China's brand
of 'State Communism' and the advent of 'free-
market' economics. It is a scenario which is bringing
modern China to a crossroads as it struggles to
create a national identity that can embrace these
opposing the ideological strands. This thesis
examines these complex inter-relationships through
the culturally hybrid built form of the shopping mall.

———Few building types are more maligned or less
understood than the shopping mall. Founded by
consumerism, the ideological imperatives of the
shopping mall do not sit easily with the dominant
socialist-humanitarian preoccupations of the
architectural profession. This study draws upon
interdisciplinary research to argue for architectural
approaches that better understand capitalism and
its social consequences.

———Through analysis of the mall in a specific
Chinese context, the study explores how it can
be understood as a socio-cultural phenomenon.

The interrelationship between cultural and
typological forms provides a number of insights into
the syntax of China's urban spaces, not to mention
the underlying structures of the shopping mall itself.

———A number of overlapping themes define the
objectives behind this study. Firstly, the study aims
to provide architectural discourse and practice
with a new set of critical tools to understand the
shopping mall typology. Secondly, the study uses
the shopping mall as a medium to engage with
modern Chinese culture in a more sophisticated
interdisciplinary manner than most contemporary
Western discourse allows. Thirdly, this study
questions the current focus of architectural debate
in China. Does the present debate really address the
most important architectural and urban forms which
are emerging in China's cities? And what lessons
might they hold for urban development globally?

———Architectural criticism has failed to address
the levels of meaning within the shopping mall.
It is, however, a building type that endures and
is now hybridising significantly in Chinese cities.
If architecture is to remain an engaged social art
then we need a more holistic understanding of this
phenomenon, one that acknowledges its place in
what is now a global condition. This thesis offers a
case study, indeed a microcosm, of what is
happening in all our cities today.

Thomas-Bernard Kenniff
A Dialogical Investigation into the Architectonics of Designing Public Space at Barking Town Square
Principal Supervisor: Dr Jan Birksted
Subsidiary Supervisor: Professor Iain Borden

This thesis is an exploration of identity, public space and design in the town of Barking, London England, where a new Town Square was produced between 2000 and 2010. Designed by muf architecture/art (public realm) and Allford Hall Monaghan Morris Architects (buildings), the Barking Town Square, as will be seen in this research, is a telling moment of urban and public space development of its period.
———The project raises significant questions about the evolving identity of its participants and publics, the value of public space in the contemporary city, and the relationship between design authority and public participation. It develops the concept of dialogue, from the Bakhtinian theory of dialogism, as a conceptual paradigm for identity, public space and design, recasting the initial investigation into an exploration of alterity (individuals and publics cannot be conceived outside of their situated relations to others), spatial heteroglossia (public space as a production of different discourses) and practical ambivalence (the blurring of boundaries to activate the social and political potential of design). The thesis thus investigates, in Bakhtinian terminology, how different voices inflect the polyphonic landscape of public space, particularly in the context of urban regeneration and the relationship between ideal projections (of publics, of public spaces, of

design concepts) and their challenge in the everyday use and management of such places. The inherent ambivalence of dialogue – particularly its openness and the way it allows contradictions to coexist – is traced throughout as a common thread uniting the questions raised by the Barking Town Square project and those of theory. The methods of investigation emphasise interviews, participant-observation and fieldwork, capturing a project that existed for the duration of my research in a state of becoming.

Brent Pilkey
Queering Heteronormativity at Home in London
Principal Supervisor: Dr Barbara Penner
Subsidiary Supervisor: Dr Ben Campkin
Honorary Supervisor: Dr Andrew Gorman-Murray,
University of Western Sydney

This thesis offers a London-based contemporary study of sexuality at home. I draw from architectural history, feminist and queer theory as well as geographies of sexualities to interrogate the stability of domesticity. Highlighting everyday homemaking practices of more than 40 non-heterosexual households in London, I seek to complicate one overarching regime of power that dominates our cultural value system: heteronormativity – the idea that normative heterosexuality is the default sexuality to which everyone must conform, or declare themselves against.

The project is a response to three decades of academic research that has looked at the spatialised ways in which sexual identity unfolds in, for the most part, peripheral zones in the 'Western' metropolis, spaces beyond the domestic realm. This thesis takes a different architectural approach; one where through interviewing 47 lesbian, gay, bisexual, transgender and queer (LGBTQ) Londoners, as well as 11 domestic tradespeople that work in these homes, agency is given to small-scale domestic interventions and everyday actions. The concept of 'queering' is important to the framework, which, in the context of the thesis, is understood as an ongoing process that LGBTQ people are engaged in through homemaking and daily living. Although some participants may not see this as a political act, I argue otherwise and suggest queering at home is a form of political activism. Through mundane domestic actions the overarching structure of heteronormativity might be challenged. I contend that queering the home unfolds in various, complex and conflicting ways.

The thesis seeks to provoke both queer theory and politics, by opening up existing approaches and remits to allow room for a domestic method. In addition, the thesis seeks to challenge assumptions within architecture but also in the wider sense. I aim to break down stereotypes surrounding non-heterosexual homemaking practices that architectural studies and media representations problematically reproduce.

María del Pilar Sánchez-Beltrán
*Tracing the Cold War in Colombian Architecture:
a Disregarded Legacy*
Principal Supervisor: Dr Barbara Penner
Subsidiary Supervisor: Professor Julio Davila Silva

Drawing on a social and cultural analysis of the architecture designed and built by the state during the Colombian military dictatorship of General Gustavo Rojas Pinilla (1953-1957), and based on original sources, including historical archives, declassified official reports, oral history, and raw blueprints, this PhD research project traces relationships between architecture, and the national and international politics of that time. In doing so, this research analyses the relation between the built environment and power, questioning concepts of representation and identity. It will be argued that as well as a materialisation of the nationalist discourse, the nationwide consolidation of modern architecture should also be seen as a camouflaged instrument of the Cold War.

———As part of the contemporary debate about the worldwide impact of the Cold War, this research focuses on the architecture of the 'National Plan of Public Works' developed during Colombian dictatorship of the 1950s. It takes as a case study one of the regime's most emblematic projects: the Naval College Almirante Padilla, using it as a methodological instrument through which larger issues can be traced: the architecture is taken to be a materialisation of the political project of a 'new state' in Latin America, according to the policies implemented across the hemisphere during the Cold War. State architecture was explicitly used as a political device of the aspiring 'welfare state' in a controversial social and governmental context. This state architecture co-opted the Modern Movement, simultaneously developing modern facilities, and following other national and international agendas. But unlike other well-known examples, this was not an attempt to create a unified national identity, or to showcase Rojas' regime. Conversely, the built environment produced by the dictatorship used common strategies of the Cold War; it embodied a 'double truth' of welfare and warfare. The legacy of this government has been almost totally overlooked. By interrogating tactics in use at the time these projects were created, what will be articulated here is a critical view of this seemingly neutral infrastructure by questioning how this shaped what I will refer to as a 'conflictual identity'.

Nina Vollenbröker
Rootedness in Mobility: Space and Spatial Practice in the Nineteenth-Century American West
Principal Supervisor: Dr Barbara Penner
Subsidiary Supervisor: Professor Jonathan Hill

Home is important to architecture. Architectural thinkers and practitioners – from Gottfried Semper to Frank Lloyd Wright, from Christian Norberg-Schulz to the Smithsons – have contemplated dwelling, belonging and rootedness. Their home-work has argued for the presence of distinct and grounding atmospheres in certain locations, underlined the importance of architectural form, and revealed the significance of everyday practice. Today's body of thought about home is thus not only inspiring and distinguished but also diverse and interdisciplinary. Its investigative angle, however, has remained surprisingly unchanged throughout the decades: virtually all scholars have approached home as a geographically locatable, static concept. Consequently, accepted understandings of home within architectural discourse are generally informed by an emphasis on enclosed, sedentarist practices and place-based roots.

This PhD considers home and rootedness through a different lens – a lens not shaped by settlement and stasis but by mobility and change. It links 'roots' to 'routes' and asks what can be discovered about home when approached from this shifted and currently under-considered angle. The thesis works with the inhabitants of the nineteenth century American West, a landscape of unrivalled physical and political mobility.

Rich and varied materials introduce a new set of questions to the longstanding architectural inquiry into home and dwelling: How might humans be at home in movement? Which spatial boundaries does mobile rootedness challenge? Which relating, non-spatial dividing lines are questioned? And what is the relationship between hybridity, fluidity and shift on one hand and stability, groundedness and stasis on the other? The diaries, mud cabins and everyday objects suggest remarkable and often unexpected answers to these questions. To some extent, they hint at the importance of architectural form and of related matters of identity, interiority and privacy. But at its core, the eighteenth century migrants' evidence underlines the porosity of the spatial and social boundaries still frequently seen to contain home and demonstrates how effortlessly and continually rootedness moves. It shows that home is not confined, static and unchangeable but nuanced, processual and able to travel across sizable territories.

Image courtesy of Nebraska State Historical Society

Pg Cert in Advanced Architectural Research

Stephen Gage

Architecture and engineering have a history where research and practice go hand in hand, where many great practices have grown as a result of fundamental research and where many research projects arise from groundbreaking design. This is especially true during periods of economic inactivity when recent models of working are called into question and new modes (sometimes based on rediscovered historical precedents) are established. This can lead to the formation of innovative practices and to the start of academic careers in research and teaching.

————The Postgraduate Certificate in Advanced Architectural Research gives students with appropriate graduate degrees the opportunity to take their work to a further stage development. Part of its production are group exhibitions, such as *Constructing Realities* held at Arup's Phase 2 Gallery in 2011, curated by Stephen Gage and Ruairi Glynn, and designed by Nick Westby. It showed how some of the best Masters portfolios and theses contain the seeds of serious design research proposals, and how these might be taken forward to create new types of place, novel interactive building elements and new façade and structural systems.

The Bartlett School of Architecture 2014

Pg Dip in Professional Practice & Management in Architecture (ARB/RIBA Part 3)

Susan Ware

The Professional Studies team aim to educate a generation of architects who are equipped to practice in an increasingly challenging environment. We do this by providing teaching and learning which encourages students to develop the skills beyond those required at threshold level by the professional criteria through reflection, appraisal, critical enquiry and research. We ask students to examine the role of the architect in the changing global construction industry to examine the effect of politics and economics on the design and procurement of the built environment in future practice.

———The programme provides the students with the skills, knowledge, ability, judgment and integrity to be competent to practice and register as an architect through ARB and obtain Chartered Membership of the RIBA. The RIBA and ARB professional criteria are used as a basis to establish evidence of candidates' fitness to practice, and threshold of competence (in terms of knowledge and ability) and professionalism (in terms of conduct and responsibility). However, the demanding programme aims to extend the students learning well beyond the minimum required for professional registration. The school draws extensively from long-standing connections with practice and the construction industry to deliver teaching and learning at the forefront of current practice

———The modular programme can be taken over 12, 18 or 24 months and is delivered through a comprehensive series of 55 lectures given by experts from practice and from within the Faculty. Its structure allows for a diversity of delivery and assessment methods replicating scenarios, roles and responsibilities from practice. A director, who is either a member of the Professional Studies team or an expert from practice, leads the teaching in each of the six modules. Students taking the final Module 6, the case study based module, are supported by a team of tutors for a series of one to one tutorials.

———In addition the professional studies team provide a range of CPD short courses and other practice/registration-orientated courses.

Summer School

Future London Home

We used to think domesticity would survive the future. The naïve charm of the 'future homes' of the 1950s and 60s is bound up in the surreal presentation of conventional families in the far off corners of the universe: under the sea, on other planets, drifting between the stars. The 'future' domestic environment was presented as resolute, an inescapable fact which technology could not subvert. Have we lost something? Can we revive domesticity in our image of the future?

———In the summer of 2014 The Bartlett School of Architecture's annual Summer School considers our current ideas of the future in the context of London. Proposals may be small interventions or larger projects. Using The Bartlett's excellent facilities and studios and UCL's associated facilities we stage a practical symposium to survey, speculate and construct.

———The Summer School is held in London at the beginning of August over a period of 2 weeks. Each year we expect to accommodate a group of participants of varying ages and differing backgrounds, including prospective university students, international students, secondary school students and those who are simply keen to develop their interest in architecture and get a taste of The Bartlett School of Architecture.

———Participants can expect to produce a range of work including drawings, models and larger scale installations. Students will work in groups and individually under the instruction of The Bartlett's teaching staff. Previous cohorts have produced boats, bridges, shadow puppet theatres, large models and a range of projects at various scales.

Summer Foundation

Welcome to London, the most populous city in Europe, a city that is constantly active and bustling. Famous for its numerous museums, theatres, musical venues, cultural events and one of the most diverse culinary cultures in the entire world. This magnificent city is the subject to study (and enjoy) during the 2014 Bartlett Summer Foundation.

The Bartlett Summer Foundation aims to introduce and prepare students for a future career in architecture and architectural education. Running for six weeks over the summer, the programme provides students with a unique creative platform to improve their design and communication skills, as well as their individual conceptual and critical thinking. Participants are of various ages and differing backgrounds, including prospective Bartlett students, international students, secondary school students and those who have a career change in mind and want to use the course as a testbed to see if they are suited to a university degree in architecture.

As well as critical design skills and conceptual thought processes students are introduced to disciplines related to architectural design practice as a means to expand their understanding of architecture. These include contemporary art practice, theatre design, fashion, drawing and photography. During the course students are also encouraged to explore London, to read widely, to visit galleries, exhibitions, concerts and to listen to lectures. The Bartlett School of Architecture offers two separate routes within the Summer Foundation. The first of these runs for four weeks from late July and focuses on developing key design skills and critical thinking. The second route offers an additional two weeks, which allows students to develop not only skills but also additional and more advanced modes of conceptual thinking which enhance their creative learning.

Students on this course begin to develop their ideas about using innovative architecture and design as tools to improve the world. To inform these speculations they are asked to investigate London's transformation within the present economic climate. Students aim to reclaim the role of design to develop scenarios to promote and celebrate a diverse and sustainable future environment.

Bartlett Springboard

Peter Cook

SOTA-Bartlett Pop-Up

'Springboard is a unique opportunity to deepen your perspective on your creative practice, gain skills, make connections and enhance your employability.'
Peter Cook

Bartlett Springboard is an exciting new studio led and directly taught by Professor Peter Cook, renowned architect and former Chair of The Bartlett School of Architecture.

———— The course is designed for architects who wish to extend the range of their work and have it tuned, reconfigured, exposed and discussed in an intensive workshop. Participants may use the course as an opportunity to develop an existing project or to embark on something completely new and unexpected.

———— During the three-month course, participants are part of The Bartlett's vibrant community. They are invited to act as critics for The Bartlett School of Architecture's review sessions, and take part in workshops and seminars. They are introduced to a group of cutting-edge London offices and their own work is reviewed by key figures from the local and international academic and architecture scenes.

Continuing a successful partnership with the School of the Arts (SOTA), Singapore, The Bartlett School of Architecture again plays host to a pop-up Summer School this year. Ten students from SOTA will visit the School, participating in workshops with Bartlett staff and students. As well as tours of The Bartlett and other UCL departments, the programme includes visits to London's museums and special collections and opportunities to experience some of London's cultural highlights. In previous years the workshop investigated London outdoors, canals, and London games; this year students will explore London and food, looking at the relationships between architecture and eating. Participants will discover how the spaces of the city and the lives of its inhabitants accommodate the production and consumption of food and drink, and produce new work, using drawing and making, which reflects and communicates their findings.

Bartlett Lectures

Featuring speakers from across the world, lectures in the series are open to the public and free to attend. This year's speakers included:

AY Architects	**Sara Franceschelli**	**Felipe Mesa**
Marie-Ange Brayer	**Usman Haque**	**Spyros Papapetros**
EcoLogicStudio	**Go Hasegawa**	**Alex Schweder**
Kees Christiaanse	**Manuel Herz**	**Julien de Smedt**
Carole Collet	**Wes Jones**	**Lars Spuybroek**
Peter Cook	**Perry Kulper**	**servo Stockholm + LA**
Verena Conley	**Ross Lovegrove**	**Tom Verebes**
Thom Faulders	**Brendan MacFarlane**	**Ma Yansong**

The Bartlett International Lecture Series is generously supported by the Fletcher Priest Trust

A range of smaller lecture series' attracted a wide range of speakers, including:

Making Buildings
Paul Bavister (BFLS), James Hampton (Egret West Architects), Dirk Krolikowski (Rogers Stirk Harbour + Partners), Tim Lucas (Price & Myers), Níall McLaughlin (Níall McLaughlin Architects), Guy Neville (Max Fordham), Matthew Potter (Wilkinson Eyre Architects)

Bartlett Plexus
Isaïe Bloch, Evan Boehm, Daghan Çam, Arthur Carabott, Benjamin Dillenburger, Mostafa El-Sayed, Jelle Feringa, John Harding, Andy Lomas, Sergej Maier, Keiichi Matsuda, Mathrioshka, Andreas Müller, Matthew Plummer-Fernandez, Davide Quayola, Gilles Retsin, Rub-A-Dub, ScanLab, Thibault Schwartz, Vicente Soler, TeamRoto, Mike Tucker, Maria E. Villafañe, Melissa Woolford

Material Matters
Bruce Bell (FACIT), Philippe Block (BLOCK Research Group, ETH Zurich), Daniel Bosia (P.ART, AKT), Ingo Ederer (voxeljet), Manfred Grohmann (Bollinger + Grohmann), Michael Hansmeyer (ETH Zurich), Benjamin Koren (One to One), Tim Lucas (Price & Myers), Ralph Parker (Price & Myers), Fabian Scheurer (Design to Production)

Bartlett School of Architecture Staff & Consultants

Chair of School

Professor Frédéric Migayrou
Bartlett Professor
of Architecture
B-Pro Director

Director of School

Professor Bob Sheil
Professor of Architecture and
Design through Production
Director of Technology

Professors, Visiting Professors and Stream Directors

Robert Aish
Visiting Professor in
Computation

Laura Allen
Senior Lecturer
Director of Publications
& Public Events

Professor Peter Bishop
Professor of Urban Design
Director of Enterprise

Professor Iain Borden
Professor of Architecture
& Urban Culture
Vice Dean of
Communications
Director of History & Theory

Professor Mario Carpo
Reyner Banham Professor of
Architectural History & Theory

Dr Marjan Colletti
Senior Lecturer
Director of Computing

Professor Peter Cook
Emeritus Professor

Professor Adrian Forty
Professor of Architectural
History
MA Architectural History
Programme Director

Professor Colin Fournier
Emeritus Professor of
Architecture & Urban
Planning

Professor Murray Fraser
Professor of Architecture
& Global Culture
Vice Dean of Research

Professor Stephen Gage
Emeritus Professor of
Innovative Technology

Professor Christine Hawley
Professor of Architectural
Studies
Director of Design

Professor Jonathan Hill
Professor of Architecture
& Visual Theory
MPhil/PhD by Design
Programme Director

Professor CJ Lim
Professor of Architecture
& Cultural Design
Vice Dean of International
Affairs

Dr Yeoryia Manolopoulou
Senior Lecturer
Director of Architectural
Research

Josep Miàs
Visiting Professor

Níall McLaughlin
Visiting Professor

Frosso Pimenides
Senior Lecturer
BSc Architecture Year 1
Co-Director

Dr Peg Rawes
Senior Lecturer
Associate Director of
Architectural Research
Coordinator of Year 5 Thesis

Professor Jane Rendell
Professor of Architecture
& Art

Susan Ware
Sub-Dean and Faculty Tutor
Director of Professional
Studies
Part 3 Programme Director

Mark Whitby
Visiting Professor in
Structural Engineering

Programme Directors/ Leaders and Coordinators

Alisa Andrasek
Lecturer in Advanced
Architectural Computation
MArch GAD Programme
Leader

Julia Backhaus
MArch Architecture
Programme Leader

Matthew Butcher
Lecturer in Architecture
and Performance
BSc Architecture Programme
Co-Leader

Dr Ben Campkin
Senior Lecturer in History
& Theory
Director of Urban Lab
Coordinator Year 3 History
& Theory

Mollie Claypool
BSc Architecture Programme
Co-Leader

Elizabeth Dow
BSc Architectural Studies
Programme Co-Leader

Dr Penelope Haralambidou
Lecturer in Architecture
Coordinator of MPhil / PhD
by Design

Dirk Krolikowski
Lecturer in Innovative
Technology & Design
Practice
Associate Coordinator of
Year 4 Design Realisation

Dr Adrian Lahoud
Reader in Urban Design
MArch UD Programme
Leader

James O'Leary
Lecturer in Innovative
Technology & Design
Practice
Coordinator of Year 4 Design
Realisation

Dr Barbara Penner
Senior Lecturer
BSc Architectural Studies
Programme Co-Leader
MPhil/PhD History & Theory
Programme Director

Frosso Pimenides
Senior Lecturer
BSc Architecture Year 1
Director

Andrew Porter
Principal Teaching Fellow
B-Pro Deputy Director

Peter Scully
Technical Director of B-Made

Dr Tania Sengupta
Lecturer in Architectural
History & Theory
Coordinator of Year 2 / Year 4
History & Theory

Mark Smout
Senior Lecturer
Coordinator of Year 5 Thesis

Patrick Weber
Senior Lecturer
BSc Architecture Year 1
Co-Director
Coordinator of Pedagogic
Affairs

Academic and Honorary Staff

Yannis Aesopos
Affiliate Academic

Abeer Al-Saud
Affiliate Academic

Dr Marcos Cruz
Reader in Architecture

Tom Dyckhoff
Honorary Research Fellow

Ruairi Glynn
Lecturer in Interactive
Architecture

Tim Lucas
Lecturer in Structural Design

Yael Reisner
Affiliate Academic
Research Fellows and
Associates

Izaskun Chinchilla Moreno
Senior Research fellow

Peter Guillery
Senior Research Associate
Survey of London

Sally Hart
Research Assistant

Helen Jones
Research Associate
Survey of London

Dr Hilary Powell
Research Fellow

Harriet Richardson
Research Associate
Survey of London

Andrew Saint
Principal Research Associate
Survey of London

Philip Temple
Senior Research Associate
Survey of London

Andrew Thom
Senior Research Associate
Survey of London

Teaching Staff

BSc Architecture Year 1
Dimitris Argyros
Timothy Barwell
Charlotte Bocci
Mary Duggan
Lucy Leonard
Brian O'Reilly
Frosso Pimenides
Sara Shafiei
Matt Springett
Patrick Weber

**BSc Architecture Year 2 /
Year 3 (Units 0-9)**
Pascal Bronner
Rhys Cannon
Ming Chung
Max Dewdney
Murray Fraser
David A. Garcia
Christine Hawley
Colin Herperger
Tom Hillier
Damjan Iliev
Jan Kattein
Julian Krüger
Chee-Kit Lai
Justin Lau
Holly Lewis
Ana Monrabal-Cook
Luke Pearson
Sabine Storp
Nick Tyson
Paolo Zaide

**BSc Architectural Studies
(Architectural &
Interdisciplinary Studies)**
Elizabeth Dow
Chee-Kit Lai
Barbara Penner
Brent Pilkey

**MArch Architecture Year 4 /
Year 5 (Units 10-24)**
Laura Allen
Abigail Ashton
Paul Bavister
Richard Beckett
Johan Berglund
Kyle Buchanan
Matthew Butcher
Izaskun Chinchilla Moreno
Mollie Claypool
Marjan Colletti
Marcos Cruz
Kate Davies
Elizabeth Dow
Bernd Felsinger
Penelope Haralambidou
Jonathan Hill
Nanette Jackowski
Carlos Jimenez Cenamor
Manuel Jimenez
Simon Kennedy
Maren Klasing
CJ Lim
Yeoryia Manolopoulou
Níall McLaughlin
Josep Mias

Philippe Morel
James O'Leary
Ricardo de Ostos
Andrew Porter
Stefan Rutzinger
Cristina Schinegger
Bob Sheil
Mark Smout
Michiko Sumi
Michael Tite
Emmanuel Vercruysse

Professional Studies
Kit Allsop
Sonia Arbachi
Elena Besussi
Elizabete Cidre
Bill Hodgson
Graciela Moreno
Simon Pilling
David Rosenberg
Susan Ware
Katy Wood

History & Theory
Tilo Amhoff
Doreen Bernath
Ben Campkin
Megha Chand
Edward Denison
Oliver Domeisen
Eva Eylers
Adrian Forty
Daisy Froud
Christophe Gerard
Jon Goodbun
Anne-katrin Hultsch
Jacob Paskins
Barbara Penner
Brent Pilkey
Peg Rawes
David Reat
Jane Rendell
Tania Sengupta
Brian Stater
Rachel Stevenson
Amy Thomas
Nina Vollenbröker
Robin Wilson

**Technology, Computing
& Open Classes**
Scott Batty
Rhys Cannon
Ed Clarke
Jean Garrett
Michael Hadi
James Hampton

Bill Hodgson
Steve Johnson
Tim Lucas
Luke Olsen
Matthew Shaw
Adam Sutcliffe
Will Trossell
Mark Whitby
Andrew Whiting
Oliver Wilton

**Dissertation, Design
Realisation and Thesis
Tutors**
Ross Adams
Hector Altamirano
Francis Archer
Paul Bavister
Jan Birksted
Iain Borden
Jason Bruges
David Buck
Ben Campkin
Daniel Cash
Mollie Claypool
Simon Dickens
Edward Denison
Christian Derix
Oliver Domeisen
Brian Eckersley
Luis Fernandez
Murray Fraser
Daisy Froud
Stephen Gage
Pedro Gil
Ruairi Glynn
Ben Godber
Jon Goodbun
Gary Grant
James Hampton
Penelope Haralambidou
David Hemingway
Bill Hodgson
Tom Holberton
Andy Hudson-Smith
Sara Klomps
Adrian Lahoud
Guan Lee
Stephen Lorimer
Luke Lowings
Tim Lucas
John Lyall
Joseph Mackey
Roberto Marin Sampalo
Anna Mavrogianni
Frédéric Migayrou
Justin Nicholls
Dean Pike

Hareth Pochee
Hilary Powell
Sophia Psarra
Rokia Raslan
Peg Rawes
Jane Rendell
Anne Schroell
Ben Sheterline
Tania Sengupta
Bob Sheil
Jason Slocombe
Mark Smout
Andy Toohey
Peter Vaughan
Nina Vollenbröker
Tim Waterman
William Whitby
Finn Williams
Robin Wilson
Oliver Wilton
Simon Withers
Brendan Woods
Manja van der Worp
Daniel Wright

B-Pro MArch Urban Design
Ross Exo Adams
Peter Besley
Hannah Corlett
Zach Flucker
Beth Hughes
Platon Issaias
Sam Jacoby
Ulrika Karlsson
Jonathan Kendall
Immanuel Koh
Adrian Lahoud
Enriqueta Llabres
Iker Mugarra
Claudia Pasquero
Godofredo Nobre Enes
Pereira
Lorenzo Pezzani
Maj Plemenitas
Marco Poletto
Eduardo Rico
Davide Sacconi
Camila Sotomayor
Emmanouil Zaroukas

**B-Pro MArch Graduate
Architectural Design**
Alisa Andrasek
Steffan Bassing
Isaïe Bloch
Daghan Cam
Moa Carlsson
Stephen Gage

Ruairi Glynn
Soomeen Hahn
Manuel Jimenez
Xavier de Kestelier
Guan Lee
Christopher Leung
Philippe Morel
Ollie Palmer
Maj Plemenitas
Giles Retsin
Thibault Schwartz
Daniel Widrig

MA Architectural History
Iain Borden
Ben Campkin
Adrian Forty
Barbara Penner
Jane Rendell
Peg Rawes
Amy Thomas
Robin Wilson

**MPhil / PhD Architectural
Design**
**MPhil / PhD Architectural
History & Theory**
Peter Bishop
Jan Birksted
Camillo Boano
Iain Borden
Victor Buchli
Ben Campkin
Mario Carpo
Marjan Colletti
Peter Cook
Marcos Cruz
Adrian Forty
Murray Fraser
Stephen Gage
Ranulph Glanville
Sean Hanna
Penelope Haralambidou
Christine Hawley
Jonathan Hill
Adrian Lahoud
Ruth Mandel
Yeoryia Manolopoulou
Sebastian Ourselin
Jayne Parker
Barbara Penner
Sophia Psarra
Peg Rawes
Jane Rendell
Stephanie Schwartz
Tania Sengupta
Bob Sheil
Mark Smout

Philip Steadman
Hugo Spiers
Neil Spiller
Philip Tabor

Short Courses
Peter Cook
Bill Hodgson
Carlos Jimenez Cenamor
Graciella Moreno
Sabine Storp

Admissions
Abigail Ashton
Adrian Forty
Jonathan Hill
Barbara Penner
Andrew Porter
Sabine Storp

Reception
Mairead Mallon

PA to Chair & Director
Meredith Wilson

**Academic Services
Administration**
Michelle Bush
Emer Girling
Eleni Goule
Tom Mole

Archive
Graciela Moreno

Research
Luis Rego

Communications
Laura Cherry
Jean Garrett
Michelle Lukins

Finance and HR
Sarah Clegg
Stoll Michael
Rita Prajapati

**Professional Studies
Administration**
Kim Macneill
Helen McKenzie
Indigo Rohrer
Naz Siddique

Facilities
Graeme Kennett
Bernie Ococ

**Bartlett Manufacturing and
Design Exchange (B-Made)**
Abi Abdolwahabi
Richard Beckett
William Bondin
Matt Bowles
Bim Burton
Inigo Dodd
Richard Grimes
Robert Randall
Peter Scully
Matthew Shaw
Paul Smoothy
Will Trossell
Emmanuel Vercruysse
Martin Watmough
Sam Wellham

Year 1 field trip to Enric Miralles' Igualada Cemetery,
Barcelona, Spain

bartlett.ucl.ac.uk/architecture

Publisher
The Bartlett School of Architecture, UCL

Editors
Frédéric Migayrou, Bob Sheil

Graphic Design
Patrick Morrissey, Unlimited
www.weareunlimited.co.uk

Editorial Coordination
Laura Allen, Laura Cherry, Michelle Lukins

Copyright 2014 The Bartlett School of Architecture, UCL

ISBN 978-0-9572355-9-5

For more information on all the programmes and modules at The Bartlett Faculty of the Built Environment, UCL, visit bartlett.ucl.ac.uk

The Bartlett School of Architecture, UCL
Wates House
Gordon Street
London WC1H 0QB

We are moving. From August 2014 we will based at:

140 Hampstead Road
London NW1 2BX
T. +44 (0)20 7679 7504
architecture@ucl.ac.uk